PICTURE BOOKS
FOR CHILDREN

PICTURE

BOOKS
for CHILDREN

third edition

PATRICIA J. CIANCIOLO

AMERICAN LIBRARY ASSOCIATION

CHICAGO AND LONDON 1990

Designed by Vladimir Reichl

Composed by Ampersand Publisher
  Services Inc. in Melior on
  an Itek IGX 7000 Imagesetter

Printed on 50-pound Glatfelter,
  a pH-neutral stock, and
  bound in 10-point Carolina
  cover stock by
  Edwards Brothers, Inc.

The paper used in this publication meets the minimum requirements of American
National Standard for Information Sciences—Permanence of Paper for Printed Library
Materials, ANSI Z39.48–1984. ∞

Library of Congress Cataloging-in-Publication Data

Cianciolo, Patricia J.
  Picture books for children / by Patricia J. Cianciolo. — 3rd ed.
    p. cm.
  ISBN 0-8389-0527-7 (alk. paper)
  1. Picture-books for children—Bibliography. 2. Illustrated
books, Children's—Bibliography. 3. Children's literature—
Bibliography. I. Title.
Z1037.C565 1990
[PN1009.A1]
011.62—dc20   89-29718
                                                        CIP

93 92 91 90 89   5 4 3 2 1

*To my mother and father
lovingly remembered*

Contents

Illustrations

Preface

It has been sixteen years between the publication of the first edition and the third edition of PICTURE BOOKS FOR CHILDREN. In that span of time, literally thousands of picture books have been published—some re-issues of old favorites, most newly created works. With these new publications have occurred some striking changes, changes resulting in more than a gratuitous parade of fashions in the literary and graphic arts. If anything, the picture books published most recently have become more conceptual, more methodological, and certainly more self-assured—many being accomplished creations, esoteric and specialized in spirit as well as in the techniques used by the authors and the book artists.

A third edition of PICTURE BOOKS FOR CHILDREN seemed quite in order. Most of the titles in the third edition are new entries. Only a very small percentage of titles from the first and second editions have been carried over; these titles were retained because they seemed as appropriate today as they were when originally selected and quite in keeping with the current trends in terms of their contents, their styles of art, and their themes.

The books included in this edition are products of our time, and they are evidence that the field of children's literature (especially that which pertains to picture books) is far from static. In fact, it is a truly dynamic field. The children who will read these books, just like the writers and illustrators who created the books, are products of their time. Thus, some of their values, interests, and needs are different from those of others who lived in the past, even as recently as five, ten, or fifteen years ago. Some of their values, interests, and needs have persisted and remain quite unchanged. These same changing and persistent values are reflected in the children's books that are published in the last years of this decade, for these books are products of their time. One can readily see that the field of children's literature, especially that which pertains to the creating and publishing of picture books, is truly dynamic.

The audience and the underlying purpose of this revised and enlarged edition remain unchanged. The work is intended to serve as a resource and guide for teachers of children from nursery school through junior high school, for day-care center personnel, for librarians in school and public libraries, for parents, and for any other adults concerned with the selection of well-written, imaginatively illustrated picture books that are of interest to children of all ages and backgrounds. This bibliography is also designed to be used as a reference tool for undergraduate and graduate courses in children's and adolescent literature offered by departments of English and by schools of library science and education.

The purpose of PICTURE BOOKS FOR CHILDREN is to identify and describe picture books that will provide children with enjoyable, informative, and discriminating literary experiences, foster the habit of reading, and initiate an appreciation for, and an understanding of, the beautiful and creative in the graphic arts. I have evaluated at first hand each of the titles listed, and I have had occasion to share some of them with individual children and with groups in school libraries and classrooms.

Like any other adult whose childhood was lost long ago, I cannot know exactly what goes on in children's minds when they read a picture book or have one read to them. However, numerous recent "response studies" (conducted under controlled situations and especially as case studies and interviews) are bringing us a little closer to this knowledge. Also, I have worked extensively in recent years with children and adolescents in school libraries and in classrooms. I have studied their responses to literature in general, but especially to picture books and to book illustrations. The selection of picture books in this publication is based on my knowledge of literature, particularly children's and adolescent literature, my experiences with young people, and my research. It is also based on written and oral testimonies of other teachers, librarians, and researchers, who have reported children's and adolescents' responses to the picture books they read on their own or had read to them. The best any adult can conclude from even the most judicious interviews or observations is that children do indeed respond to certain books (to certain elements of literature and to certain kinds of book art) and that their responses vary in intensity and in degree, from favorable to unfavorable. In all fairness, we have to admit that no adult can select books from the child's point of view. We must remember that children are ultimately the consumers of the books we select. With this in mind, I have tried to identify and include in this publication the picture books that I am convinced will please children, that will help them look at picture books (and, by extension, literature, painting, and the other graphic arts) as something expandable, fulfilling, and pleasurable. It was my intention to include titles that will help individual children realize that picture books (and again, literature, paintings, and the other graphic arts) offer new ways of "seeing" the panorama of existence.

All selections in this bibliography are hardbound editions, although many are also available in paperback. The cutoff publication date was March, 1989.

In addition to the annotated bibliographic list, PICTURE BOOKS FOR CHILDREN includes an introduction and an index of authors, illustrators, and titles. The introduction, Choosing Picture Books, explores the values and uses of the variety of picture books being produced today, examines and describes current trends in writing and illustrating picture books, and discusses criteria for evaluating them. The main body of the work consists of annotated entries categorized to reflect the basic concerns of all people, regardless of age or culture. Each of the four categories includes fiction, nonfiction, and poetry. The entries in each category are arranged alphabetically by author. They include the title of the book, the illustrator, the publisher, and the year of publication. The age range of reader appeal or interest is also indicated. The annotations comment on the story or theme as well as the style of art and the media used in creating the illutrations. In some instances a statement points out possible classroom use or special reader interest.

There is no doubt that another specialist in children's literature would create an entirely different bibliography. That is as it should be. My judgments about the picture books are based on my knowledge, my philosophy of art and literature, accepted principles of child growth and development, and established educational goals and practices. They are also largely influenced by my affective response to a piece of literature and must, to some extent, be considered an affective endeavor. Thus, in many respects, the bibliographies in this book, while based on extensive professional experience, reflect a consistent set of principles developed from personal judgments.

I am indebted to Sylvia Royt, former editor at the American Library Association, for her help in the preparation of the first two editions of PICTURE BOOKS FOR CHILDREN. I will be forever grateful for her thoroughness and enthusiasm. It was my privilege and good fortune to have her as my editor.

Also, I thoroughly appreciate the words of encouragement from Herbert Bloom, senior editor, ALA Books, and Helen Cline, managing editor, in all phases of preparing this edition.

Choosing Picture Books

The picture book, because of its unique blending of illustrations and words, is considered a genre apart from any other kind of literature. (The genre also includes wordless stories told entirely by the sequencing of pictures.) Among the many books published over a period of time are to be found a respectable number of picture books that are examples of high quality writing and illustration. This is literature that communicates and appeals to children, that enriches, extends, and expands their background of experiences, their literary and aesthetic interests, tastes, and preferences by providing a variety of sensory images and vicarious experiences, plots, characters, and themes.

Children's literature today is extremely cosmopolitan and diverse. Picture books, which make up so large a segment of what is published for children, tend to be more expansive and varied in scope and subject than the other types of literature produced for children. One may find a picture book (in English) on almost any topic for readers ranging from toddlers to mature and sophisticated adults. The stories told in picture books may be classified as modern realistic fiction, as here-and-now stories, as historical fiction, and as fanciful fiction. Picture books may also include poetry, biography, and concept or informational books. Among the picture books published in any one year, some will be new and some reissues of old favorites. They will be illustrated in diverse styles of art, many written and illustrated by people who come not only from different nations and cultural backgrounds, but also who obviously differ in their understanding of and expectations from their target audience.

SOME TRENDS

It has been eight years since the last edition of PICTURE BOOKS FOR CHILDREN, and it seems quite safe to say that literature for children is very much alive and prospering. There is no dearth of picture books for children from infancy (as young as six months of age) through young adulthood (age eighteen and beyond). Among this abundance of picture books, can be found those which provide children with simplified and really quite static pictures, most of which are in bright primary colors. Children as young as six months through age two-and-one-half or even three years will be attracted to them and discover easily manageable images of people and objects that are immediately familiar. Often these images are presented in concept books, counting books, or alphabet books. Usually these books are accompanied by a very minimal amount of text. Occasionally, one can find some simple nursery rhyme collections for that age reader, too. The pictures and words are printed on cloth or stiff board (usually with a glossy finish) that can withstand children's vigorous use and can be wiped off with a damp cloth.

In contrast, one can find picture book stories where neither text nor illustrations play a subordinate role to the other. The appeal of these stories ranges from the three-year-old child, unable to read but quite capable of listening to and understanding the story, to the mature and sophisticated young adult (age eighteen or older) who is an experienced and accomplished reader. In these picture books the illustrations are superbly accomplished works of visual and graphic art, and the texts are written in beautifully expressive language. Of particular significance is the fact that the illustrations are not merely an attractive reiteration or elaboration of what is obvious in the text; in addition to bringing out and emphasizing the text, they convey other meanings and impressions that readers would not have envisioned from the verbal information on its own. They encourage higher-level thinking and imaginative thinking. Readers can and do grasp their meaning and significance and can go well beyond what the illustrator and author suggested. Unlike the picture books for infants in which the content (topics or subject matter) is limited to the children themselves, close members of their family, and their very immediate world, the picture books for children from ages three through eighteen and older depict concepts and stories that enable these readers to concentrate more broadly on aspects that are well established parts of their experiential background and are about things they know well. But these picture books can take the readers well beyond the familiar. Staying within the children's capacity to understand, these picture books can help them view themselves in a different and more informed manner than they did previously and introduce them to more complicated, mature, and remote aspects of the real world (in the past, present, and future), as well as the world of make believe. In addition to those alluded to above, some interesting trends can be observed in picture books published currently. These trends are discussed briefly below.

An increasing number of picture books are now being published in full color or four-color instead of just black-and-white or with pages alternating full color or four color and black-and-white. It appears that when the national economic picture is fairly healthy and stable, picture books are printed in full color. When the economy slips, black-and-white illustrations are more apparent. At present, the economy seems to be in good shape; so the book-buying public is more willing and able to pay the higher price for picture books illustrated in full-color art. Two picture books in which full-color illustrations were reproduced most effectively are *Heckedy Peg*, written by Audrey Wood and illustrated by Don Wood, and the 1988 Caldecott Honor book *Mufaro's Beautiful Daughters*, written and illustrated by John Steptoe. In *Heckedy Peg* somber, dark tones are used when an unpleasant or frightening person (specifically, the witch Heckedy Peg) is present or an unpleasant event happens (such as when the children are kidnapped by Heckedy Peg and turned into different kinds of food); in contrast, glowing, rich, warm colors are used when the members of this loving family, respectful and always sharing and giving to one another, are shown. In *Mufaro's Beautiful Daughters*, a Cinderella-type story set in Zimbabwe, Steptoe recreates the lush, strong colors one associates with the flora and the fauna, the very atmosphere, of the forests and terrain of this African country. The illustrators of both of these beautiful picture books used full-color to advantage, creating a definite sense of place and mood.

Relatively little experimentation is apparent in aspects of book illustration, especially in the use of media, styles of art or story (in terms of plots, motifs, or structure). One finds mostly established, conservative authors and illustrators and the tried-and-true stories (especially folktales and classics) being published. Each publishing season there will be *some* examples of innovative picture books. Currently, these prove to be the exception rather than the rule, and I have included as many of them in this edition of PICTURE BOOKS FOR CHILDREN as I could. This seems to be an era in which specialization in graphic arts and past accomplishments in either writing or illustrating are often rewarded more than innovation and experimentation. I have no explanation for this trend, but I will hazard some guesses. Perhaps the trend is a reflection of the fact that this is a fairly conservative era in the United States. Liberalism and free spiritedness in thinking and behavior are not exactly welcomed in many facets of our society. Since writers and illustrators (and publishers) tend to be products of their times, the literature they create (and publish) tends to reflect their values and attitudes. Since the book-buying public is also a product of the times, it too will buy the books that reflect the values it holds. It will look for the conservative books, the tried-and-true titles and motifs. A 1987 Caldecott Honor book was *Rumpelstiltskin,* retold and illustrated by Paul O. Zelinsky. Although one cannot deny that the oil paintings, which strongly suggest those of the Renaissance, are beautiful in every respect and the graphics are masterfully crafted, there was little or no gamble on the book being a "sure sale." For one thing, "Rumpelstilt-skin" is a well-known folktale, so even the most uninformed book purchaser would not hesitate to buy it; furthermore, the illustrator is well-known; he won a 1985 Caldecott Honor book award for the illustrations he created for Rika Lesser's retelling of *Hansel and Gretel,* and he illustrated Beverly Cleary's 1984 Newbery Medal book *Dear Mr. Henshaw,* as well as many other critically acclaimed books. Thus, he would not have to prove himself to the book-buying public; in fact, there is little doubt that many professional book selectors would buy a book illustrated by him sight unseen, and they would be more inclined to examine a book he illustrated before examining one by an illustrator unknown to them. The 1989 Caldecott Medal book was *Song and Dance Man,* written by Karen Ackerman and illustrated by Stephen Gammell. The colored pencil, highly stylized, expressionistic drawings border on the cartoon style. They are quite in keeping with the upbeat, exuberant personality of the ex-vaudevillian who charms and delights his grandchildren with his dancing, jokes, and tricks. Yet, in comparing the illustrations Gammell prepared for this book with those that he prepared for some of his other picture books, it immediately becomes apparent that they are all quite similar—in style of art, use of media, choice of colors, and even the facial expressions of the characters. The illustrations he created for *Old Henry,* written by Joan W. Blos, and the 1986 Caldecott Honor book *The Relatives Came,* written by Cynthia Rylant, come to mind.

Picture books for older readers (ages ten through eighteen or nineteen) are increasing. Although the story is presented in the picture-book format, there are many things about these picture books that appeal to the interests of adolescents and challenge them cognitively and affectively. The stories (in prose or verse) challenge readers to think seriously about important ideas or issues; both text and pictures offer a complexity of meanings that are obviously for older and accomplished readers. There are also many picture books in which only the most literal readers will be unable to find more than a simple story. Children gain new insights, different from what they had before reading these books. Often, authors will make use of literary devices such as satire, irony, cultural allusions, idioms, and dialects; illustrators will use the most sophisticated forms of expressionism or impressionism, illusionary art, or visual puns. Books vary from one another in style, format, and level of sophistication.

The Wedding Ghost, a stunning and very sophisticated book by the talented author-illustrator team of Leon Garfield and Charles Keeping, comes to mind immediately. This original fantasy is presented in an oversized, profusely illustrated book, a format that was traditionally associated with a reading audience much younger than the audience this book obviously addresses. Indeed, the story that is depicted is really very mature. It is rich in Freudian symbolism and alludes to aspects of Shakespeare's Twelfth Night and the traditional fairy tale "Sleeping Beauty"; and the plot strongly suggests a nineteenth-century Gothic. It is a haunting account of what happens to a groom-to-be before his wedding night when he sets out to follow a map sent anonymously as a wedding gift, quite certain it was sent by an old nurse who was not invited to the wedding. Charles Keeping's expressionistic, black-and-white, pen-and-ink drawings detail, extend, and enrich Garfield's impeccable text. Together, words and pictures offer a narrative that is sensuous, mysterious, eerie, and haunting, offering the mature reader an artful balance between the real, the ugly, and the beautiful. The Wedding Ghost is a picture book that could stimulate the imagination and provoke thinking by the experienced and mature young adult reader.

There is a proliferation of books for children ages six months through three years, especially concept books and toy books. In most instances the pictures in these books are of objects or static scenes rather than action scenes, and they are printed on cloth or glossy board. Some parts of the pictures may be textured or have moving or detachable parts. They encourage the children not only to look at the books but also to touch and handle them. By playing with fastenings such as press studs, cord, and buttons, children learn to tie and untie, push and pull, fasten and unfasten. Thus, they not only learn to associate books as a source from which they can learn about themselves and their world, but also as a source of considerable pleasure. In addition, these books can help them learn how to do things by following directions and manipulating things, and help them develop eye and hand coordination and the large and small muscles in their hands and fingers.

This trend is in direct response to an increased awareness among young parents and educators of the benefits derived from exposing children to books before they start school. By the age of six months, children become interested in and obviously enjoy pictures in a book; they will sit on a lap and look, often touching the pictures as some older person turns the pages. In only a few months they will turn the pages themselves and be quite delighted that the picture of a favorite or familiar object is still there. With continued exposure to these kinds of picture books, babies will notice details and point to special features in the picture that are of particular interest to them; soon they will even make noises that are associated with the animal, machine, or person pictured. It is not until they are approximately sixteen months old that they will listen long enough and enjoy having a book read through, rather than looking at only one or two pictures at a time. It is around this age that they can understand and appreciate action-type pictures that depict short, here-and-now stories and poems. The little books (6 by 6-1/2 inches) that are included in the What I Like series: *Eating, Getting Dressed, Going to Bed,* and *Taking a Bath,* written by Marcia Leonard and illustrated by Deborah Michel, are quite typical of the books for the infant and toddler. In these books the toddler is shown participating and accomplishing some aspect of the activities commonly associated with those suggested by the titles of the books. The illustrations are full-page, rather simple line and watercolor expressionistic paintings. Another good example of a picture book for the very young child is *Numbers,* written and illustrated by Sara Lee Anderson. In this attractive picture book, objects, grouped together sequentially from one to ten, appear on brilliantly colored cardboard pages that get bigger as the number of objects grouped together get bigger.

There is a proliferation of pop-up books for readers of all ages. Some of the most accomplished paper engineering has gone into creating the contemporary pop-up books—the Pop-Up Field Guide series, written and illustrated by Cecilia Fitzsimons, includes *My First Butterflies* and *My First Fishes and Other Waterlife,* to name but two. Pop-ups are just the thing to use to introduce children ages 5–9 years to reference books as a special resource for identifying and classifying things they see in their environment; they are also fine books to alert young children to things in their environment, to help them notice and question what is commonly found around them. A pop-up book that won international acclaim for its paper engineering is *The Facts of Life,* written by Jonathan Miller and David Pelham and illustrated by Harry Willock. Readers as young as age eight and as old as eighteen and even beyond can hardly help being impressed with this picture book. It presents aspects of human reproduction and gestation in technical terms, yet the text is not at all difficult to read or understand. Incredibly accomplished three-dimensional pop-up pictures, moving diagrams, and lift-up flaps, plus realistic pictures embellish the well-written text.

There is a proliferation of books traditionally associated with pedagogic aims. These books are also of interest to nonprofessional book selectors such as parents, grandparents, relatives, or friends who go into a book shop to buy a book for a favorite child who is about to celebrate a birthday or special occasion. They are the types of books teachers and school librarians can use to great advantage in connection with all aspects of the curriculum, enabling them to implement the current emphasis on using multiple resources in the instructional programs and using literature across the curriculum. Thus, one will find that *Me, Molly Midnight* and the sequel *Runaway Molly Midnight,* Nadja Maril's picture books about the famous watercolorist and oil painter Herman Maril, would be of interest to a number of book purchasers. There is little doubt that all of them would be very pleased with the wealth of information in these books—the descriptions of Maril's studio, the working materials he used, his techniques for using color, form, and space—just as they would appreciate that so many of his most important paintings are reproduced in full color in these picture books. Over and above being pleased with the contents of these books, any number of purchasers would identify a very different reason or purpose for using the picture books with children. And that, of course, is just fine, for it only serves to demonstrate the wonderful potential for such picture books. I was delighted to see Lisbeth Zwerger's picture-book interpretation of O. Henry's "The Gift of the Magi." This popular classic short story about the sacrifices a couple made to buy each other Christmas presents is now available in hand calligraphy with Zwerger's full-page, expressionistic, watercolor paintings. All aspects of the format of this book lend an aura of elegance to the charming and romantic story. It is a perfect picture book for adolescent and adult readers.

Internationalism in publishing picture books is a major and important development. Picture books are co-produced or co-published in foreign countries. This means that they were published originally or simultaneously in English-speaking countries with the same or only some minor changes in the illustrations and texts; or they originate in non-English-speaking countries and were published in English-speaking countries with the same illustrations and a text translated into English. (It should be mentioned, too, that picture books which originate in the United States or other English-speaking countries are very often translated into other languages and published in foreign countries with the original pictures.) This is a very fine development especially if we point out the international aspects of these picture books to children and help them recognize how the elements of the stories and the illustrations are similar and different from those in books that are created and published originally in the United States. Such an approach can serve to foster the development of an international literary heritage. It will help our children become more aware and appreciative of the accomplishments of the literary and graphic artists from other parts of the world and realize that children from other parts of the world enjoy the same kinds of stories that they do. In the long run, it will help them be more cosmopolitan and less provincial in their outlook and knowledge of other people. Picture books created by the British award-winning author-illustrator Shirley Hughes are good examples of books internationally co-published in English-speaking countries. Her books about Alfie, a feisty and exuberant little boy are much loved by children in the United States, England, and Australia, and any other English-speaking country for that matter. All of the picture books about Alfie—*Alfie Gets In First, Alfie's Feet, Alfie Gives a Hand,* and *An Evening at Alfie's*—are illustrated with action-filled, realistic pictures done with ink and watercolor. The text and the illustrations in each convincingly depict Alfie's emotions and predicaments, most of which are quite like those experienced by faithful readers. One of the most stunning and accomplished picture books to originate in a non-English-speaking country and subsequently translated into English and published in the United States is *The Painter and the Wild Swans,* written by Claude Clément, translated from the French by Robert Levine, and illustrated by Frédéric Clément. It is a haunting, multi-level story about Teiji, a famous Japanese painter, who stops painting after he sees a flock of exquisitely beautiful swans fly overhead. Convinced he has to see the birds again in order to capture their beauty on canvas, he follows them across a treacherous lake to the island where they gathered. Unfortunately, Teiji's boat capsizes, and although he manages to swim to shore and see the birds again, he does not paint them, for his brush and paints are lost when his boat capsizes. He dies convinced that just seeing the birds is enough, for "Such beauty is rare and impossible to capture on canvas." The illustrations, done in acrylic paintings in tones of blue, gray, and white, with hints of red and yellow, are quite like classic Japanese brush paintings. Teiji's transformation from a man into a swan that flies away "with his brothers" where winter is milder is depicted most effectively by this amazingly talented artist's combination of poetic prose and truly striking paintings. Teiji's story, told from his perspective long after he is transformed into a swan, is in the form of a poem, which is included in English in its entirety at the back of the book as well as line-by-line and page-by-page in delicate, Japanese calligraphy. Originally published in France under the title *Le peintre et les cygnes sauvages,* the picture book received the French Foundation Grand Prize for Children's Literature.

There is a proliferation of picture-book stories depicting innocent victims of war and other anti-war themes. As expected, picture books on such mature topics would most probably be of interest to readers at least age nine through the young adult years, age eighteen or nineteen. *Faithful Elephants: A True Story of Animals, People, and War* was written by Yulio Tsuchiya, translated by Tomoko Tsuchiya Dykes, and illustrated by Ted Lewin. It is a highly emotional and disturbing portrayal of grief, fear, and sadness produced by war. The zookeeper of Tokyo's well-known Ueno Zoo relates why and how, during World War II, three famous performing elephants were allowed to starve to death and all the other animals in the zoo were poisoned to death. The illustrations for this true story are expressive watercolor paintings. Published originally in Japan as a narrative poem under the title *Kawaiso no zo,* and with entirely different illustrations, it is read on the Japanese radio every year to mark the anniversary of Japan's surrender. *The Miracle Tree,* written by Christobel Mattingly and illustrated by Marianne Yamaguchi, focuses on a pine tree on Christmas Day as the symbol of hope and happiness. This is a fascinating story about three people who were separated by World War II, each suffering the devastating effects of the atomic bomb dropped on the city of Nagasaki. The relationship between these three people and the role the tree played in reuniting them twenty long years after they had been separated by the bombing is artfully developed through exquisite language and striking, black-and-white, charcoal drawings.

Many series are available including picture books about the same story characters, prequels and sequels, as well as picture books on comparable themes or subjects. Over the years Ernest Raboff has written a number of factual picture books about the great masters, such as Marc Chagall, Paul Klee, Leonardo daVinci, and others. Each is entitled with the name of the person whose life story is told and whose art (media, style of art, symbolism, etc.) is discussed. Each is illustrated generously with full-color reproductions of the artist's work, smaller drawings and designs in black-and-white, and, in some instances, photographs. Mairi Hedderwick's picture-book stories about Katie Morag— *Katie Morag Delivers the Mail, Katie Morag and the Two Grandmothers, Katie Morag and the Big Boy Cousins,* and *Katie Morag and the Tiresome Ted*—are much enjoyed by children, who delight in her predicaments; they find them (and Katie herself) both humorous and upsetting. But unlike Katie, children, especially those who have read a number of books about this lovable little Scottish girl, know that somehow Katie will come out the winner. The illustrations are detailed, expressionistic, watercolor paintings that seem as uninhibited as the protagonist they depict.

In the main, almost everyone who reads, regardless of age, educational background, or experience with literature, tends to choose books or reject them on the basis of some aspect of their content. A person's interest in a particular topic is a reflection of a desire, conscious or unconscious, to learn more about the human condition. Instinctively people want to know more about themselves and their world. It is the content of the picture book, and the quality of the literary and artistic amalgam resulting from the combination of words and illustrations used to express that content, that facilitates the development of the reader's imaginative, creative, and critical thinking, satisfying his or her basic need to know or fulfilling an innate craving for the beautiful.

THE PICTURE BOOK AS LITERATURE

The Sharing of Important Experiences

The subject of literature comprises aspects of the human condition. It may pertain to any human experience, everything which has to do with people—their actions, their needs and desires, their strengths and frailities, their response to the world in which they live. Writing literature, be it fiction, poetry, or drama, is not the same as writing a script for a documentary movie or television report or writing a newspaper article. The writers who view them as comparable will make little use of their imagination. And imagination is the human faculty that lends the writer (or illustrator) to create a literary work of art, art at its finest and most memorable.

When literature is viewed as one of the humanities, one tends to read a literary selection to find out how the author interprets people's responses to certain social issues or to aspects of the human condition. Literature is used as a source through which one gains an understanding of oneself and one's relationship to other people and things. It is used to find out what an author offers the reader in relation to the perpetual and universal human questions common to people of all ages: "Why am I like I am?" "Who am I?" "What is my world?" "What else might it be?" This approach to literature is jusitifed if one remembers that literature, as an art form, should not be read on the literal level for actual or even partial answers to these persistent human concerns, nor should it be read as a source for factual information. No attempt should be made to read into these stories or poems or even to judge them on terms of eternal standards, such as "truth," as though they were factual or informational writings.

Picture books can be used to help children of all ages realize that their wishes, feelings, and actions are normal and merely a part of growing up or occur because they are functioning people. The stories and illustrations of many contemporary picture books emphasize basic human emotions and human frailities that, to some extent, are common to all people regardless of race, creed, sex, or national origin. The text and illustrations in picture books should depict individuals from diverse cultures participating and functioning as all people do, regardless of their cultural background. In other words, they should depict individuals involved in universal experiences. Finding picture books that meet this criterion should present little or no problem.

All of Shirley Hughes' picture-book stories about Alfie *(Alfie Gets In First, Alfie Gives a Hand, An Evening at Alfie's)* are refreshingly upbeat and highlight the range of emotions that this rambuctions little boy, his family, and friends feel when he gets into his predicaments. Most young readers of these books know all too well that Alfie's predicaments (often viewed as crises by Alfie) are really very common. Just like Alfie, they might have been accidently locked in (or out of) their homes or put their boots on the wrong feet. The exuberant illustrations, done in ink and watercolor, reflect and extend these very credible stories that "tell it like it is," but with just the right amount of exaggeration to make them interesting and artful. They help children to see themselves in proper perspective, to laugh at themselves, and to gain a better understanding of everday life and growing up.

Another book that may help children see themselves in proper perspective and not take themselves too seriously (perhaps even learn to laugh at themselves) is Judith Viorst's *Alexander and the Terrible, Horrible, No Good, Very Bad Day,* illustrated by Ray Cruz. Well on its way to becoming a classic, this is a refreshing account of the disasters that befall Alexander from the moment he wakes up in the morning with gum in his hair until he goes to bed wearing pajamas he does not like—after his bed lamp burns out and he bites his tongue. The cross-hatched drawings in this picture book highlight Alexander's reactions to his traumas.

Our self-concepts are shaped largely by the way we believe significant others view us. Thus children who believe that parents, siblings, other relatives, and closely associated persons respect and accept them will be more likely to have a better opinion of themselves. For that reason, picture books that portray aspects of family life with significant members of the family, immediate and extended, may affect a child's view of self. They also can provide children with a frame of reference and some insights into human relationships. Almost as important, they can provide a source of amusement.

Eloise Greenfield's polished text and Carole Byard's stunning charcoal drawings combine to tell the story of *Grandmama's Joy,* a tender and heartwarming portrayal of how little Rhonda, orphaned when her parents are killed in an automobile accident, brought joy to her grandmama and her grandmama brought joy and security to the little girl. There is no doubt about the mutual feelings of love and respect the two have for each other, which provide them with a strong sense of security and self-respect regardless of the problems and stresses they are confronted with daily.

Any number of picture books depict children and elderly relatives or friends relating with one another in a positive manner. Among them is *Wilfrid Gordon McDonald Partridge,* a very special picture book originally published in Australia, written by Mem Fox and illustrated by Julie Vivas. This is a story of a small boy with a long name (see the title of the book) who lives next door to a home for the elderly and visits frequently with the people who live there. During his visits he discovers that the elderly are fun to be with, and he notices also that each person has some special quality. The one person he especially likes is a lady who, like himself, has a long name. He is determined to help her "find" her memory. The full-color, expressionistic paintings and the accomplished writing with its frequent use of figurative terms make this story of friendship between the elderly and a child a truly memorable and insightful one. Children (and adults) will think about this book long after the covers are closed. *Two Piano Tuners,* written and illustrated by M. B. Goffstein, is another well-crafted picture book depicting a similar relationship that shows the elderly as functioning and worthwhile people in their own right. In *Two Piano Tuners*, by way of very simple line drawings and brief text, readers meet Debbie Weinstock, an engaging and determined little girl who wants to become a piano tuner—a good one like her grandfather, Ruben Weinstock— despite the fact that her parents have other plans for her avocational future. There is no doubt in Debbie's mind, or in the mind of the reader of this perceptive little book, that Ruben Weinstock (or one's own grandfather or great-grandfather) is a fine model for young people.

Picture books can help children realize that, while life is sometimes unpleasant or difficult, they need not crumble because of it. The picture-book stories by Vera Williams are good examples of books that put forth such a theme. *Music, Music for Everyone* addresses what happens when a beloved relative becomes ill and is bedridden and paying for their care may put a strain on the family's finances. In this story Rosa sets out to help pay the medical bills for her ailing grandmother by playing her accordion in a combo at parties. In *A Chair for My Mother*, the family's belongings are destroyed by fire, and Rosa determinedly saves loose coins in a huge jar to buy a new chair for her mother. And in *Something Special for Me*, readers learn that though parents want to celebrate their child's birthday or other special occasions, they can do it only within the limits of their budget. In this award-winning picture book, Rosa has a tough time picking out her birthday present, knowing very well she has to stay within the amount of money her mother allocated for this special occasion. Few other books address a family's struggle against hardship and adversity in such a forthright yet upbeat and appealing manner.

Any number of picture-book stories focus on children's adjustment to change and meeting new friends, most assuredly a universal concern of all persons regardless of age. Worthy of note are stories about the adjustment of immigrant children to new customs and associates, especially those pertaining to their classmates in their new school. Both *Angel Child, Dragon Child*, written by Michele Maria Surat and illustrated by Vo-Dinh Mai, and *Molly's Pilgrim*, written by Barbara Cohen and illustrated by Michael Deraney, are sensitive portrayals of children's concerns about these matters when they and their families emigrate to the United States. The combination of the accomplished text and the impressionistic drawings in *Angel Child, Dragon Child* provide a memorable story of the challenges that confront a Vietnamese girl's adjustment to life in the United States. Readers are presented with diverse interpretations of the term "pilgrim" in *Molly's Pilgrim*, which tells what happens when Molly is told to dress a doll as a Pilgrim for a Thanksgiving display in school and her mother dresses the doll as she herself dressed before emigrating to America from Russia to seek religious freedom, stating that she is a modern pilgrim. In both stories the authors and illustrators convincingly depict how the immigrant children's relationships with their schoolmates affect their self-concepts and their relationships with their parents.

If one is to offer books to help children understand and value the cultural puralism that characterizes this nation, individuals from the diverse groups of which it is constituted should be depicted participating in or functioning according to the traditions and shared experiences most commonly related to the members of that culture group. For example, in the research conducted by Rosalie Black Kiah[1] it was found that among the salient shared experiences of black people, strong kinship bonds are valued, but protective attitudes toward kin and others who are not blood related are also exhibited. Often blacks augment the nuclear family by taking kin and people not related by blood into their homes. Furthermore, there is considerable flexibility in the roles assumed within the family, the emphasis being on the importance of the role rather than on who performs it. Thus, in stories about blacks, traditions should be portrayed so that the reader will recognize the positive and negative consequences these traditions and attitudes have upon the people who are forced or choose to retain them in their lifestyle or code of ethics.

It should be pointed out that the illustrator can and should present appropriate traditions and shared experiences, too. Unfortunately, research solidly demonstrates that there are proportionately few books in which authors or illustrators actually portray and come to grips with the salient shared experiences and traditions of any one minority people. Most of the books about minorities depict members of these diverse groups in universal experiences. However, there are some fine examples to be found among the contemporary books for children in which the illustrators do depict the salient shared experiences and traditions of minorities.

Noteworthy is the technique used by book illustrator Carole Byard to

1. Rosalie Black Kiah, "A Content Analysis of Children's Contemporary Realistic Fiction about Black People in the United States to Determine If and How a Sampling of These Stories Portrays Selected Shared Experiences of Black People." Unpublished Ph.D. dissertation, Michigan State University, East Lansing, Michigan, 1976.

simulate the impression of a dream in Eloise Greenfield's *Africa Drea-min* which young readers vicariously experience the same dream the black child in the story has about the people and places of Africa long ago. It is a technique that is really quite sophisticated, actually almost surrealistic. Nonetheless, the thoroughly accomplished blend of ex-pressionistic, grease-pencil drawings and well-written text offers young readers an insightful and convincing portrayal of African life and culture, past and present. Readers are bound to recognize and appreciate this commentary about the heritage of black people and treasure the basis for ancestral pride. In *Cornrows* by Camille Yar-brough, yet another fine book illustrated by Carole Byard, one finds an artistic dramatization of warm family relationships and some distinc-tive facets of African heritage and traditions. Each night the children's Mama and Great-Grammaw told "some se-ri-ous, dy-no-mite stories" that explained how the symbols used in the design of the royal stools and sculptured ware, the ritual masquerades, and how hair was braid-ed indicated one's clan, village, social status, and gods.

Terry Latterman, author and illustrator of *Little Joe, a Hopi Indian Boy, Learns a Hopi Indian Secret,* reveals *some* (not all) aspects of initiation of young Hopi Indian males into the Powamu society, a ceremony that is the first step a child takes on the path to adulthood. (Notice I emphasized that only some aspects of the initiation rights are revealed; there are some aspects of these rights that Powamu traditions and beliefs restrict to members of their society only and, thus, may not be revealed to non-Indians.) The illustrations, which are pen-and-ink sketches with earth- and turquoise-color overlays, depict in a very general way some of the things that one might associate with this Native American group from the southwestern United States, for ex-ample, their architecture and the designs and symbols on their pottery, clothing, and weaving.

Shared Experiences and Literary Forms

Children can be introduced to the diversities of humankind in stories, poetry, and factual accounts of the events and accomplish-ments that occurred in years past or that are now taking place, but in distant, foreign lands. Admittedly, children live in the present, in the here and now, with little appreciation or understanding of what the future may offer—except for the span of a day, a week, or perhaps a season. And, as the noted historical fiction writer Eric Haugaard said in a speech to the participants of the eleventh Loughborough International Seminar on Children's Literature at Framingham (Massachusetts) State College on August 5, 1978, a child's life is divided into periods. For example, everything that has taken place before the child was born is put into a time frame—not unlike the academicians' prehistoric times—that, in fact, is difficult for the child to think of as a reality. This response would explain why literary forms are useful when such a lack of imagination prevents us from learning from the experience of others. Literary forms enable us to learn from experience by providing messages that give meaning to the clutter in everyday and expressions.

The concept of cultural pluralism, supported (at least in theory) by a growing number of people in the United States and throughout the world, is fostered by the present trend to publish specific kinds of picture books.

Modern Realistic Fiction. Modern realistic fiction (also called contemporary realistic fiction and here-and-now stories) is set in contemporary times; everything that happens in the story could indeed happen or has happened to someone in today's world. The experiences depicted may be universal experiences—they could happen to anyone in today's world regardless of social class, ethnicity, race, or gender. In contrast, they could be salient shared experiences—experiences that are quite likely to occur to people in today's world *because* of their social class, ethnicity, race, or gender. Children seem to enjoy picture books in the modern realistic fiction genre because, in many respects, the characters seem so much like themselves. They can easily identify with the characters and experience vicariously, to a significant extent, feelings and thoughts comparable to those the characters had in response to particular conflicts or circumstances. Identification and personal involvement with the book characters are essential if readers are to gain even the least bit of pleasure and enjoyment from reading literature. In these stories readers will find characters who tend to have interests and problems comparable to their own. Thus, they might realize that their problems and their responses are not unique. A fine example of modern realistic fiction in the picture book form is *I Need a Lunch Box,* written by Jeannette Caines and illustrated by Pat Cummings. Preschoolers are bound to identify with the little boy in this story who, though not yet in school, wants to own a lunch box like his older sister, who is going to start first grade. The full-color, realistic illustrations seem just right for this credible here-and-now story. Modern realistic fiction can also extend children's horizons, for it can be used to broaden their background of knowledge about human behavior and show them how they might deal with unforeseen events or conflicts in their own lives. *The Accident,* written by Carol Carrick and illustrated by Donald Carrick, depicts a boy's response to the death of his much loved dog when it is hit by a truck. The impressionistic, line and watercolor-wash illustrations seem to add even more emotional intensity to the realistic story. Readers who have experienced the death of a beloved pet will fully recognize the depth of feeling and range of emotions depicted in this very credible here-and-now story. Merely reading such a story might not lessen one's anguish should something comparable happen, but a story like *The Accident* might at least prompt children to recognize that their feelings and emotions about their pet's death are not abnormal.

One will notice that the illustrations in the modern realistic picture books are truly varied, ranging from the almost photographic representational or realistic style to the fairly abstract impressionistic art style, from the stylized, expressionistic to cartoon-style drawings and the naive-art-style illustrations. This is a good trend, for it serves as an effective way to expose children to the various styles of art. Logic suggests that this exposure would help the children to become more appreciative and perhaps even more discriminating in their response to book art in particular and the visual arts in general. Another value of the diversity of art style used in modern realistic fiction is that it dramatizes the fact that not only do individuals respond to life's experiences in diverse ways, but they also express their responses to these experiences in diverse ways. As subtle as this message may be, thoughtful readers of the words and pictures in these picture books can indeed grasp that very message. Catherine Deeter's meticulous, realistic acrylic paintings accompany Alice Walker's haunting, first person story *To Hell with Dying,* which is about a special relationship between a girl and man who was a neighbor and close friend of her family. In contrast, one will notice that accomplished, impressionistic watercolor paintings by Chihiro Iwasaki heighten the emotions inherent in the innermost thoughts expressed by the small heroine of *Staying Home Alone on a Rainy Day* when she is home alone for the first time during a rain storm. Karen Barbour's expressionistic paintings in *Flamboyan* are done in rich, warm colors with watercolor and gouache and suggest an uninhibitedness and vitality quite in keeping with the exuberant, free-spirited heroine from the Caribbean that Arnold Adoff describes in his imagery-filled, poetic prose. Cartoon art, always popular with children, is the style that Caroline Bucknall uses in her illustrations for *One Bear in the Picture;* it seems to add just the right touch of exaggerated to this story about the series of frustrations the young hero experiences when his attempts to keep clean for the class photograph are foiled. Naive-style paintings were created by Frane Lessac for Charlotte Pomerantz's *The Chalk Doll,* a convincing account of a mother telling her bedridden child about growing up in Jamaica in a poor and loving family. One will discover an amazing array of surprises in the surrealistic pictures that Anthony Browne made for Annalena McAfee's *The Visitors Who Came to Stay,* a believable account of a child's feelings of resentment when her divorced father's girlfriend and her young son move in with them. Folktales from almost any national, religious, or ethnic group are now being adapted, illustrated, and published as picture books. Effective also in transmitting this concept of cultural pluralism are the many modern literary pieces that are being created as picture books, be these historical fiction, modern realistic fiction, modern poetry, fantasy, or informational literature.

Historical Fiction. In some picture books, one finds stories in which there is a healthy blend of fiction and history that permits the reader to view the past as vital, dramatic, and emotionally significant. In picture books about the past, the reader's interest should focus on the historical person, the period, or the event itself, not on the story per se. Historical stories should be typified by a realistic spirit, factual accuracy, and an imaginative (not a preordained) unfolding of events.

It is hoped the stories about people, periods of time, and events of the past may help children to discover that history generally consists of people doing things, reacting to environmental conditions, and seeking ways to solve problems in the face of truly insurmountable or challenging circumstances. Most often the illustrators of this kind of picture book are scholarly and respect themselves and their audience to the extent that the graphics they produce to accompany the stories authentically recreate the historical period, person, or event.

A very special historical fiction book for the younger reader is *The Leatherman,* written and illustrated by Dick Gackenbach. This true story, told with feeling and sensitivity, is about an eccentric traveler who, for thirty-one years in the late 1800s, came to Mill City every thirty-four days, always on schedule, always clad in a leather suit, and speaking to no one. This odd behavior made people curious about who he was and why he continued his endless wandering, traveling in a circle throughout the Connecticut hills, into New York State, and back again. The reader, too, is intrigued by his ways and some answers to these questions about the Leatherman are given. However, like so many other historical matters, some questions have to be left unanswered.

A unique historical event is recorded in *Joshua's Westward Journal*, written by Joan Anderson and illustrated with black-and-white photographs by George Ancona. Numerous, vivid details describe the realities of the family's courageous, challenging, and sometimes frightening trip westward on the National Road in 1836 in a horse drawn Conestoga wagon from their home in Indianapolis to a small town in Illinois. Words and photographs in this informative book offer an insightful and thought-provoking comment about some of the people that helped make America (especially the Midwest) what it is today. One might enjoy comparing *Joshua's Westward Journey* with *Cassie's Journey: Going West in the 1860's,* which was written by Brett Harvey and illustrated by Deborah Kogan Ray. This is an historical fiction picture book story about hardships, dangers, and pleasant experiences a little girl and her family had as they traveled as part of a wagon train from Illinois to California. Black, grease-pencil sketches illustrate this memorable story, and a very simple topographical map is included to show the route that Cassie and her family followed during the westward migration.

There are informational books about aspects of the past as well as books about contemporary people and things far removed from the child's here-and-now world. In any informational book, facts are presented. In the main, these facts should be specific in nature and should be presented in a manner that is logical, simple, and direct. If interpretation of these facts is ambiguous or debatable, the reader should be alerted. Furthermore, the material in factual picture books should be presented in a manner that will motivate the reader to seek more information about the subject.

The text and the illustrations in *A Peaceable Kingdom: The Shaker Abecedarius*, written and illustrated by Alice and Martin Provensen, offer children a fascinating and insightful glimpse of Shaker life in New England during the period from 1774 through the late 1800s. The illustrations are naive-style paintings, a style of art often found in the pictures painted by the people living in New England during this time. In this ingenious, exquisitely designed alphabet book one finds mouth-filling names of real and fanciful animals in the first line of each of the twenty-six lines of rhymed verse, just as there were in the abecedaries used by the Shaker children when they were taught to read. The pictures, showing the various routines and activities typical of the people living in the Shaker community, are informative and portray the attitude of devotion, industry, and compatibility that pervaded this religious community.

In *The Way to Start a Day* by Byrd Baylor, a deceptively simple statement about how people all over the world in times past started the day, Peter Parnall has created precise and elegant, expressionistic, line-and-wash illustrations for his interpretations of this very sophisticated picture book. One will notice that the shapes created by the lines and color—or lack of color—within each double-page picture are smaller pictures that are creatively integrated; the drawings of the people have a graceful, flowing quality and their smallness is in perfect proportion to the natural surrounding. The contents and themes of both of these factual books are for readers well beyond what we used to think of as picture book age range; they would be enjoyed and appreciated most by children ten and older.

Distant Places. There are many picture books about people who live in distant lands and who, because of isolation or conditions of climate, governmental rule or religious beliefs, for example, have lifestyles dramatically different from those of children in the United States. Very comparable to the task of bridging the gap between the past and the present is the task of learning about and coming to terms with "other people," whose lifestyles, beliefs, and values differ from ours due to geographical, sociological, and cultural factors.

In one, an autobiographical account entitled *Peter Pitseolak's Escape from Death,* the story of people's struggle with adverse weather and a harsh environment is elegantly depicted. Translated by Eva Keleotak Deer and Lucy Carriere, and edited by Dorothy Eber, this is an engrossing, authentic account of a harrowing walrus hunt during which Eskimo artist Peter Pitseolak and his stepson Ashevak were caught on a huge ice floe that was swiftly moving out to sea. The naive-style drawings made with felt pen, crayon, and pencil, combine with the moving story to provide readers with a rare glimpse of a slice of contemporary life vastly different from what they have experienced—one worth knowing about if only to contrast it with their own.

Author-artist Ted Harrison created two choice informational books in *Children of the Yukon* and *A Northern Alphabet.* Both books are illustrated with flat, bright, and full-color, naive-style paintings. In *Children of the Yukon,* the illustrations and the authoritative text offer an array of thought-provoking facts about the year in various Yukon settlements. The book emphasizes how the climate and the geography of the Yukon region influence the lifestyles of the people who live there. In *A Northern Alphabet* Harrison depicts cultural aspects of the people living across North America north of the sixtieth parallel, and in some cases as far south as the fifty-fifth parallel. Each picture contains things beginning with a single letter of the alphabet pertaining to life in the Yukon. The text consists of a literal statement about the picture that appears to serve primarily as a story starter, for each picture tells so much more than the text does. Each picture is framed with a strip of more words that pertain to the Yukon but are not shown in the picture. So, readers are encouraged to seek other books to find out what these enrichment words included in the frame mean, thus continuing to learn even more about the Yukon.

Literature can alert children to their immediate world and can also serve as a vehicle to new and more expansive environments. Thus, picture books may explain, in terms young readers can understand and identify with, what is happening in their world—why and how and when it really happens. Works of fiction, prose, and nonfiction offer young readers different ways of learning the meanings and possibilities of life and nature, encouraging them to actively respond not only to what they see, hear, smell, taste, and touch in the immediate world, but also, to some extent, to learn how and why they respond as they do to these sensory experiences. Picture books can help children become vitally alert and more fully functioning human beings.

Informational Writing. The children's world and their responses to it can be viewed through informational writing. In the main, fiction and poetry permit readers to know by experiencing their world through their emotions, by presenting responses to interpretations of existence that readers infer from the story's events, and with which they can identify. In other words, facts are placed within a setting of personal significance and elicit responses by means of affective domain. Informational writing, on the other hand, primarily presents facts and ideas directly and logically. Responses tend to be cognitive and less personal, even though factual picture books may present, directly or indirectly, an attitude toward the significance of the existence (or lack of existence) of a fact or idea.

The forms and patterns in nature are celebrated in *To Look at Any Thing,* a unique collection of poetry Lee Bennett Hopkins compiled to accompany the black-and-white photographs by John Earl. In yet another, Byrd Baylor not only alerts readers of *Guess Who My Favorite Person Is?* to the many facets of their world, but she also emphasizes that they are to respect the different ways each of us responds to the sights, sounds, smells, tastes, and textures we encounter.

So many of the concept books for children in the two- to four- or five-year-age range are simplistic and patronizing, hardly worth the paper they are printed on. Some excellent concept books are available, though. An example of one that never talks down and is written and illustrated in a manner that even the toddler can enjoy and understand is *Look Around! A Book about Shapes* written and illustrated by Leonard Everett Fisher. This stunning concept book is well within the comprehension and interest level of the toddler and nursery-school-age children; it can also stretch their thinking and their interests and make them more alert to what is in the world around them. The text presents a thoroughly accurate and understandable description that defines each of the basic shapes. Each shape is shown alone and then in a familiar scene. In each case readers are asked to compare and contrast one shape with another and are encouraged to look for more examples of these shapes after they have finished reading the book. To stretch readers even more, Fisher includes some of the less common shapes at the back of the book and the names (but not the descriptive definitions) that accompany each of these shapes. One hopes that this will motivate readers to remember the names of each of these shapes, to look for them in things around them, just as they did with the easier, more commonly seen shapes.

Picture books that present factual information about the basic characteristics of people, plants, and animals are also being produced. With this information youthful readers may come to realize and appreciate the value and beauties that life has to offer; they are not so likely to be thwarted by what may be viewed as unreasonable expectations or shocked by the unexpected. Perhaps, such books will help children learn to adapt to nature in ways that are compatible rather than in conflict with it.

Awe of and reverence for life are evident in *Panda* by Susan Bonners, a captivating and hauntingly lovely picture book in which the author-artist details the life cycle of the panda. The antics of this animal, the scenes of the icy mountains, the wildflowers, and much more are depicted with artistic excellence in blue, black, and white watercolor on wet paper.

To help children grasp the full meaning and significance of the assorted facts presented about the panda in this book, Bonners has made many comparisons with aspects of the reader's own world. Nancy Larrick's exceptional compilation of poems in *Cats Are Cats* and Ed Young's superb, impressionistic illustrations, done in charcoal and pastel on wrapping paper, capture the very essence of so many aspects about cats. This is one of the most elegant picture books I have seen, and even though elegance is hardly popular, this is bound to be an exception. Even readers of *Cats Are Cats* who are not cat-lovers can hardly help appreciating the beauty of cats, their grace, intelligence, charm and so much more. Wouldn't it be nice if such an elegant picture book about dogs were available, too?

Imagination and Fantasy. A great many educators view the development of imaginative thinking as a major goal of the educative process, and fanciful fiction, whether in the form of folktales, myths and legends, or modern fantasy, is recognized as an important means of nourishing a child's imagination. The ability to think imaginatively is important for various reasons. It is, first of all, a crucial ingredient of all creative endeavors which, in turn, are necessary for the continued progress of civilization. Imaginative thinking evoked by reading enables children to develop a notion of credibility about themselves and their immediate world. It helps them view the real world in better perspective, understand why and how things happen, and cope with life in a wholesome and positive manner. Fanciful fiction also affords readers a temporary but actual escape from the tedium and pressures they frequently face. Finally, fantasy is important for its own sake—for the enchantment, excitement, and exhilaration it provides.

Beautifully illustrated versions of familiar and unfamiliar folktales abound. A traditional form of expression handed down through the ages, each folktale links present-day young readers with the culture of past generations. In folktales are to be found commentaries on humanity's dreams, aspirations, frailties, basic strengths, and emotions. Some identify the absurdities of life and help children to laugh at themselves and their condition. Reading and thinking about the themes of folktales will help children find some answers to their questions about themselves and about the human experience in general.

Most folktales contain elements of fantasy along with the morals, beliefs, ideals, traditions, and humor espoused by the peoples or cultures from whom such stories have evolved. Currently, a proliferation of folktales from these multifarious sources is being published, books that can help young readers to appreciate folkways other than their own. Consider, for example, how a child might respond to the statement, "When we die, all that remains is the story," a point of view rooted in Taoist tradition and the theme of *White Wave*, the Chinese folktale told by Diane Wolkstein and illustrated with Ed Young's elegant, impressionistic, black-and-white drawings.

The humorous cumulative narrative verse by Audrey Wood and the full-page, animated, oil paintings by Don Wood are most expertly blended in *The Napping House*. Children are absolutely delighted when people and creatures literally accumulate on a cozy bed in a napping house and by the commotion and turmoil that occurs when a wakeful flea bites the slumbering mouse. Be assured, it will take little or no time before children listening to *The Napping House* read aloud will join in the litany about people and creatures piling on one another, then removing themselves as they wake each other up.

Variants of folktales on the same theme can be useful in our pluralistic society to help children see that people everywhere are much alike in some ways, even when they are obviously different in others. One might have the children compare and contrast the "Cinderella" motifs as they originated in different countries, noting how the various ethnic aspects from each of these culture groups influenced the details of the stories: What character held the magic power? How did the two main characters meet? How were they separated? What did the Cinderella figure lose? How were they reunited? What happened to the Cinderella figure's family after she married the man she grew to love? Thus, one could use these and other questions when comparing and contrasting the French variant of this motif found in *Cinderella* (based on Perrault's retelling), retold in English and illustrated by Errol LeCain; the German variant found in the Grimm brothers *Cinderella,* retold in English and illustrated by Nonny Hogrogian; the Chinese variant, Ai-Ling Louie's retelling *Yeh-Shen* which is illustrated by Ed Young; and the Vietnamese variant, *In the Land of the Small Dragon*, retold in English by Ann Nolan Clark and illustrated by Tony Chen. John Steptoe tells an African version of the Cinderella motif in *Mufaro's Beautiful Daughters.*

A fairly large number of stories in picture-book form may be classified as modern fantasy. Actually, only a small percentage of these are typified by good storytelling and lively imagination, two important qualities that must be evident in a tale of fantasy or whimsy if it is to stimulate the reader to engage in imaginative and creative thinking to any significant extent. Magic of one kind or another may be the principal ingredient of fanciful stories in picture-book form. Most often picture-book fantasies present familiar animals or inanimate objects that are endowed with human qualities and extraordinary as well as ordinary creatures that possess remarkable powers. In still other fantasies, new and unusual worlds are created.

Personification of animals is perhaps the most common kind of modern fantasy in picture books, but one will also find many stories in which objects (especially toys) are given human qualities. An excellent example of story in which an animal is given human qualities is *Pos-*

sum Magic, written by Mem Fox and illustrated by Julie Vivas. Hush, a young possum, became invisible when she was fed "people food" by Grandma Poss. When Hush wanted to become visible Grandma Poss realized that she had forgotten the spell to make Hush reappear. The cartoon-style drawings and the carefully written but easy-to-read text help readers keep up with Grandma Poss and Hush as they travel all over Australia in search of the right food. The very names of the foods mentioned in *Possum Magic* will intrigue most American children, but just in case they want to know what a vegemite sandwich is, or what pavlova and lamington are, they need only refer to the glossary at the back of the book. Better yet, they can get a copy of *Grandma Poss Cookbook,* which contains some easy-to-make recipes for the tasty people foods that Hush ate in her attempt to be visible again.

There is no paucity of fanciful tales about extraordinary creatures or even ordinary creatures who possess extraordinary powers. A fun-filled fantasy about how a leprechaun outsmarted a man who thought he had put this solitary fairy in a position that would force him to reveal the hiding place of his gold is found in *Clever Tom and the Leprechaun,* written and illustrated by Linda Shute. The cartoon-style watercolor paintings give this slight fantasy a specific setting and reiterate nicely the theme of oneupmanship and the upbeat mood.

Marilee Heyer's *The Forbidden Door* tells an unusual and haunting adventure set in an extraordinary world. The detailed text and the elaborate, full-page, fantasy-art display the underground world in which an evil monster has imprisoned a little girl and her relatives. The child has some harrowing adventures when she discovers the Forbidden Door to the Outside, but she manages to shatter the power of the evil monster and thus free herself and her relatives from their long imprisonment underground.

The Picture Book as Art

Webster defines art as the conscious skill and creative imagination in the production (or creation) of aesthetic objects. So, *literary* art is the conscious skill and creative imagination in the creation of a novel, a picture book, poem, or drama. The author and book illustrator are literary artists: authors tell their stories and create images with skillful and original use of words; book illustrators tell their part of the story and create images with skillful and original use of line and shapes, color and shading. Each kind of literary artist can stimulate the reader to extract from the images new meanings about aspects of the human condition that the author or illustrator choses to represent in the images created through carefully selected words or pictures.

If one agrees that literature is an art, then one must consider that whatever image of reality or aspect of the human condition is depicted in a novel, picture book, poem, or drama is an *illusion* of that reality. The image cannot be a mere mirroring if any aspect of life in it is truly a work of art. Artistic excellence is never identical with photographic accuracy, with a mirror reflection of aspects of the realities of the human condition. In a work of literary art (in the novel, picture book, poem, or drama), the writer or the book illustrator uses words or lines and shapes to create images that amount to a *selective interpretation* of the reality. The result of this selective interpretation is an *illusion* rather than a miniature reproduction of the reality that is depicted in or associated within the story. The illusionary image must be thoroughly identifiable and believable, yet it must not be exactly like life.

Inherent in an illusion is some amount of reality, for if it were ommitted entirely there would be complete abstraction; there certainly would be no story. The literary artist seldom portrays life as it is heard about or actually experienced. It is portrayed as the literary artist *wanted* to portray it—bigger or weaker perhaps, or more dramatic or tragic than it would be in real life. And that is as it should be.

The technique of selective interpretation to create an illusion might be likened to the view one gets when looking through windows in different rooms and from different sides of a building. Each glimpse of the outside world is limited by the shape and the placement of each of the windows. Likewise, the content, images, and themes that are depicted in the stories, poems, or drama by an author and the pictures of each book illustrator will be limited and shaped as the artists (writer or illustrator) engage in selective interpretation of aspects of the reality they choose to depict. Selectivity of interpretation evokes in the reader judgments about values and preferences.

What constitutes the "best" in literature for one person by no means coincides with another's idea of the best. The fact that one's response to literature is personal and subjective has repeatedly been made quite clear to me when my university-level students share their evaluations of the books they have read. I have also been reminded of this fact a number of times when I have served on various committees of professional organizations whose charge it is to identify titles that are distinguished or at least notable in one way or another. Members of each of these committees use specific criteria pertaining to the aspects of literary or graphic excellence when they evaluate the books. The people who have made up any one of these committees differ from one another in various ways: in personality and disposition, in professional experience and academic preparation, in their concepts of childhood, and in their own familiarity with adult and children's literature. Often each of us has named completely different titles as excellent. It is not too unusual, either, to have one committee member identify a selection as a great piece of literature and another committee member declare it to be quite ordinary or even mediocre.

The subjectivity of what constitutes the best in literature may be dramatized further by considering the diverse responses of literary reviewers and critics to *Harriet and the Promised Land*, written and illustrated by Jacob Lawrence. This picture book is a landmark among juvenile books dealing with black history and among picture books in which expressionistic paintings are used to illustrate the text, which is a narrative poem. Among the reviewers and critics who decided this book was addressed to a young reading audience and who were inclined to interpret the art as well as the text at the literal level, the responses were devastatingly negative. On the other hand, among those who recognized that the intended reading audience included mature and thoughtful juveniles and adults, the responses were very positive. Their comments indicated that they perceived that Jacob Lawrence expressed ideas and intense emotions and feelings by way of sophisticated, expressionistic paintings; that the narrative verse and the illustrations pertained to and commented about aspects of black history, the Old Testament in particular, and the human condition in general; and that the book's symbolism was associated with the intolerable, dehumanizing circumstances many present-day people face daily, as well as with the brutal conditions blacks endured during slavery.

We Be Warm Till Springtime Comes, written by Lillie Chaffin and illustrated by Lloyd Bloom, is one of the best picture books of this decade. The black-and-white, impressionistic, oil paintings, combined with the expressive, poetic prose, depict most convincingly the piercing cold winter, the family's love and respect for one another, as well as the sense of responsibility and courage that motivated the young boy to go out in the storm to gather fuel from a deserted coal mine so his family would have enough fuel for the fire to last through the night. At least one reviewer said that she and her staff would not recommend this picture book because it showed "a weak woman," that the mother should have gone out in the storm herself to gather the coal instead of depending on the male in the family, namely her young son. In other words, she said that *We Be Warm Till Springtime Comes* is a sexist book. This charge is without foundation. It is quite clear that the mother could not go out into the storm; she did not have a pair of warm shoes, and her son did. Such realities exist! One does not find a weak woman in this story. One finds a woman without the necessary kind of clothing. Furthermore, one might well ask, even if she were fortunate enough to have had the right kind of shoes to go out into the storm, what is wrong with a child, as old as the boy in this story obviously was, assuming responsibility? *We Be Warm Till Springtime Comes* depicts some definite possibilities in life; indeed, realities that some people could well (even do) experience. Whether or not they are caused by circumstances that are due to sexism is not the issue. They could and do exist and are part of the human experience. They are, therefore, proper fare for literature. Unfortunately, the issue of sexism in literature is not one that can be discussed at great length here, but I would like to discuss it briefly.

What constitutes "the correct" or "proper" image of the female (or of the male) is a timely topic, and it is not a question for which one will find a simple answer. Sexism is a concern that book selectors must be informed about and should consider when selecting books for use with children. I would like to think that by this point in time we are sensitive enough and possess enough knowledge about the damaging affects of sexism to reject it as much as possible—in life and in the language and illustration included in the literature we offer children. But let us not label something sexist unless it really is! Sexism is not just a woman's issue, it is a human issue. In this context we must be well aware of the implications and the ramifications of our language with reference to the images of girls and boys, women and men created in literature (or elsewhere). Both our language and the images created must enable persons to see themselves and others as free, unique human beings. With the change in the concept of femaleness there has occurred a change in the concept of males; these changes affect the extent to which common needs of men and women are polarized, differentiated, or viewed as substantially the same in terms of human (not sexual) needs. The tough, strong, aggressive, macho male has become one who is self-confident, successful, willing to fight for family and beliefs with warmth, gentleness. These men, like women, can at times be vulnerable, frightened, and capable of using their inner resources to cope and adapt, and thus survive. They do not have to be rugged and domineering to be heroic; they can, at times, be weak and submissive, and at other times be independent, self-assertive, compassionate, sensitive, and evidence the gamut of human emotions, feelings, and needs. A woman on the other hand, does not need to live and act like a macho male. Nor does she have to be self-obsessed, headstrong, and difficult. She does not have to succeed in areas once thought to be strictly areas for the opposite sex to be considered a successful woman.

Criteria for Evaluating a Picture Book

More than story, illustration raises questions of aesthetics. These, too, are debatable. There is no surefire recipe for looking at and evaluating book illustrations. There is, nonetheless, a fundamental approach one can follow to examine book illustration. First and foremost, one must consider book illustrations works of art. (*Art* as described on pages 25-26.) From that point, it might be well to follow the procedure below, as described by Roger Fry in *Last Lectures* (Beacon Press, 1962), which calls for confining one's attention to the very basic aesthetic qualities and then comparing a number of different works to see to what extent they possess or lack these qualities. Keep in mind that although the qualities are discussed below as separate entities, they are interdependent and interactive. These basic qualities are *sensibility* and *vitality*. Marcia Brown elaborates on them in *Lotus Seeds: Children, Pictures, and Books* (Scribner, 1986) as does Lyn Lacy in *Art and Design in Children's Picture Books* (American Library Association, 1986).

Sensibility. When considering the quality of sensibility, look at the composition of the illustrations, that is the relationship of the artistic elements (line, color, light and dark, shape and space) to each other and to the whole. These elements are combined to determine such characteristics as order and harmony, and are evidenced in the overall design of the picture. Style, which will be discussed below, comprises the patterns that order and harmony can take. Sensibility also includes the characteristics of variety and the uniqueness that express the artist's feelings and sensitivity in executing the overall design and idea. An artist will not so much adhere to styles as adapt them. To get at these aspects of the quality of sensibility, ask questions such as the following when examining the illustrations:

How appropriate are all of the artistic elements in the illustrations to the spirit that pervades throughout the story? Do they comply with the mood, pace, or attitude of the human experience that is depicted and commented upon in the story?

Do the artistic elements reveal something new or evoke a more intense response every time one looks at the illustrations?

Do treatments of the illustrations vary from page to page? Especially important here, is whether or not the illustrations vary in content, size, shape, use of color, and placement from page to page.

Is there a pleasing interplay and balance between pictures and type?

Admittedly, one's response to color and color harmony is very personal; nonetheless, are the choice and use of color appropriate to the mood of the story and are they interesting? How effectively does the contrast or graduation of value in colors and color forms (tones, shades, and tints) imply contour, texture, and depth to the shapes in the pictures.

Is there discernible buildup in the dramatic interest of the pictures? Does it reflect the buildup of tension around the conflict? Does this buildup of tension also reflect the changes in mood or personality of the characters if the story requires it?

Do the illustrations of the characters evidence observable, individual qualities of all people, including minorities, so that stereotyping is avoided?

Vitality. When considering the quality of vitality, look for characteristics that focus on the timelessness or the lasting quality of the details of the illustrations, the aura or mood that lingers in one's mind after the illustrations have been viewed. To leave a distinct impression, artists must be original. Only this way can they be authentic. In this lies their strength. To get to these aspects of the quality of vitality, ask questions such as the following when examining the illustrations:

Is there rhythm of line, of movement, of shape and mass in each of the drawings? How has the rhythm been adapted to keep with the tenor and pace of the text?

Do the illustrations not only encourage the reader to look at them, but also add more to the readers' minds and imaginations than the readers would have been able to gain from the text alone? This means that the illustrations should not be too sophisticated or photographically perfect.

Is each picture alive and complete by itself on the page, yet when combined with the other illustrations in the book, does it amount to something much more?

Focusing on these questions when looking at picture books, or any illustrated books for that matter, will give readers the potential to develop powers of discrimination and enrich their literary experiences. Children (even as young as age three) can be taught how to look at the illustrations in their picture books to find answers to these questions. The questions must be worded, of course, so that the children can understand them and should be asked after the children have had numerous experiences enjoying stories for the satisfying and pleasant literary experiences they offer.

So with these considerations in mind, criteria were formulated to select the titles identified in this revised and enlarged edition of PICTURE BOOKS FOR CHILDREN. The four general criteria guiding the selection of the picture books listed in this edition were excellence in overall literary quality; excellence of execution in the artistic techniques employed; excellence of pictorial interpretation of story elements; and excellence of presentation for the intended audience—children. The more specific criteria applied to the evaluation of the books were as follows: that pictures that illustrate a literary selection must convey and enhance the author's meaning, ideas, and moods beyond the merely literal approach to visual communication, stimulating and encouraging the individuality and imagination of the viewers of the book art; that the book art in turn has to exhibit the individuality—the personal style—of the illustrator. It is important that the result of this union between the author and the book artist should be a oneness (like partners in a marriage), that oneness occurring as a result of becoming wholesome contrasts or blissful and compatible similarities. Whatever the combination of individual entities of words and illustrations, the union must result in something that is typified by a unique and beautiful whole. Neither partner in this marriage may be more or less important than the other; each must contribute a full share to the literary work, namely the picture book.

Since these criteria, general and specific, seem objective enough and even readily implementable, one might suppose that whoever used them to evaluate books for inclusion in a collection would identify the same titles. This has not yet happened nor is it likely to, for interpretation and implementation of these or any other criteria are ultimately personal and subjective. Frequently, disagreements that book selectors might have about the quality of a picture book rests on their response to what the well-known artist and illustrator Ben Shahn referred to as "the shape of the content"—that is to say, the style of art that is used to create the pictures rather than the picture's content.

Striking contrasts in art styles (to say nothing of the topics dealt with, the writing styles, themes, and moods of these books) are immediately apparent when one compares books published in any one period of time—especially when comparing those published at other, differing times. Children's books are being and have been illustrated in a variety of art styles, ranging from straightforward photographs and the realistic to the surrealistic, from the naive- and folk-art styles to the highly sophisticated, expressionistic, and abstract impressionistic art styles. Such variety is fine and should be encouraged. It dramatizes the existence of a wholesome diversity in artistic tastes as well as a wide range of sophistication and appreciation of literary art and fine art, too. This is as it should be, for total conformity in taste may be considered a vice rather than a virtue. To foster conformity suppresses development of independent thinking and inhibits development of talent and ability to express one's experience and feelings.

This is not to suggest that, by valuing diversity in taste rather than conformity, there are no generalizations, values, precedents, and traditions to keep in mind when evaluating children's literature. What I am saying is that there is considerable room for personal and individual response when deciding about the worth and beauty of the visuals and text of picture books, for there are many books currently available to today's children, which, if they are made available in our schools and libraries, will help foster a wholesome diversity in taste and cultivate positive images of self and of others in the children who read them.

Images of Minorities

Seldom if ever does one actually see in the real world firmly fixed attributes for all persons of a particular cultural, racial, national, or ethnic group. Therefore, the illustrations in a book about a single cultural or ethnic group should depict all types of people within that group. All black people do not reside in inner-city ghettos, all Mexican-Americans are not migrant workers, all Italians do not own and work in shoe repair shops or fruit stands, nor do all Chinese operate hand laundries or chop suey parlors. Although the features of most ethnic and racial minority groups are often identifiable, nonetheless, within each of these groups, individuals will display a wide variety of facial traits. What the illustrator must do is highlight both common and unique features when depicting ethnic or racial characters. Between blandness and sterotyping there lies the artistic realm of authenticity. If one is to view oneself in an adequate and positive manner, it is important that the self and others one sees portrayed in books should be depicted in a manner that will permit one to recognize the self or other as a member of a particular racial or ethnic group as well as an individual with unique features, stature, and body build. For that reason, there should be illustrations that offer each member of each of our diverse cultural groups a fair abundance of models upon which to build a valid and positive self-image. There are numerous picture books about diverse ethnic and racial groups included in this edition of PICTURE BOOKS FOR CHILDREN, although the percentage of all the picture books about minorities that have been published in recent years is shamefully miniscule. We are indeed fortunate to have such books as *Flamboyan, Now Sheba Sings the Song,* and *Aekyung's Dream.* In *Flamboyan,* the reader meets a modern Caribbean Island girl through Arnold Adoff's imagery-filled, poetic prose and Karen Barbour's large, vibrant, expressionistic, watercolor and gouache paintings. (This book should be read aloud to get the full benefit of Adoff's exquisite, figurative and rhythmic language). Maya Angelou's sensuous poem in *Now Sheba Sings the Song,* which celebrates the strength and complexities of black women the world over, was inspired by drawings that Tom Feelings made of black women at random over the course of twenty-five years. Together the poem and his illustrations, more than any other picture book that I am aware of, show black women, as Feelings said, "as different, separate, and individual." The features of various members of the Korean family, as well as their cultural traditions, are depicted most aptly in Min Peak's *Aekyung's Dream.*

It is also vital that the reader's concept of others be positively strengthened by seeing an individual of any race or ethnic group portrayed in a variety of realistic situations, at the same time exhibiting features and qualities unique to that person. Such illustrations permit the reader to react to and identify with each book character as an individual and help to avoid any unconscious preconditioning that could lead to stereotyping and scapegoating. When children learn to understand, respect, and accept diversity, they will neither fear nor view with disdain differences in color, status, or lifestyle.

Research has amply demonstrated the effect illustrations have on their viewers, that book illustrations are important and effective means by which readers may learn facts, attitudes, and values—not only about self, but also about others. An illustration can show readers new ways of seeing; it can sharpen (as well as shape) their point of view; it can help provide a deeper understanding of the relationships between people who may have backgrounds similar to or different from the readers. It is important, therefore, for book selectors to keep in mind that the illustrations in the books should portray facts, attitudes, and values that will offer readers acceptable, authentic, positive images of individuals who are members of the many and diverse cultural, ethnic, and racial groups making up our society.

Style

Style is a term which refers to the configuration or gestalt of artistic elements that together constitute both a specific and a characteristically identifiable manner of expression. Style refers to the personal character or form that is recognizable in an artist's work because of his or her particular and consistent treatment of details, composition, and handling of a medium. Also, style refers to the manner that has developed and become standard within a culture or during a particular period of time. It is often difficult to identify a specific artistic character or style which is used by an individual artist or even by people in a particular era or culture. It is upon these broad characteristics that various styles of art have been labeled as surrealistic, representational, expression istic, impressionistic or as folk art, cartoon art, or naive art. Whenever the illustrations in a book are strongly suggestive of one of these art styles, I mention it in my description of that book. Following are brief statements describing each of these styles of art, along with one or two titles of picture books in which are to be found illustrations exemplifying these art styles.

Representational, or Realistic, Art. In representational, or realistic, art artists offer direct observations of the reality they have observed or experienced. To obtain a realistic visual interpretation, the artist strives for a somewhat photographic exactitude of detail, conveyed in recognizable shapes that are in proper perspective and proportion, though often actually not as detailed as the reality being depicted. Pat Cummings realistic pictures in rich, bright colors add vitality to Jeannette Caines *I Need a Lunch Box,* making even more credible all aspects of the here-and-now story that focuses on a little boy, not yet in school, who insists on having a lunch box like his older sister, who has started first grade. Realistic illustrations seem quite in keeping with the action and setting of *William and Boomer,* written and illustrated by Lindsay Barrett George. Double-page paintings in full-color watercolor, dyes, and colored pencil detail this account of how a little boy and a deserted baby goose become fast friends. The boy, the goose, the flora, and the fauna near and in the water where the two swam are depicted in striking graphics.

Surrealistic Art. Surreal pictures are composed to suggest the kind of images experienced in dreams, nightmares, or a state of hallucination, yet presented in as graphic a manner as possible. Most of the books published by Harlin Quist, the talented, advant-garde editor-publisher, are illustrated in this style of art. One title which is especially exemplary of surrealism (in the illustrations and in the text) is Eugene Ionesco's *Story Number 1,* translated by Calvin K. Towle and illustrated by Etienne Delessert. This is a wonderfully zany book that will often confuse adults, but it is just the thing for the "brand of humor" that is typical of three- or four-year-olds. Children to whom I have read this story delight in the marvelously zany play with words and the oversized, equally zany fantasy-oriented illustrations done in warm, bright colors.

Anthony Browne implemented surrealism to perfection with his illustrations for the Grimm brothers' *Hansel and Gretel.* He brought a modern setting to a story that one ordinarily envisions as happening long ago and far away. His story characters are drawn in a detailed, representational style, and they are clothed in contemporary dress (for example, the stepmother is shown wearing a fake fur coat and smoking a cigarette). The objects on the furniture and the furniture itself are associated with contemporary times—there is a television set, a bottle of Olay lotion is on the dresser, and a ladies nylon stocking is falling out of the dresser drawer. All this is presented in a straightforward manner rather than in a fantastic manner that Delessert used in the story discussed above. The unexpected juxtaposition of the setting creates a feeling of anti-realness, evoking unfamiliar feelings and a sense of unrealness. One will notice any number of visual images suggesting (according to Freudian psychology) children wanting to be independent of their parents (especially their mother), yet reluctant to let that happen: the ever-present birds throughout the book are used as a symbol for the children's development and progression; the cage and the patterns of bars (seen so obviously in the back of the dining chair, in the other pieces of furniture, and in the huge tree trunks, for example) are used as metaphors for the children's passive dependence. It is uncertain what, if any, effect all this visual symbolism will have on children, but Browne's use of it must be acknowledged and it all fits in with the surrealistic approach he used to illustrate this well-known fairy tale. He has certainly illustrated it with great originality.

Impressionist Art. Recognizing that the properties of light and color in the atmosphere permit one a view of nature that constantly changes, the impressionist artist strives to make fixed for all time that which was originally momentary, spontaneous, and transient. In impressionist art the composition is somewhat informal, the figures frequently appear marginal, colors are broken and juxtaposed and caused to mingle and thus mix in the eye of the viewer. The result is that the contours of the reality (be that reality a person, an object, or even a landscape) are softened and the illusion of mass bulk diminished. One is given the *impression* of a certain aspect of the reality rather than a sharp, detailed description of it. Chihiro Iwasaki's impressionistic illustrations are readily recognizable. In *Staying Home Alone on a Rainy Day* she applied her medium well. She highlights the most aqueous quality of her medium, using it as semi-transparent and varied in hue and carefully modulated. It is this very use of her medium that gives form to her images. There is only the impression or suggestion of the figure and facial features of the forms in her pictures—a balloon and the child playing the piano are all viewed from above or, in the case of the fish in the bowl or the child's face, are viewed at eye level. Also in the impressionist style are the fresh, bright, full-color paintings created by Susan Bonner to depict the sights Sarah and her mother see and talk about in *Sarah's Questions*, written by Harriet Ziefert. Bonner's paintings capture the instantaneous, personal impression that an alert and curious individual might well get when taking a leisurely walk on an open and spacious area on a sunny summer afternoon.

Expressionistic Art. Expressionism leans heavily toward abstraction in that it is intended to highlight the form of the reality, the essential or structural quality of the reality. Not only is it counter to academic or realistic art, but it is also concerned primarily with expressing the artist's subjective, emotional response to the reality that is seen or experienced. Often expressionistic art appears somewhat sophisticated and mature in its subjectivity and abstraction.

Examples of clearly expressionistic illustrations for *The Way to Start a Day,* the 1979 Caldecott Honor book written by Byrd Baylor, are elegant in their simplicity. Peter Parnall's free-flowing, uninhibited line drawings and flat colors are perfect accompaniments to and interpretations of Baylor's brief but profound verbal comments about the ways that people all over the world in times past and present welcome each new day. In sharp contrast are the elegant, expressionistic pictures that Lisbeth Zwerger made for O. Henry's "The Gift of the Magi." The full-page illustrations for this much loved, romantic classic short story are done in watercolor and reflect an early 1900s setting. Indeed the choice of colors and the fine, graceful lines that form the elongated and sharp features of the characters' faces and bodies are strongly suggestive of the Austrian expressionist artists of that era.

Naive Art. One gets the impression from a painting done in the naive style that the artist is ignorant of the technical aspects of depicting a reality in his or her painting. One also may be led to conclude that the artist rejects or is at least removed from artistic traditions, for in the art produced, no particular line of stylistics is developed. Instead, naive artists present the essence and the appearance of objects and scenes out of their own experience. Characteristic of naive art are simplification of what is seen and experienced, vitality and often awkward spontaneity, candidness, and intensity. The art of the naive is a pre-perspective art. The viewer notices that there occurs an almost universal adherence to frontal posture or profile and a disregard for anatomy and perspective that suggests either a fairly undeveloped level of consciousness or a lack of skill in expressing a consciousness, if indeed it exists.

Exemplary of naive book art is the work of Barbara Cooney and Peter Pitseolak, two artists with very different cultural backgrounds. Cooney's naive-style paintings in *Island Boy* are in full-color gouache and are perfectly compatible with the life style a small boy followed on the small island out in the bay of New England—from his childhood years well into his later years, when he was an old man and the grandfather of a boy who was not only named after him, but also followed the same lifestyle, loving the island and the sea that surrounded it. The naive drawings made by Peter Pitseolak, the well-known Eskimo artist, to illustrate a narrow escape from death that he and his son experienced while walrus hunting, are recorded in an autobiographical account entitled *Peter Pitseolak's Escape from Death*. Both books discussed above are illustrated in the naive-art style, yet each artist's drawings are starkly dissimilar in style, in content, and use of medium.

Folk Art. Folk art is a broad designation for the artistic expression of folk cultures found among isolated environments or communities in a geographical area inhabited by a dominant ethnic group. Evident in the artwork of any one folk culture would be identifiable traditions, motifs, symbols, treatment of line, modeling, color, volume, and space. There are as many folk art styles as there are folk cultures. With the proliferation of adaptations of folktales published each year, one will often find that the artists have included in their illustrations many of the characteristics found in the art of that particular folk culture who's variant of a folktale they are illustrating. In several of the books illustrated by Ed Young, are to be found thoroughly authentic graphic interpretations of Persian folk art and Chinese art. For example, one will find exotic Persian miniatures in *The Girl Who Loved the Wind*, an original tale written in the style of a folktale by Jane Yolen. Typical of the Persian miniatures, the perfected draftsmanship in Ed Young's collage pictures has much in common with children's drawings. The pictures contain a wealth of interesting detail, but the kinds of things that are detailed and the perspective and sense of proportion given to them are reminiscent of the way children portray things—with figures that are placed in different planes, in the "high horizon" convention, so that each is seen separately, and human figures, animals, and natural objects are portrayed as idealized symbols. In other words, they are presented in an elaborate but uncomplicated way. That beauty of line, the rich, warm tones in the colors used, and, most of all, a perfectionism typical of Persian art are seen in Ed Young's illustrations, too.

Young's illustrations for *Yeh-Shen: A Cinderella Story from China* retold by Ai-Ling Louie are done in pastels and watercolor. The jewel tones used throughout are really quite stunning. His pictures of the clothing, hairstyles, and jewelry worn by the Chinese nobility place the action for this story shortly before the time of Chin (200–206 B.C.). The illustrations are placed on panels, like those of the Chinese folding screen and an image of a fish or a portion of a fish is alluded to on each page. In this variant of the Cinderella motif, it is the bones of the fish, which Yen-Shen loved and her stepmother killed, that possess the source of magic.

Cartoon Art. In cartoon sketches the artist resorts to such techniques as slapstick, exaggerations, and absurdities depicting incongruities and incompatible characteristics or situations to the extent that laughter, or at least a smile, is evoked. There is no paucity of illustrations done in the cartoon style. One can count on Steven Kellogg to create detailed, whimsical cartoon-style illustrations for the original, humorous, and thoroughly fantastic adventures he creates. Especially noteworthy are the pencil line and watercolor-wash, cartoon-style illustrations he made for the chaotic adventures about the nutty Great Dane, named Pinkerton. These include *Tallyho Pinkerton!; Pinkerton, Behave; A Rose for Pinkerton;* and most recently, *Prehistoric Pinkerton*. He is also known for the ever favorite, science-fantasy picture book *The Mysterious Tadpole*. This is a cleverly written story of what happens when Louis receives what he thinks is a tadpole sent by his uncle from Loc Ness. The tadpole grows and grows and grows but never does turn into a frog as Louis' teacher said it would. The cartoon illustrations warrant careful and repeated examination!

THE ORGANIZATION OF THIS BOOK

The subject categories in PICTURE BOOKS FOR CHILDREN—Me and My Family, Other People, The World I Live In, and The Imaginative World—reflect such basic and common questions children may ask as "Who am I?" "Why am I like I am?" "What is life?" "What is the human experience?" and "What is my (the) world?" These are fundamental concerns of all children (of all humankind, for that matter) and are reflected in the categories making up this publication. Each category mixes realistic fiction and fanciful tales, informative books, and verse, for a child does not necessarily choose a book for the genre of literature it exemplifies. Rather, unwittingly or consciously, a child chooses a book perhaps for the mere appeal of its format, but more often because its title or content reflects a particular reading need or interest and suggests that the book might possibly bring the child closer to an answer to one or another of the questions mentioned above.

Literature can inform young readers about people who are like themselves in many ways but who look different, who live differently, and who subscribe to different moral, ethical, and religious codes. A picture, being a visual medium, constitutes an obvious and especially powerful means of illustrating the fact that all members of any one group of people are alike in some ways and different in some ways, too; that people are to be viewed as individuals and not lumped together under one faceless anonymity. We are all familiar with the metaphor "every picture is a window." It is this window provided by picture-book illustrations, together with the details in the text, that teaches the reader to respect simultaneously the likenesses as well as the uniqueness and diversities that typify people. Picture books can instill in the reader an appreciation for the challenge and exhilaration of being different from other human beings and, at the same time, provide comfort and a feeling of unity with everyone else who is part of our pluralistic society. Books in all sections show people as part of one family consisting of (1) individuals who, because they are alike in some ways, share universal experiences; and (2) individuals, who, though they are different from most people, still share these differences with other people (and thus have salient shared experiences). The participants in the Dartmouth Seminar, who were literature and language scholars from English-speaking countries, recommended that literature be used to introduce children to the paradoxes, complexities, and incongruities of life. To a large extent this can be accomplished by making accessible to children picture books that depict individuals engaging in and responding to universal experiences and salient shared experiences.

A gentle reminder is required here. The reader of the picture book must enjoy it in order to identify with and respond to its story line and characters. Furthermore, such emotional identification is likely to occur only when text and illustrations of the book radiate sincere human emotions, warmth, and hope, and when the aspect of the human condition being depicted is comparable to the readers' own experiences or are within their ability to understand. If emotional identification and enjoyment are experienced from the literary selection, then the reader may consciously (or, more likely, subconsciously) continue to read in order to find answers to basic human questions and concerns. Responsive children given a picture book that stimulates them to think beyond the literal level of the text and illustrations can have reading experiences that open boundless vistas to new thoughts and new worlds.

People do not become self-actualized and are not likely to come even near to realizing their actual potential, free to be individuals in the best sense, unless their very basic aesthetic and intellectual needs are met. Unfortunately, unless these needs are satisfied early, during one's developing years, one's cravings for knowledge and the beautiful are too often suppressed. Indeed, the levels of one's thinking powers will not be advanced nor one's aesthetic tastes be raised to any significant extent unless one has opportunities to experience the thought-provoking and the beautiful repeated in many different ways.

Thus, the development of "good taste" and the ability to recognize what is "best" or "beautiful" is acquired and dependent upon exposure to the best and the beautiful. Children, in their search for beautiful and satisfying literature (and picture books are a major genre of literature), will read whatever is at hand. Should they fail to find fine literature among the picture books accessible to them at home or in school and public library collections, their craving for it will soon wane; it is that easily extinguished. In all probability, the young people in whom this occurs will eventually read little, if any, literature except that which is required of them. On the other hand, it is quite likely that children will become avid and discriminating readers if satisfying, exciting, and quality literary selections are made readily accessible to them. For this reason, the concern that parents, teachers, and librarians have about making the best literature (including the best picture books) attainable to children is more than justified.

It is up to the book selectors, then, to make accessible to young people the best that is available, so that, although children will continue to choose books on the basis of their content, what they select from will be of merit—well written and fittingly illustrated.

Me and
My Family

Ackerman, Karen   *5–9*
SONG AND DANCE MAN   *YEARS*
    Illus. by Stephen Gammell. New York: Knopf, 1988.

An entertaining and refreshingly upbeat story, the 1989 Caldecott
Medal book, depicts a grandfather showing his grandchildren the
equipment he used when he was "a song and dance man": tap shoes,
bowler hats and top hats, bow ties and matching vests, a cane. To their
delight he performs parts of his vaudevillian acts, tapdancing, singing,
and cracking jokes to demonstrate what he so enjoyed doing "back in
the good old days." The highly stylized, expressionistic, colored pencil
drawings appear in full- and double-page spreads, aptly mixed
throughout the book. They are in full color and transmit the upbeat
mood as well as the warm feelings and respect the children and their
grandfather have for each other.

Adoff, Arnold   *5–9*
FLAMBOYAN   *YEARS*
    Illus. by Karen Barbour. San Diego: HBJ, 1988.

Imagery-filled, poetic prose depicts a little Caribbean island girl's
real world and fantasy world. Large, vibrant, expressionistic, watercolor and gouache paintings aptly reflect the essence of the island
setting—the climate, flora, and fauna.

Aleichem, Sholem   *4–8*
HANUKAH MONEY   *YEARS*
    Trans. and adapted by Uri Shulevitz and Elizabeth Shub. Illus. by
        Uri Shulevitz. New York: Greenwillow, 1978.

A masterpiece in which text and colorful illustrations tell a nostalgic
Yiddish story of a shtetl family's celebration of Hanukah, the Feast of
Lights. The two children and their family enjoy customs such as lighting the Hanukah lamp, eating the traditional pancakes, playing a game
called dreidel, and collecting Hanukah money as they celebrate this
holiday, which commemorates the rededication of the Temple in Jeru-
salem by Judas Maccabeus in 165 B.C.

Allen, Robert Thomas   *7–13*
THE VIOLIN   YEARS
    Photos by George Pastic. New York: McGraw-Hill-Ryerson, 1976.

44   Based on the award-winning motion picture of the same name by Andrew Welsh and George Pastic, this is a heartwarming, sentimental story about a young boy who learns, with the help of an old man, that the violin makes lovely music and that "nobody ever says goodbye who leaves the world beautiful music." The story includes the musical score for "Reminiscence," the old man's song, and more than fifty black-and-white photographs that were taken during the making of the film. The book was awarded the Ruth Schwartz Memorial Foundation Award by the Canadian Bookseller's Association in 1976.

Andrews, Jan   *6–9*
VERY LAST FIRST TIME   YEARS
    Illus. by Ian Wallace. Vancouver, Canada: Douglas & McIntyre, 1985.

A little Inuit girl is allowed to gather mussels alone for the very first time, on the seabed, under the ice, when the tide is out. She has no trouble filling her pan with mussels but gets so carried away with the shadows of the various creatures darting and skittering around her that she fails to realize she has overstayed her visit and the tide is coming in. The last few harrowing minutes are quite something for Eva (and the reader) to experience. The full-color, realistic paintings are very detailed and transmit a fine sense of place and ethnicity. All of the scenes of the little girl walking on the floor of the sea are double-page spreads. There are seven of them. The other scenes pertaining to aspects of this unique tale are full-page pictures. The illustrator was awarded the 1986 Amelia Frances Howard-Gibbon Medal by the Canadian Library Association.

Angelou, Maya   *11–18+*
NOW SHEBA SINGS THE SONG   YEARS
    Illus. by Tom Feelings. New York: Dutton/Dial, 1987.

Maya Angelou's sensuous poem celebrates the strength and complexities of black women the world over. It was inspired by an incredibly astute collection of drawings that Tom Feelings made of black women at random, wherever he happened to travel over the course of twenty-five years. The drawings, done in black line and sepia tones, accomplish what Feelings said he hoped to accomplish: to show black women as "different, separate and individual, real women," and to show the fluid energy of their rhythmic movements, "and in almost all

Illus. 1. From *Now Sheba Sings the Song* by Maya Angelou, with art by Tom Feelings. Art copyright © 1987 by Tom Feelings. Reproduced by permission of the publisher, Dial Books for Young Readers.

of them the strong presence of a definite dance consciousness in their lives." From the collective portraiture shown in illustration 1 we gain an appreciation of the individual strengths of black women.

Aragon, Jane Chelsea   *4–8*
WINTER HARVEST   *YEARS*
    Illus. by Leslie Baker. Boston: Little, Brown, 1988.

46   Stunning, impressionistic watercolor paintings capture the very essence of a cold snowy winter night in the country, the setting for this
narrative poem about a little girl and her father who scatter grain, sweet
corn, and apples around a salt lick for the deer that gather each evening
on the frozen pond near the family's house.

Baillie, Allan   *6–9*
DRAC AND THE GREMLIN   *YEARS*
    Illus. by Jane Tanner. New York: Dial, 1989.

Two Australians combine their talents to create this story of how a
girl and boy use the things in their backyard (foilage, a garden hose, a
charcoal grill), their pets (a dog and cat), and a beautiful white butterfly
as bases for their fanciful, dramatic play about how bold Queen Drac
and the Gremlin of Groaning Grotto rescue the benevolent White Wiz-
ard from imminent danger. The full-color realistic paintings depict the
real world that provoked the wonderful imagining described in the
text. A unique picture book in every respect.

Bernbaum, Israel   *10–16+*
MY BROTHER'S KEEPER: THE HOLOCAUST THROUGH   *YEARS*
THE EYES OF AN ARTIST
    Illus. New York: Putnam, 1985.

MS,
SAPAR

Because "the language of art can leave a more lasting impression than
words and has a universal appeal," the author, who is a famous canvas
painter, has used elements of his paintings from his series "Warsaw
Ghetto, 1983" to tell the story of the Warsaw Ghetto in World War II.
He explains how he used his art—his choice of colors, use of symbolism, and style—to tell this horrendous story. A number of photographs
from newspapers and other sources were incorporated with full-color
reproductions of his paintings and a well-written, informative text.
Bernbaum said that he wrote this fine book so that, through his art,
people would learn "to be your brother's keeper." I have little doubt
that readers will learn that lesson well.

Birdseye, Tom   *5–8*
AIRMAIL TO THE MOON   *YEARS*
    Illus. by Stephen Gammell. New York: Holiday, 1988.

A riotously humorous story of a spunky, mouthy child's frustrating search for her missing tooth. Stephen Gammell's illustrations highlight this outrageous, but convincing story exceptionally well.

Blegvad, Lenore   *4–7*   47
RAINY DAY KATE   *YEARS*
    Illus. by Erik Blegvad. New York: Margaret K. McElderry, 1987.

Crisp, full-page expressionistic paintings rendered in pen and ink and watercolor and a very easy-to-read, rhymed text (for beginning readers) are combined to tell a satisfying rainy day story about a bored, highly creative boy, who, disappointed because his friend Kate cannot come and play, makes his own "Kate" out of pillows, old clothes, paper, string, paints, and glue.

Bontemps, Arna   *12–16*
LONESOME BOY   *YEARS*
    Illus. by Felix Topolski. Boston: Houghton, 1955.

A haunting story about a New Orleans trumpet player's passionate devotion to playing jazz. Black-and-white, impressionistic line drawings are beautifully appropriate for the off-beat, perceptive tale. Compare with *Ben's Trumpet* (Greenwillow, 1979) by Rachel Isadora.

Bornstein, Ruth   *6–10*
THE DANCING MAN   *YEARS*
    Illus. by Ruth Bornstein. New York: Clarion/Seabury, 1978.

Poetic prose combines with black-and-white pencil drawings to tell this enchanting mood tale about Joseph, an orphan boy from a poor village on the shores of the Baltic Sea, who is given a pair of silver shoes that enable him to laugh and dance with the world. One hopes that young readers will see Joseph's wisdom many years later when he tells another small boy, alone on the seashore, that he is the Dancing Man and has a "gift" for him. Compare and contrast the text and illustrations in *The Dancing Man* with the 1989 Caldecott Medal book *Song and Dance Man,* written by Karen Ackerman and illustrated by Stephen Gammell (Knopf, 1988).

Browne, Anthony   *6–9*
LOOK WHAT I'VE GOT!   *YEARS*
    Illus. by Anthony Browne. New York: Knopf, 1980.

Jeremy tries to outdo his age mate Sam, but no matter how hard and how often he tries, Sam still manages to come out the winner. The full-color expressionistic pictures go beyond the literal interpretation of the brief and easy-to-read text, offering numerous clever and extraneous things to see. Be prepared for outbursts of laughter as children notice something new or enjoy these pictures for the umpteenth time.

Bucknall, Caroline   4–6
ONE BEAR IN THE PICTURE   YEARS
   Illus. by Caroline Bucknall. New York: Dial, 1988.

Try as he does to keep clean for the class photograph, luck is against him. The cartoon-style, ink and watercolor pictures, reproduced in clear bright colors, portray the frustrating experiences of an exuberant character who will interest and charm his readers immediately.

Bunting, Eve   6–9
HOW MANY DAYS TO AMERICA? A THANKSGIVING   YEARS
STORY
   Illus. by Beth Peck. New York: Ticknor & Fields, 1988.

Except for a few instances when the illustrations do not interpret the statements of the text accurately, this is a competent picture-book account of the dangerous boat trip made by refugees from a Caribbean island to the United States. Taken alone, the illustrations are quite beautiful. Most of them are double-page, impressionistic, chalk and grease pencil drawings in full color. Each picture reflects the tensions and dangers of the people as they escaped through the secret streets of their homeland at night and traveled across the treacherous sea.

Bunting, Eve   6–9
THE WEDNESDAY SURPRISE   YEARS
   Illus. by Donald Carrick. New York: Clarion/Houghton, 1989.

Seven-year-old Anna teaches her illiterate grandmother how to read. Both of them delight in offering this accomplishment as a happy birthday surprise to Dad. Expressive, telling watercolor paintings in full color illustrate this satisfying, realistic story.

Burningham, John   8–11
JOHN PATRICK NORMAN McHENNESSY: THE BOY WHO   YEARS
WAS ALWAYS LATE
   Illus. by John Burningham. New York: Crown, 1988.

When John Patrick Norman McHennessy, a meek, innocent, and guileless boy, explained that his tardiness was due to outrageous, but true adventures, his teacher did not believe him. The boy exacts a richly deserved retaliation when the teacher himself becomes the victim of an unbelievable happening. Effectively illustrated with cartoon-style illustrations. Compare and contrast with Dr. Seuss' *And to Think I Saw It on Mulberry Street* (Random, 1937) and Ellen Raskin's *The World's Greatest Freak Show* (Atheneum, 1971).

Caines, Jeannette   *3–6*
I NEED A LUNCH BOX   *YEARS*
   Illus. by Pat Cummings. New York: Harper, 1988.

Though he is not yet in school, a little boy definitely wants a lunch box so he can be like his older sister, who is going to start first grade. He dreams about having not one, but five lunch boxes—one for every school day—and even knows what he will put in each of them. The ending of this believable, here-and-now story is bound to surprise and please young readers. The realistic pictures, in rich, bright colors, add considerable vitality to this easy-to-read, very credible story.

Caines, Jeannette   *4–8*
CHILLY STOMACH   *YEARS*
   Illus. by Pat Cummings. New York: Harper, 1986.

Sandy is fondled and touched by her Uncle Jim in a manner she does not like. In fact, she gets "a chilly stomach" when he touches her, but she does not want to tell her parents because she is afraid they won't believe her and won't like her any more. She finally does tell her friend Jill, who, in turn, says she will tell her own mother and that Sandy should tell her parents, too. Double-page, realistic drawings, done in full-color pastels, help to make this story about confusing relationships more understandable and credible.

Carrick, Carol   *5–8*
THE ACCIDENT   *YEARS*
   Illus. by Donald Carrick. Boston: Clarion/Houghton, 1976.

A believable and poignant account of young Christopher's response to the death of his dog Bodger, who was hit by a pickup truck. The impressionistic line-and-wash illustrations contribute significantly to the depth of feeling evoked by the realistic story. The sequel to this story is *The Foundling* (Clarion/Houghton, 1978). Other books about Christopher and Bodger are *Sleep Out* (Clarion/Houghton, 1973) and *Lost in the Storm* (Clarion/Houghton, 1974).

Carrick, Carol   *5–8*
LEFT BEHIND   *YEARS*
   Illus. by Donald Carrick. New York: Clarion/Houghton, 1988.

A credible story of how Christopher got separated from his class-mates when coming back from a trip to the aquarium. The full-color, line and watercolor wash, expressionistic paintings add just the right amount of detail to the subway scenes and the boy's response to being lost.

Chaffin, Lillie D.   *5–9*
WE BE WARM TILL SPRINGTIME COMES   *YEARS*
   Illus. by Lloyd Bloom. New York: Macmillan, 1980.

A superb picture book that offers a convincing demonstration of a young boy's sense of responsibility and family love. Nicely crafted, poetic prose combines with absolutely stunning, impressionistic paint-ings done in black-and-white oils to tell how Jimmy Jack Blackburn went out into the piercing cold winter storm to gather coal from a deserted coal bank so his family would have enough fuel for the fire at least through the night.

Clifton, Lucille   *4–6*
AMIFIKA   *YEARS*
   Illus. by Thomas D. Grazia. New York: Dutton, 1977.

Amifika overhears his mother tell his aunt that his daddy is coming home from the Army and that to make room for him in their two-room apartment she will have to get rid of something he would not miss, something he would not remember. Because Amifika cannot remember his father, he is convinced his father cannot remember him, and with childlike logic concludes that his mother intends to get rid of him. All ends well. As soon as his father comes home and gives him a warm, loving hug, the little boy remembers him and his love. He no longer has doubts that his dad remembers him, and both Amifika and the reader of this believable here-and-now story are convinced that all members of this loving family will remain together. The monochromatic pencil drawings are in the realistic style of art.

Cohen, Barbara   *6–10*
THE DONKEY'S STORY   *YEARS*
   Illus. by Susan Jeanne Cohen. New York: Lothrop, 1988.

   A retelling of the Old Testament story in which Balak, King of Moab, calls on the prophet Balasam to curse the Israelites, but Balasam's *51* donkey, Sosi, forces him to listen to the word of God, and Balasam blesses them instead. The realistic full-color gouache paintings aptly capture the mood and setting of this well known Bible story.

Cohen, Barbara   *6–9*
MOLLY'S PILGRIM   *YEARS*
   Illus. by Michael J. Deraney. New York: Lothrop, 1983.

   Diverse interpretations of the term *pilgrim* are presented in Cohen's sensitive story. A little girl is told to dress a doll as a Pilgrim for the Thanksgiving display at school; her mother dresses the doll the way she dressed before emigrating to America from Russia to seek religious freedom, stating that she is a pilgrim, a modern pilgrim. The realistic black-and-white illustrations reflect the era and the changing moods that are so important to the story. Compare the way the same theme was developed in the 1984 Academy Award–winning film, *Mollie's Pilgrim.*

Collington, Peter   *3–8*
MY DARLING KITTEN   *YEARS*
   Illus. by Peter Collington. New York: Knopf, 1988.

   A "precious" book (in the best sense of the term), this almost wordless book depicts a kitten waking up its sleeping owner only minutes after the kitten itself has wakened. The sequence of the full-page pastel drawings could easily facilitate independent, creative storymaking by even the youngest "reader" of the visuals.

Cooney, Barbara   *4–8*
ISLAND BOY   *YEARS*
   Illus. by Barbara Cooney. New York: Viking/Kestrel, 1988.

   Accomplished, naive-style paintings in clean, full-color gouache create a definite sense of pace and appreciation for the lifestyle of a small boy who loves an island in the bay of New England. His love grows and persists into his later years, when he becomes an old man and the grandfather of a boy, named after him, who also loves the island and the sea around it.

Egger, Bettina   5–9
MARIANNE'S GRANDMOTHER   *YEARS*
52   Illus. by Sita Jucker. New York: Dutton, 1987.

After her grandmother's death, a little girl remembers the good times they had together, the stories her grandmother told her, and how well the grandmother listened to whatever the child had to say. The alternating full- and double-page, expressionistic watercolor paintings convey the deeply emotional and compassionate aura of this story.

Ehrlich, Amy   5–8
ZEEK SILVER MOON   *YEARS*
    Illus. by Robert A. Parker. New York: Dial, 1972.

Expressionistic paintings in full color emphasize and extend the mood and action expressed in Ehrlich's story about the everyday activities of a warm, loving family.

Feelings, Tom   9–16
BLACK PILGRIMAGE   *YEARS*
    Illus. by Tom Feelings. New York: Lothrop, 1972.

A personal, partial autobiography offers the readers an astute view of the heritage of African Americans. Superb drawings and paintings from various periods of Feelings' life, some in full color, others in black and white, help the reader to gain deeper insight into the evolution of black consciousness.

Fields, Julia   5–9
THE GREEN LION OF ZION STREET   *YEARS*
    Illus. by Jerry Pinkney. New York: Margaret K. McElderry,
        1988.

In verse suggestive of a black vernacular and folk traditions, the reader finds a first-person account of older children frightening younger children when they all pretend the green stone lion statue in a nearby park has come alive. Using ink, graphite, and watercolor to create the full-color realistic paintings, award-winning book illustrator Pinkney depicts to perfection the children's emotions and actions as they move from the real world to the world of make-believe and back to the real world again. Excellent for reading aloud and for independent, private reading.

Fleischman, Sid   *4–8*
THE SCAREBIRD
  Illus. by Peter Sis. New York: Greenwillow, 1988.

A lonely old farmer comes to value the companionship and friendship of a young orphan who came to help him with his farm. Full-page, expressionistic oil paintings in rich, full color embellish the mood and sense of place of this captivating story.

Flournoy, Valerie   *4–8*
THE PATCHWORK QUILT   *YEARS*
  Illus. by Jerry Pinkney. New York: Dutton/Dial, 1985.

A quilt "can tell your life story," said Tanya's grandmother. Indeed, the quilt this grandmother made with the help of the whole family did just that, bringing joy to everyone as well. The full-color art for the illustrations, which were rendered in pencil, graphite, and watercolor, adds to the feeling of love and respect that pervades among the members of this black family. Compare the grandmother's motivation for making the quilt and her family's responses to the quilt-making with a different family's response to a grandmother who weaves as depicted in *Annie and the Old One*, written by Miska Miles and illustrated by Peter Parnall (Little, Brown, 1971).

Fox, Mem   *5–8*
WILFRID GORDON McDONALD PARTRIDGE   *YEARS*
  Illus. by Julie Vivas. New York: Kane/Miller, 1985.

A small boy with a long name lives next door to a home for the elderly. During his many visits there, he discovers that the older people are fun to be with, each one having some special quality worthy of note. The one person he especially likes is a lady who, like himself, has four names. This account of his attempt to help her "find" the memory she "lost" is a genuinely moving and insightful story. The full-color expressionistic paintings and the marvelous use of figurative language express the joy of the young and old in each other's company. (See illustration 2.) Compare the images of the elderly and their need to communicate as portrayed in this book with those in *Happy Birthday, Grampie*, written by Susan Pearson and illustrated by Ronald Himler (Dial, 1987).

Illus. 2. Illustration from *Wilfrid Gordon McDonald Partridge* by Mem Fox; illustrated by Julie Vivas, copyrighted © 1985; reprinted by permission of Kane/Miller publishers.

Freeman, Don   5–8
DANDELION   *YEARS*
    Illus. by Don Freeman. New York: Viking, 1964.

    Cartoon drawings illustrate this amusing story of a vain but winsome lion who learns to be himself after he arrives at a come-as-you-are tea party so overdressed that no one recognizes him and he is turned away.

George, Lindsay Barrett   4–7
WILLIAM AND BOOMER   YEARS
   Illus. by Lindsay Barrett George. New York: Greenwillow, 1987.

   Double-page, realistic paintings in full color and rendered in watercolor, dyes, and colored pencil combine with a brief, easy-to-read text   55
to offer young readers a convincing and interesting account of how a
little boy and a deserted baby goose become friends and almost con-
stant companions. When the little boy learns how to swim, the two
swim together every day the whole summer long.

Goble, Paul   6–10+
BEYOND THE RIDGE   YEARS
   Illus. by Paul Goble. New York: Bradbury, 1989.

   In this beautiful picture book, Paul Goble combined his knowledge
about the culture of the Plains Indians with his talent as a storyteller
and a graphic artist to tell an original story that incorporates Native
American beliefs about what happens to people after their life on earth
has ended. Family members are shown preparing a deceased person's
body for her trip to the Spirit World, placing her on a platform among
the branches of an old cottonwood tree so the earth will take her body
and her spirit will be free to live forever. The few Plains Indian prayers
that are included add further to the authenticity of Goble's statement.
Be certain to notice how the details of the people's clothing, their hair
styles, and their teepees, as well as the variety of the flora and fauna of
the Great Plains contribute to the sense of ethnicity and locale of this
picture-book story.

Goffstein, M. B.   6–12+
AN ARTIST   YEARS
   Illus. by M. B. Goffstein. New York: Harper, 1980.

   Miniature, naive-style paintings done in pen and ink and full-color
watercolor wash combine with sparse, precise, poetic prose to offer
children and adults a message that they can ponder: an artist, "small,
strong, and with limited days . . . tries to make paint sing." The simplicity of the illustrations helps to dispel the view that artists are
"different" and "strange." The young reader will see and understand
that artists are a functioning and creative part of society. (See illustration 3.) For other especially affecting picture books that offer equally
sophisticated and perceptive statements about other types of creative

persons, see *A Writer* (Harper, 1984) and *An Actor* (Harper, 1987), both by M. B. Goffstein.

Goffstein, M. B.   *4–6*
SLEEPY PEOPLE, 2nd ed.   *YEARS*

56   Illus. by M. B. Goffstein. New York: Farrar, 1979.

A family of Sleepy People, miniscule people (some of whom, the author-artist says, may live in our old bedroom slippers) prepare for bed, partake of a bedtime snack, listen to their sleepy mother sing a sleepy song, and then fall sound asleep. The tiny ink-and-wash, naive-style sketches are perfectly delightful and exactly right for this ingenuous story!

Goffstein, M. B.   *7–11*
TWO PIANO TUNERS   *YEARS*
Illus. by M. B. Goffstein. New York: Farrar, 1970, 1977.

Illus. 3. Illustration from *An Artist* by M. B. Goffstein. Copyright © 1980 by M. B. Goffstein.

Debbie Weinstock, an engaging and determined little girl, wants to become a piano tuner, a good one like her grandfather, Ruben Weinstock. Very simple expressive line drawings illustrate this humane and simply told story—a plain but thoughtful piece of literature that effectively expresses the idea that people should be allowed to decide for themselves what avocation they will follow.

Gould, Deborah   4–8
BRENDAN'S BEST-TIMES BIRTHDAY   *YEARS*
   Illus. by Jacqueline Rogers. New York: Bradbury, 1988.

   This author and the illustrator both know children. There's no doubt about it! Brendan's father gives him a digital watch with a stopwatch for his birthday. From that moment on Brendan times absolutely everything—the length of time it takes to follow a cake recipe and spread the frosting, blow up the balloons for his party, open the gifts from each of his guests, and other party activities. The action-filled, full-color sketches done with ink, crayon, and watercolor capture the mood of the gala occasion.

Graham, Bob   3–6
BATH TIME FOR JOHN   *YEARS*
   Illus. by Bob Graham. Boston: Little, Brown, 1985.

   Bath time for toddler John means playtime for him—splashing, dumping water on his energetic dog Theo, playing with his windup frog. When Theo picks up the frog and runs away with it, more adventures follow for John, his sister Sarah (who is taking care of him), and Theo. The line and watercolor-wash sketches add to the rollicking fun. Other books in this popular series by the Australian author-artist are *Here Comes John* (Little, Brown, 1983) and *Here Comes Theo* (Little, Brown, 1983).

Gray, Nigel   5–9
A BALLOON FOR GRANDAD   *YEARS*
   Illus. by Jane Ray. New York: Orchard Books, 1988.

   Momentarily upset when his red-and-silver balloon blows out of the back door of his house and glides up and away into the distance, Sam comforts himself by suggesting that perhaps the balloon is headed to North Africa where his Grandad Abdulla lives. Adventures the balloon has on the way to Sam's beloved relative are illustrated with stunning, full-color, expressionistic paintings, executed from various perspectives and filled with authentic representations of the flora and fauna, terrain, and architecture of this part of Africa. The illustrations warrant repeated examination, for each examination will reveal many more things of interest.

Greenfield, Eloise   6–9
AFRICA DREAM   *YEARS*
   Illus. by Carole Byard. New York: John Day, 1977.

Expressionistic drawings made with grease pencil effectively depict a black girl's dreams about the people and places of long-ago Africa. The accomplished blend of text and pictures should contribute significantly to helping black children take pride in their heritage and should help all children, regardless of their racial origin, grow in their knowledge about and understanding of some aspects of African culture in the United States today.

Greenfield, Eloise   4–9
GRANDMAMA'S JOY   *YEARS*
   Illus. by Carol Byard. New York: Philomel, 1980.

Greenfield's tender, heartwarming, competently written account of how Rhonda brings joy to her grandmama is illustrated with masterfully executed charcoal drawings that were printed using a special two-color technique. A unique and memorable picture book!

X   Greenfield, Eloise   3–9+
UNDER THE SUNDAY TREE   *YEARS*
   Illus. by Amos Ferguson. New York: Harper, 1988.

JAPAR

  Brightly colored, naive-style paintings and free verse depict the vitality, dignity, and the aesthetic sensitivity typical of persons living in the Bahamas. A beautifully sensitive statement for children and adults to ponder over and over. To realize the full power of these poems, be certain to read them aloud.

Grimes, Nikki   6–18
SOMETHING ON MY MIND   *YEARS*
   Illus. by Tom Feelings. New York: Dial, 1978.

  Reportedly, Feelings' portraits of children provided the inspiration for these "prose poems" based on the thoughts and feelings universal to childhood and the black experience. A fine variety of elegant, mono-chromatic, line-and-wash drawings, and pen-and-ink sketches are artistically combined with enough white space to highlight the well-placed text and the illustrations. This is an exceptional book in content and appearance.

Hayes, Sarah   3–7
EAT UP, GEMMA   YEARS
  Illus. by Jan Ormerod. New York: Lothrop, 1988.

A truly credible glimpse of the eating habits of Baby Gemma depicts her throwing her breakfast on the floor, squashing grapes, banging her spoon on the table, crying to eat the fake fruit off a lady's hat, and so on. Those who have younger siblings will be certain to acknowledge the "truth" about Baby Gemma's antics; those who have no younger siblings will, no doubt, find it enlightening. All will delight in the ingenious way Baby Gemma's brother finally gets her to eat how and what she should.

Hearn, Michael Patrick   4–8
BREAKFAST, BOOKS, AND DREAMS: A DAY IN VERSE   YEARS
  Illus. by Barbara Garrison. New York: Warne, 1981.

Each of the twenty poems included in this delightful collection of poetry about children's daily activities and concerns is illustrated with an intaglio print, printed in sepia. The poems, written by some of America's foremost contemporary poets, offer impressionistic thoughts and comments about such things as a crazy quilt, eggs, the library, the classroom, antics of friends, cafeteria lunches, homework, and so much more.

Hedderwick, Mairi   5–8
KATIE MORAG DELIVERS THE MAIL   YEARS
  Illus. by Mairi Hedderwick. Boston: Little, Brown, 1984.

Once again Katie Morag gets into a predicament, a humorous one for readers and upsetting, to say the least, for Katie Morag! This time Katie's mother asks her to deliver the mail to four of the villagers, one of whom is her feisty grandmother. Unfortunately, when Katie stops to play in a pool of water, she slips on a slippery stone, and falls into the water, mailbag and all. With the addresses on the packages smudged (except for the one addressed to her grandmother), she gets them mixed up, much to the annoyance of all who receive them. The detailed, double-page, expressionistic illustrations are done in watercolor. They bring this uninhibited heroine and her family to life and establish a fine sense of the fictitious Isle of Struary, which is strongly suggestive of Coll, a real island off the west coast of Scotland. Note the endpapers. Those at the front of the book consist of a pictorial map of the village populated with people going about their business during the day; those at the back of the book offer an aerial view of the village at night with almost everyone in their well-lighted homes. Other stories written and illustrated by Mairi Hedderwick that are about this popular heroine are *Katie Morag and the Two Grandmothers* (Little, Brown, 1985); *Katie Morag and the Tiresome Ted* (Little, Brown, 1986); and *Katie Morag and the Big Boy Cousins* (Little, Brown, 1987).

Hendershot, Judith   5–9
IN COAL COUNTRY   *YEARS*
    Illus. by Thomas B. Allen. New York: Knopf, 1987.

Spare prose combines with full-page illustrations in pastels and charcoal, reproduced in full color to depict the life of a miner's family as seen through the eyes of a young girl. The girl vividly recalls some of the things that happened to her and to her family, the things they did and saw through the seasons of one year when she was growing up in a small Ohio coal mining town during the 1930s. This beautiful picture book is a fine memorial to the hardships and excitements one finds in a life affected by a local industry.

Henkes, Kevin   3–7
✗ GRANDFATHER AND BO   *YEARS*
    Illus. by Kevin Henkes. New York: Greenwillow, 1986.

SAPAR

Young Bo and his grandfather have a wonderful time together when the two spend the summer at the grandfather's home. They play ball, work in the kitchen, cook their dinner on a grill and eat outside, listen to old stereo records, make crafts, work in the garden, go for long walks, tell stories, go fishing, and celebrate Christmas (because Grandfather will not be able to join Bo and his family for the forthcoming Christmas). The full-page expressionistic pencil drawings, printed on a warm, yellow background, highlight the congenial mood that is so pervasive in this satisfying here-and-now story. Compare the relationship between grandfather and grandson, the general mood, as well as the effect of the style of art and use of color in *Grandfather and Bo* with *Dawn*, written and illustrated by Uri Shulevitz (Farrar, 1974).

Henry, O. (pseud. of William Sidney Porter)   *11–16+*
THE GIFT OF THE MAGI   *YEARS*
    Illus. by Lisbeth Zwerger. Calligraphy by Michael Neugebauer. Natick, Mass.: Neugebauer Pr., 1982. Distributed by Alphabet Pr.

An elegant picture book edition of the classic short story about the   *61*
sacrifices a couple make to buy each other Christmas presents. She cuts her beautiful golden brown hair and sells it to buy her husband a chain for his watch; he sells his watch to buy his wife a set of expensive combs for her hair. Although the theme is timeless, the full-page, expressionistic watercolor paintings reflect the early 1900s setting that is suggested in the text. The hand calligraphy of the text adds to the elegance and romantic aura of the book.

Hines, Anna Grossnickle   *4–7*
GRANDMA GETS GRUMPY   *YEARS*
    Illus. by Anna Grossnickle Hines. New York: Clarion/Houghton, 1988.

A convincing portrayal of what happens when five young grandchildren stay overnight with their grandmother. The colored-pencil illustrations add to the humor and credibility of this here-and-now story.

Hoban, Russell   *4–6*
BEDTIME FOR FRANCES   *YEARS*
    Illus. by Garth Williams. New York: Harper, 1960.

Frances, a charming little badger, tries practically everything she can think of to stay up when bedtime comes. Illustrated with realistic pen-and-ink sketches. Other books about Frances (all published by Harper) are *Baby Sister for Frances* (1964), *Bread and Jam for Frances* (1964), *Bargain for Frances* (1970), *Birthday for Frances* (1968), *Best Friends for Frances*, (1969).

Howard, Elizabeth Fitzgerald   *5–8*
THE TRAIN TO LULU'S   *YEARS*
    Illus. by Robert Casilla. New York: Bradbury, 1988.

Although the train ride described in this story takes place in the late 1930s, the children's reactions to traveling alone on a commercial transportation vehicle would undoubtedly be the same today. The realistic, full-color watercolor paintings capture the moods and the experiences of the two girls traveling alone from Boston to Baltimore and offer a nice variety of scenes they would be likely to see from the windows of the fast moving train. The map at the beginning of the book, which shows the route the girls follow, should give the story immediacy and make it more interesting.

62

Hughes, Shirley   3–7
ALFIE GETS IN FIRST   *YEARS*
    Illus. by Shirley Hughes. New York: Lothrop, 1981.

SAPAR

    Alfie races ahead of his mother and sister, Annie Rose, as they return home from shopping and smugly waits for them on the top step of the porch in front of their house. As soon as his mother unlocks the door, he dashes in ahead of her, proudly announcing that he is the winner again. Unfortunately, when his mother goes back outside to get Annie Rose out of her stroller, Alfie accidently locks them out—and he is unable to reach the latch to let them in or put the key through the mail slot. The commotion the crisis causes outside as the neighbors try to help is awesome, but eventually Alfie calms down and solves the problem in his own way—to everyone's relief and satisfaction. The animated, realistic line and full-color wash illustrations are done with ink and watercolor. They highlight the range of emotions Alfie and all the others feel during this not too uncommon predicament extremely well. (See illustration 4.) Other Alfie books (all published by Lothrop) are *Alfie's Feet* (1982), *Alfie Gives a Hand* (1983), and *An Evening at Alfie's* (1984).

Hughes, Shirley   4–8
DAVID AND DOG   *YEARS*
    Illus. by Shirley Hughes. New York: Prentice-Hall, 1978.

    Thanks to the help and generosity of his older sister, Dave is able to trade her large Teddy bear for Dogger, his well-loved toy dog, who was found, and also cherished, by another little boy. Dave's trials and tribulations are depicted in detailed, action-filled, line and full-color wash paintings. This picture book, entitled *Dogger* (Bodley Head, 1977) in England, was the 1978 Kate Greenaway Medal winner.

Hughes, Shirley   4–8
GEORGE, THE BABYSITTER   *YEARS*
    Illus. by Shirley Hughes. New York: Prentice-Hall, 1977.

Illus. 4. From *Alfie Gets In First* written and illustrated by Shirley Hughes © 1981 by Shirley Hughes. Reprinted by permission of Lothrop, Lee & Shepard (a division of William Morrow & Co.).

George, a teenager, gets more than he bargained for when he babysits for three children. Nonetheless, he proves himself quite capable of handling each challenge. Realistic illustrations in full-color detail this pleasant, humorous, believable story, which, entitled *The Helper* (Bodley Head, 1975) in England, was named a runner-up for the Kate Greenaway Medal in 1975 and given The Other Award by the Children's Rights Workshop in 1976.

Ionesco, Eugene   *3–6*
STORY NUMBER 1   YEARS
  Trans. by Calvin K. Towle. Illus. by Etienne Delessert. New York:
    Harlin Quist, 1968.

Marvelous plays on words tell a zany story about a three-year-old
who wants the attention of her parents and the maid early in the
morning. Illustrated with moderately surrealistic paintings that effectively extend the text.

Isadora, Rachel   *5–10*
BEN'S TRUMPET   YEARS
  Illus. by Rachel Isadora. New York: Greenwillow, 1979.

  A sophisticated and thoroughly modern picture book about a little
boy enamored with the jazz he hears coming from the Zig Zag Jazz
Club. The illustrations are black-and-white, pen-and-ink drawings,
and the style used to create each picture changes from page to page, a
technique reflecting the unpredictable and uninhibited elements typical of the improvised jazz that prevailed in the 1930s and 1940s, the
time frame for the story. A 1980 Caldecott Honor book. Compare with
Lonesome Boy, written by Arna Bontemps and illustrated by Felix
Topolski (Houghton, 1955).

Isadora, Rachel   *5–8*
THE PIRATES OF BEDFORD STREET   YEARS
  Illus. by Rachel Isadora, New York: Greenwillow, 1988.

  A straightforward account of a little boy obsessed with retelling the
movies he sees by drawing his own pictures of them—first with chalk
on the sidewalk, stoops, and his apartment building, then on sheets of
a drawing pad with crayons that were given to him by an understanding landlady. Full-color, realistic watercolor paintings embellish the
easy-to-read text.

Iwasaki, Chihiro   *4–8*
STAYING HOME ALONE ON A RAINY DAY   YEARS
  Illus. by Chihiro Iwasaki. New York: McGraw-Hill, 1968.

  Beautifully evocative impressionistic illustrations and poetic text
reveal the innermost thoughts of a small child, home alone for the very
first time when a thunderstorm occurs.

Johnson, Angela   *3–8* X
TELL ME A STORY, MAMA   *YEARS* SAPAR
    Illus. by David Soman. New York: Orchard Books, 1989.

    Double-page watercolor paintings in full color enrich this collection
of Mama's childhood experiences that her daughter knows by heart, *65*
but obviously likes to hear Mama tell again and again.

Johnston, Tony   *4–7*
YONDER   *YEARS*
    Illus. by Lloyd Bloom. New York: Dial, 1988.

    Told in verse, this narrative is a tribute to traditions in rural America.
With each event marked by the planting of a new tree, readers see the
farmer get married and establish a homestead, watch his family grow
and mature, and years later see the farmer die. Impressionistic paintings, in rich, full color, mark these important nostalgic events, many of
which are associated with seasons. The text and illustrations present
an interesting array of literal and symbolic statements.

Kalman, Maria   *4–6*
HEY WILLY, SEE THE PYRAMIDS   *YEARS*
    Illus. by Maria Kalman. New York: Viking/Kestrel, 1988.

    Alexander, unable to sleep, wakes up his older sister Lulu in the
middle of the night to ask her to tell him some stories. She moves over
to his bed, gets comfortable, and proceeds to tell him five stories, then
five more, and then just one more. Each story is short, childlike, and
inventive. Some are realistic, others outrageously impossible; some
involve clever plays on and with words. The full-color, expressionistic
illustrations are as zany and childlike as the stories.

Kennedy, Richard   *9–14*
THE DARK PRINCESS   *YEARS*
    Illus. by Donna Diamond. New York: Holiday, 1978.

    The princess, born totally blind, thought she was loved only for her
beauty, not for herself. To prove to her that his love was sincere, the
Court Fool looks into her face, knowing he too would become blind by
doing so. When he stumbles backward over a cliff's edge, the princess
leaps into the water to save him. They both drown, yet they know of
their love for each other. The delicate, full-page illustrations, in alter-

nating spreads of full color and black and white, highlight the ethereal and romantic mood of this bittersweet Romeo-and-Juliet story.

Khalsa, Dayal Kaur   5–7
I WANT A DOG   YEARS
66   Illus. by Dayal Kaur Khalsa. New York: Potter, 1987. Distributed by
        Crown.

For years May tries to convince her parents that she should be allowed to have a dog. But her parents are as adamant in their opposition as May is single-minded in her pleading and scheming. This refreshingly off-beat story, which ends to the satisfaction of all concerned, is illustrated with brightly colored, naive-style paintings that reflect the protagonist's energetic and undaunted attitude.

King, Larry L.   3–6
BECAUSE OF LOZO BROWN   YEARS
        Illus. by Amy Schwartz. New York: Viking/Kestrel, 1988.

A perfect example of the adage that people fear the unknown is nicely demonstrated in this story about a little boy who is afraid to meet his new neighbor, Lozo Brown. The exaggerated, cartoon-style illustrations effectively dramatize how outlandish the boy's fears are, for once he meets Lozo, the two become friends.

Kraus, Robert   4–7
PHIL THE VENTRILOQUIST   YEARS
        Illus. by Robert Kraus. New York: Greenwillow, 1989.

Young readers are in store for a great bit of fun with this story. Phil uses his ability to throw his voice so often that he annoys people, especially his mother and father. Then comes the night when he uses this ability to frighten away a burglar who breaks into his house. Finally, his parents admit they are lucky to have a ventriloquist in the family! The cartoon-style illustrations—rendered in watercolor paints, colored markers, and pen-and-ink—effectively add to the humor of the easy-to-read text.

Lager, Claude   3–8
JEANETTE AND JOSIE   YEARS
        Trans. from the French. Illus. by Claude K. Dubois. New York: Vi-
        king/Kestrel, 1988.

What starts out as a very bad day (Jeanette breaks a lamp when she falls out of bed, spills hot chocolate on a fresh tablecloth while eating her breakfast, and is unable to think of anything to do) turns out to be a good day after all. When she goes outside with her sled to play in the freshly fallen snow, she meets a new neighbor, equally bored and looking for a friend. The line and watercolor-wash paintings reflect this pleasant and credible tale of the power of friendship to relieve boredom. First published in Belgium in 1988 as *Babbette et Virginne* by Pastil, an imprint of Lecole des Loisirs.

Lasky, Kathyrn   *6–9*
SEA SWAN   *YEARS*
  Illus. by Catherine Stock. New York: Macmillan, 1988.

Feeling that life is passing her by and longing for independence and self respect, Elizabeth Swan decides on the morning of her seventy-fifth birthday, to learn something new. So, she takes swimming lessons, then she enrolls in a water ballet class, teaches herself how to cook and scuba dive, draws up plans for a new house in the country, and even plants a vegetable garden on her new property before she moves. She continues to plan for the future. In anticipation for forthcoming visits by her grandchildren, she decides she had better learn how to bake chocolate cake. Full-page, impressionistic paintings in colored pencil and watercolor embellish this upbeat story.

Latterman, Terry   *8–12*
LITTLE JOE, A HOPI INDIAN BOY, LEARNS A HOPI   *YEARS*
INDIAN SECRET
  Illus. by Terry Latterman. Gilbert, Ariz.: Pussywillow, 1985.

Pen-and-ink sketches with turquoise and earth color overlays are skillfully combined with an elaborate text to reveal only as much as the white man is allowed to know about young Hopi Indian males' initiation into the Powamu society, a ceremony that is the first step a child takes on the path to adulthood. Especially interesting to children is Latterman's revelation of some of the mysteries and the purpose of the Kachinas, one aspect of the Hopi Indian culture visible almost everywhere in the Southwest, even today. Compare and contrast the aspects of the Hopi Indian culture here with those apparent in the text and illustrations of *The Mouse Couple,* a Hopi folktale translated by Ekkehart Malotki and illustrated by Michael Lacapa (Northland, 1988).

Lee, Jeanne M.   *5–8*
BÁ-NÁM   *YEARS*
   Illus. by Jeanne M. Lee. New York: Holt, 1987.

68   Elegant, crisp, full-page illustrations in full color and an easy-to-read
text tell an interesting and exciting story in which a little Vietnamese
girl and her family visit the gravesites of their ancestors and present
offerings on Thanh-Minh Day, a special day reserved each year for that
practice. The little girl's reaction to this practice and to the grave-
keeper, Bá-Nám—an old wrinkled woman whose body was twisted and
bent and whose teeth were stained black to stop decay—provide a
thoroughly credible and memorable story that offers a message well
worth heeding without being didactic.

Leonard, Marcia   *Infancy–3*
What I Like series: EATING, GETTING DRESSED, GOING   *YEARS*
TO BED, and TAKING A BATH
   Illus. by Deborah Michel. New York: Bantam, 1988.

SAPAR

   Each of these little books (6 by 6½ inches) depicts a toddler or
nursery-school-age child taking pride and delight in participating and
accomplishing aspects of the everyday activities suggested in the titles
cited above. In each case the child is shown doing as much as he or she
can do alone or gracefully accepting help from a parent. Also, questions
are addressed to the readers (or listeners), encouraging them to talk
about and to take pride in participating and accomplishing the same
activities as the children pictured in the books. Full-page, unsophisticated, line-and-watercolor, expressionistic paintings add to the pleasant tone of the involving texts. Their simplicity, brightness, and scale
reflect the way the toddler sees his world. (See illustration 5.)

Levinson, Riki   *6–9*
OUR HOME IS THE SEA   *YEARS*
   Illus. by Dennis Luzak. New York: Dutton, 1985.

   Large, expertly crafted acrylic paintings, some in the realistic others
in the impressionistic art style, give a sense of immediacy and excitement to the mixture of old Chinese traditions and modern ways that the
Hong Kong family in this beautiful picture book live with daily. Sky-
scrapers, decorated with ornate signs in red and gold and occupied to
capacity with families and businesses; bustling, crowded, narrow
streets; open markets where fish, fruits, vegetables, clothes, and so

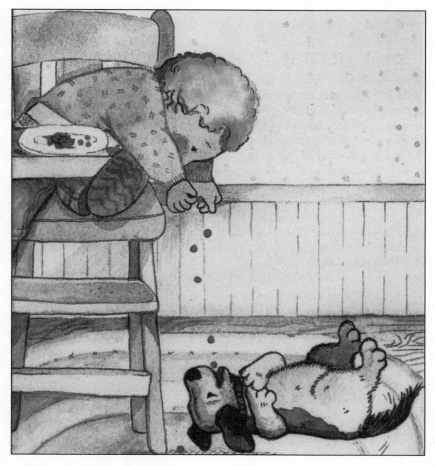

Illus. 5. Illustration by Deborah Michel from *Eating* by Marcia Leonard, © 1988 by Small Packages, Inc., published by Bantam Books.

much more is sold; innumerable junks and sampans jammed together in the harbor; and little parks where caged birds are aired and children play are among the sights readers see as they follow the young narrator. Finishing the last day of the school year, he hurries home (a houseboat in the Hong Kong harbor), looking forward to spending his vacation fishing with his grandfather and to pursuing fishing as a profession instead of becoming a teacher, as his mother has said he will be when he gets older.

Lindgren, Astrid   5–9
THE GHOST OF SKINNY JACK   YEARS
    Trans. from the Swedish by Yvonne Hooker. Ilus. by Ilon Wikland. New York: Viking/Kestrel, 1987.

70   Two children walk through the meadows, fields, and tree-covered hills to visit their grandmother whose cottage is in a hollow below a ridge. They enjoy visiting her and look forward to the gifts she always manages to find for them in her attic; they especially enjoy the exciting stories she tells them. During this particular visit, they ask her to tell them a ghost story about Skinny Jack, a ghoulish tale they have heard many times before but always delight in hearing again. With each retelling they are titillated and frightened, and this time is no exception. With gifts in hand (a guitar for the boy and a backpack full of illustrated magazines for the girl), they say goodbye to their beloved grandmother and head for home. The boy, walking far ahead of his sister and happily playing his guitar, is totally unaware that she is still thinking about Skinny Jack, who she is convinced has followed her and grabbed her from behind, to hold her fast. (In actual fact, the strings of her backpack have gotten stuck on a hazelnut tree branch.) She is terrified and screams hysterically. As the girl says as she narrates the story, "Miracles do happen," and readers will appreciate the "miracle" that comes to her rescue. The full-color, impressionistic illustrations, rendered in ink, crayon, and paint, expertly enhance this ghost story. This picture book was published originally in Swedish under the title *Skinn Skerping bemskast ay alla spoken i Smaland* by Rabén & Sjögren (Stockholm, 1986).

Linn, Margot   3–6
✗ A TRIP TO THE DENTIST   YEARS
SAPAR
    Illus. by Catherine Siracusa. New York: Harper, 1988.

    Simple, grease-pencil line and full-color, watercolor-wash drawings, in the expressionistic style, combine with a clear, simply-written text to answer the kinds of questions children are likely to have before they visit a dentist. *A Trip to the Doctor* (Harper, 1988) by the same author
also ← and illustrator team is another informative and comforting book about what, to some children, often amounts to a frightening or unpleasant experience.

Lionni, Leo   5–9
FREDERICK   YEARS
    Illus. by Leo Lionni. New York: Pantheon, 1967

Frederick the mouse is able to recreate the beauty of the seasons through the magic of words in a story in which simple text and collage pictures dramatize the importance of respecting an individual's talents and imaginative spirit.

Lisowski, Gabriel
6–10 *YEARS*
ON THE LITTLE HEARTH
  Trans. by Miriam Chaikin. Illus. by Gabriel Lisowski. New York: Holt, 1978.

This is an illustrated version of a Jewish lullaby that was sung in Eastern Europe in the late nineteenth century. The melody was intended to lull children to sleep, to encourage them to learn the alphabet so they could study the Torah (God's law) and be knowledgeable, and to learn to comport themselves correctly. The crosshatched pencil illustrations in black and white highlight aspects of shtetl life that are mentioned in this traditional Jewish song. Included at the end of this book are the musical score for the song, created by Mark Warshowski, and four refrains of the song in English, Hebrew, and Yiddish. In Yiddish the song is known by the title "Oif'n Pripitchik."

Little, Lessie Jones and Eloise Greenfield
4–6 *YEARS*
I CAN DO IT MYSELF
  Illus. by Carole Byard. New York: Crowell, 1978.

A comforting, satisfying account of a little boy named Donny who goes to the store alone to buy his mother a special plant with bell-like, pink flowers for her birthday. Along the way he manages to overcome several obstacles, including a frightening bulldog. Grease pencil sketches with splashes of yellow wash nicely depict the truly believable incidents and relationships portrayed in the story.

Livingston, Myra Cohn (compiler)
4–9 *YEARS*
POEMS FOR MOTHERS
  Illus. by Deborah Kogan Ray. New York: Holiday, 1988.

An excellent collection of poems highlighting the many roles played by mothers and stepmothers. Written by many poets including the compiler herself, the poems are illustrated with line-and-wash impressionistic paintings that enrich and extend the themes of love and care that pervade the volume.

Lloyd, David   *3–5*
X DUCK   *YEARS*
   Illus. by Charlotte Voake. New York: Lippincott, 1988.

SAPAR

72

Lloyd knows about children's language development! A little boy
calls all animals "duck" and all vehicles "truck." Eventually, with the
help of his grandmother, he sorts them out. Although the illustrations
are a bit too much like John Burningham's cartoon-style line and watercolor-wash paintings, they are quite appropriate for this convincing
here-and-now fiction.

Locker, Thomas   *6–10*
FAMILY FARM   *YEARS*
   Illus. by Thomas Locker. New York: Dial, 1988.

A well-written text and accomplished impressionistic oil paintings
in full color convincingly depict some of the problems of a family
trying to make a living on a small farm that is threatened because of the
low prices of milk and corn. The determined, resourceful family save
their farm by growing and selling pumpkins and flowers. Each full-
page painting reveals some of the intimacies of farm life—its scenic
aspects as well as its ever present responsibilities and chores—through
one calendar year. (A portion of the proceeds from this book will be
donated to Farm Aid.)

Maiorano, Robert   *6–11*
A LITTLE INTERLUDE   *YEARS*
   Illus. by Rachel Isadora. New York: Coward, 1980.

This author-and-artist team offers the reader a satisfying glimpse of
a pleasant and rewarding encounter between Jiminy Cricket, an elderly
stagehand, and Bobby, a small boy. Arriving backstage at the theater
long before the performance of "The Nutcracker Ballet" in which he has
a small role, Bobby hears Jiminy Cricket improvising at the piano. The
two make a bargain: the man will teach the boy how to play the piano
and the boy will teach the man some ballet steps. The black-and-white,
pen-and-ink sketches are beautifully expressive. They superbly dramatize the setting, the action, and the genuinely warm feelings of
respect the boy and man have for each other, as well as their love for
music and dance. A small picture book that is truly special.

Mathis, Sharon Bell   *8–12*
THE HUNDRED PENNY BOX   *YEARS*
   Illus. by Leo and Diane Dillon. New York: Viking, 1975.

Although this is a profusely illustrated short story rather than a picture book, the ten full-page, representational watercolor paintings are too exceptional and too much a part of the believable story to leave the book out of this publication. Great-great-Aunt Dew has a story to go with the year stamped on each of the one hundred pennies in her box, and Michael loves to hear her tell them. The conflict that arises because of Aunt Dew's presence in the house and Michael's mother's resolve to dispose of the old box and replace it with a new one makes for a warm and touching story.

Mayer, Mercer (compiler)   *7–up*
A POISON TREE AND OTHER POEMS   *YEARS*
    Illus. by Mercer Mayer. New York: Scribner, 1977.

A poignant anthology of twenty poems that present an array of human feelings—emotions about oneself and one's relationship to significant others. Impressionistic, monochromatic drawings effectively dramatize the astute and perceptive poems about the human condition.

McAfee, Annalena   *5–9*
THE VISITORS WHO CAME TO STAY   *YEARS*
    Illus. by Anthony Browne. New York: Viking/Kestrel, 1985.

Katy is quite content with the pleasant routine that she and her father established after her parents were divorced. When her father's girlfriend and young son move in with them, Katy resents the change in lifestyle that takes place, and also resents having to share her father's affection. The father's solution to the conflict proves to everyone's liking. The full-page, surrealistic illustrations dramatize perfectly a kind of crisis that is common in families today. Katy's inner turmoil is externalized through the bizarre objects that appear in the pictures, and the physical tension is apparent in all four members of the household. (See illustration 6.)

McKissack, Patricia C.   *6–9*
MIRANDY AND BROTHER WIND   *YEARS*
    Illus. by Jerry Pinkney. New York: Knopf, 1988.

Beautiful, double-page watercolor illustrations done in the realistic style decorate this rather lengthy story about a little girl's scheming to get Brother Wind to help her win the Junior Cakewalk contest. Named a 1989 Caldecott Honor book and given the 1989 Coretta Scott King Award for its illustrations.

Illus. 6. From *The Visitors Who Came to Stay* by Annalena McAfee with illustrations by Anthony Browne. Illustration copyright © 1985 by Anthony Browne. Reprinted by permission of Viking Penguin, a division of Penguin Books, USA, Inc.

Miller, Jonathan, and David Pelham   *8–16+*
THE FACTS OF LIFE   *YEARS*

    Illus. by Harry Willock. Paper engineering by John Strejan, James
    Diazz, David Rosendale, and David Pelham. New York: Viking/
    Kestral, 1984.

A masterpiece in paper engineering offering a precise, comprehensive, well-written text that includes technical terms about life before birth. Three-dimensional, pop-up pictures, moving diagrams, and lift-up flaps, plus realistic pictures embellish the text to describe in detail aspects of human reproduction and gestation—the human male and female reproductive systems, the fertilization of the egg, and the development of the baby.

Miller, Margaret   *6 mos.–2*
MY FIRST WORDS: ME AND MY CLOTHES   *YEARS*

    Illus. with photographs. New York: Crowell, 1989.

A fine concept book for the toddler, in which familiar items of clothing are shown and named (mitten, slipper, sock, etc.) along with the part of the body on which each is worn. Notice that the child pictured on the cover is a black toddler, but the hand and the foot shown along with the mitten and slipper are those of a Caucasian child! (See illustration 7.) The photographs are crisp and clear, and are in

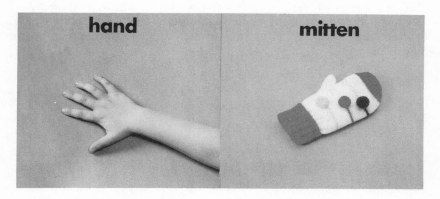

Illus. 7. Photograph from *My First Words: Me and My Clothes* by Margaret Miller (Thomas J. Crowell), Copyright © 1989 by Margaret Miller. Reprinted by permission of Harper and Row Publishers, Inc.

rich, full color. Other books in "My First Words" series are *In My Room, At My House,* and *Time to Eat.* All are about familiar things to touch, eat, wear, or play with in the children's here-and-now world. In each case the child is made to feel a close part of that world.

Moore, Elaine.   5–8
GRANDMA'S PROMISE   *YEARS*
   Illus. by Elise Primavera. New York: Lothrop, 1988.

A genuinely loving and respectful relationship is depicted in this account of how a little girl and her grandmother enjoy midwinter and attend to the wild animals who cannot find their own food because it is covered with snow and ice. Realistic, double-page watercolor paintings embellish the idyllic rural images of the inside and outside that are referred to in the text.

Morgan, Michaela   4–6
EDWARD HURTS HIS KNEE   *YEARS*
   Illus. by Sue Porter. New York: Dutton, 1988.

The line and watercolor-wash, cartoon-style illustrations are a perfect match for this story of a walk an accident-prone child and his mother take to visit grandmother. Children might well appreciate Edward's response to his scratched knee as well as his fantasies as his mother carries him and then encourages him to continue on his own. They will no doubt be far more sympathetic about Edward's mom's bruised and hurting foot than Edward and his grandmother were. Poor mom! See other picture books about this interesting little boy (all published by Dutton): *Edward Gets a Pet* (1987), *Visitors for Edward* (1987), and *Edward Loses His Teddy Bear* (1988).

Naylor, Phyllis Reynolds   3–6
THE BABY, THE BED AND THE ROSE   *YEARS*
   Illus. by Mary Szilagyi. New York: Clarion/Houghton, 1987.

Colored pencil drawings in soft, full color document this family's delight and preoccupation with the baby sister's every need and antic.

Nelson, Vaunda Micheaux   5–9
ALWAYS GRAMMA   *YEARS*
   Illus. by Kimanne Wheeler. New York: Putnam, 1988.

This child's account of the gradual change in her once communicative, fun-loving and mentally alert Grandmother—her confusion, progressive loss of memory, and withdrawal, all manifestations of Alzheimer's disease—is authentically and sensitively presented. The realistic, full-color watercolor illustrations are a fine complement to the realistic story.

Nixon, Jean Lowery　　　　　　　　　　　　　　　　　　*5–9*
IF YOU WERE A WRITER　　　　　　　　　　　　　　　　*YEARS*
　Illus. by Bruce Degen. New York: Four Winds, 1988.

A mother who is a successful writer describes the writing process and offers some suggestions to her young daughter when the child says that she would like to be a writer, too. The characterized, realistic illustrations rendered in pen and ink and full-color, watercolor wash interject a relaxed, humorous aura to a credible introduction to the craft of writing. Compare this interpretation of the writing process with that presented by M. B. Goffstein in *Writer* (Harper, 1984).

O'Brien, Anne Sibley　　　　　　　　　　　　　　　　　　*1–5*
IT HURTS!　　　　　　　　　　　　　　　　　　　　　　*YEARS*
　Illus. by Anne Sibley O'Brien. New York: Holt, 1986.

A short, simple story and precise, realistic watercolor paintings forthrightly and believably express a little girl's feelings when she falls down and hurts her knee as well as her response when her mother treats the cut. Other here-and-now stories in this series of board books about child and parent relationships when daily crises occur are *I Want That*, about sharing; *Where's My Truck?* about putting toys away; *I'm Not Tired*, about taking a nap; *I Don't Want to Go*, about leaving a playground, *It's Hard to Wait*, about feeling neglected; *Don't Say No!* about feeling frustrated. All were written and illustrated by Anne Sibley O'Brien and published by Dutton in 1986.

Ormerod, Jan　　　　　　　　　　　　　　　　　　　　　*3–7*
101 THINGS TO DO WITH A BABY　　　　　　　　　　　　*YEARS*
　Illus. by Jan Ormerod. New York: Lothrop, 1986.

Brief text (mostly captions) and more than one hundred watercolor pictures of assorted sizes and shapes and arranged in varied ways on the pages, alert a six-year-old girl (and young readers) to one hundred and one things to do with a new baby in the family.

Oxenbury, Helen   2–4
✗ TOM AND PIPPO AND THE WASHING MACHINE   YEARS
JAPAR   Illus. by Helen Oxenbury. New York: Aladdin Books/Macmillan,
         1988.

78   A perfectly charming book! Tom tells how shocked and worried he
is when Pippo, his toy monkey, has to be put in the washing machine
after playing in the mud with him. The simple, witty, expressionistic
illustrations, which alternate between uncolored line drawings and
line drawings heightened with watercolor-wash, are absolutely delightful, each adding depth of feeling to this easy to read but well-written
text. Printed in large type, it is perfect for the beginning readers to read
aloud to younger siblings or for them just to read alone and "remember
when they were as little." Other books about Tom and Pippo in this
series, all of which were published by Aladdin/Macmillan in 1988 are
Tom and Pippo Go for a Walk, Tom and Pippo Make a Mess, and *Tom
and Pippo Read a Story.*

Paek, Min   5–9
AEKYUNG'S DREAM   YEARS
    Trans. from Korean by Min Paek. Illus. by Min Paek. San Francisco:
    Children's Book Pr., Revised edition, 1988.

Having been in America only six months, Korean-born Aekyung is
self-conscious about her inability to speak English very well. She is
also reluctant to go to school because her fellow classmates tease her
about her "Chinese" eyes. Inspired by a dream about the beloved
Korean King Syong of the fifteenth century Yi Dynasty, she grows more
determined to learn to speak English better, make friends with her
classmates, and make use of her own talents and individuality, especially her cultural heritage. She gradually adjusts to her new country
and to her new friends. Illustrated with simple, pen-and-ink line and
clear, brightly colored overlays, the text of this convincing story about
a child's adjustment to a new country and new culture is presented in
handwritten English lettering and Korean calligraphy. The clarity and
directness of the illustrations show Aekyung's strength and determination as she struggles with life in a new country. (See illustration 8.) This
is a fine story to use with immigrants as well as with native-born
Americans. Compare and contrast the immigrant child's experience in
this story with *Molly's Pilgrim,* written by Barbara Cohen and illustrated by Michael J. Deraney (Lothrop, 1983).

Illus. 8. *Aekyung's Dream* by Min Paek, published by Children's Book Press, San Francisco.

Panek, Dennis
BA BA SHEEP WOULDN'T GO TO SLEEP
   Illus. by Dennis Panek. New York: Orchard, 1988.

3–6
YEARS

Ba Ba Sheep stayed up all night and played with his building blocks and toys. The next day he struggles to keep awake, hardly able to wait until it is time to go to bed where the sheets are smooth, the pillow soft, and the blanket warm. The cartoon-style illustrations, done in crisp line and flat, rich colors, add just the right amount of humor and charm. The result is an endearing bedtime story that will be asked for many times.

Pearson, Susan   5–9
HAPPY BIRTHDAY, GRAMPIE   YEARS
   Illus. by Ronald Himler. New York: Dial, 1987.

   Martha loves her grandfather very much. She loved him when he was old but spry and seemed to enjoy life; and she loves him now that he is older and blind, somewhat withdrawn, and has reverted to speaking Swedish, his native language, instead of English, which he no longer seems to remember. His reaction to the birthday greeting card she makes for him out of raised letters and different textured materials will most certainly move every reader, regardless of age. The art consists of fourteen large, full-page, impressionistic paintings (and a few small ones) in rich, full color; they are nicely compatible with the sensitive and positive tone that pervades throughout this realistic story. Compare the image of the elderly presented in this book with that in *Wilfred Gordon McDonald Partridge*, written by Mem Fox and illustrated by Julie Vivas (Kane/Miller, 1985).

Plotz, Helen (compiler)   3–6
A WEEK OF LULLABIES   YEARS
   Illus. by Marisabina Russo. New York: Greenwillow, 1988.

X

SAPAR

   Fourteen stylized, gouache paintings in bright, full color illustrate the same number of poems grouped by days of the week—lullabies and bedtime poems by such authors as Elizabeth Coatsworth, Nikki Giovanni, Gwendolyn Brooks, and Elizabeth Shub.

Pomerantz, Charlotte   5–8
THE CHALK DOLL   YEARS
   Illus. by Frane Lessac. New York: Lippincott, 1989.

   Rose, sick in bed with a cold, is enthralled as her mother tells her about growing up in Jamaica in a poor and loving family. Especially fascinating to the child is her mother's story of the wonderful fun she had playing with a rag doll she made herself and a store-bought "chalk doll" with a missing arm and broken nose that was given to her. The full-page, up-beat, naive-style paintings in bright colors seem just perfect for this convincing account of one person's simple, childhood joys.

Rabe, Berniece *3–8* ✗
WHERE'S CHIMPY? *YEARS* SAPAR
 Photographs by Diane Schmidt. Niles, Ill.: Albert Whitman, 1988.

81

 A realistic story of a little girl with Down's syndrome who, with her father, searches for the toy monkey that is her bed companion. This is one of the few stories about a child with Down's syndrome who is involved in activities, interests, and feelings that all children can iden- tify with, whether or not they have this disorder. The full-color illustra- tions that show the little girl and her father searching, first for the beloved stuffed animal, then the father's glasses, superbly capture the typical play activities of a young child and the happy, loving relation- ship between the father and daughter—real-life persons about whom Berniece Rabe wrote this upbeat, memorable story.

Raskin, Ellen *6–10*
SPECTACLES *YEARS*
 Illus. by Ellen Raskin. New York: Atheneum, 1968.

 Nearsighted Iris Fogel sees some really strange things when she does not wear her glasses. Together, the brief text and cartoon drawings provide an amusing and highly imaginative picture book.

Rockwell, Anne *4–9*
HANDY HANK WILL FIX IT *YEARS*
 Illus. by Anne Rockwell. New York: Holt, 1988.

 A beautifully positive attitude is put forth in this story about a very competent handyman—competent in repairing practically everything for anyone that calls him to service and competent in keeping things in proper and efficient order in his own home. The flat and bright full- color, cartoon, line and watercolor-wash illustrations, readily identi- fiable as those of this prolific author and artist, add consider- able detail and interest to this account of a busy and successful handyman.

Rockwell, Anne *4–7*
HUGO AT THE WINDOW *YEARS*
 Illus. by Anne Rockwell. New York: Macmillan, 1988.

 A satisfying and multi-dimensional story about Hugo, the dog who waits and waits at the window (not too patiently) for his friend and master to come back home. Return the master does, eventually, with a wonderful surprise for Hugo. Be certain to look *very carefully* at the details of the cartoon-style illustrations, which were rendered in pen and ink and watercolor. Had Hugo looked carefully in the windows of the buildings directly across the street from him as he watched and waited, he would have known exactly where his friend went *and* what he did. He also would have seen any number of other interesting sights, and other stories would have unfolded before his eyes. Compare the treatment of this theme with the classic *Nothing Ever Happens on My Block,* by Ellen Raskin (Atheneum, 1970).

Rogers, Jean   *4–6*
RUNAWAY MITTENS   *YEARS*
   Illus. by Rie Muñoz. New York: Greenwillow, 1988.

   A truly believable saga of the varied places a little boy manages to lose (and find!) the new red mittens that his grandmother made especially for him. The brightly colored and simply shaped figures in the paintings, which so effectively illustrate this story of people braving the artic cold, are strongly suggestive of Inuit (Alaskan) felt appliqués and drawings.

Russo, Marisabina   *3–6*
THE LINE UP BOOK   *YEARS*
   Illus. by Marisabina Russo. New York: Greenwillow, 1986.

SAPPR

   This satisfying, realistic story of how a little boy lined up his toys and objects all the way from his room to his mother in the kitchen is illustrated in bold, full-color, gouache paintings. *The Line Up Book* was given the 1987 International Reading Association Children's Book Award.

Rylant, Cynthia   *5–8*
MR. GRIGGS' WORK   *YEARS*
   Illus. by Julie Downing. New York: Orchard, 1989.

   Mr. Griggs loved his work in the post office and when he was not there everything he saw reminded him of it. The full-color pastel drawings highlight the old man's dedication, pride, productivity, and interest in his work and the people he served so faithfully.

Schotter, Roni   *5–9*
CAPTAIN SNAP AND THE CHILDREN OF VINEGAR LANE   *YEARS*
   Illus. by Marcia Sewall. New York: Orchard, 1989.

Oversized illustrations in firm, flowing line-and-wash paintings, done in a resist technique, blend with the well-written text to present this account of how children befriended grumpy old Captain Snap, who they discovered, quite by accident, had some very fine talents: he could make amazing sculptures out of bits of scrap and was an excellent storyteller.

Schwartz, Lynne Sharon   *5–10+*
THE FOUR QUESTIONS   *YEARS*
  Hebrew calligraphy by Lilli Wronker. Illus. by Ori Sherman. New
     York: Dial, 1989.

The four questions that begin the Seder are focused on in this picture book explanation of the Passover traditions and its celebration of freedom. Hebrew typography highlights what is told in art and pictures. The animal figures in each of the full-color, split-frame illustrations are suggestive of the techniques used in medieval Hagaddahs that were specially selected to avoid the biblical proscription against creating images. The last picture depicts the order of the Passover Seder in twelve parts. Turn the book upside down to get a better view of the Hebrew calligraphy and the split-frame pictures. The gouache paintings are filled with the symbols and rituals of this major Jewish holiday; each picture offers a talented blend of the traditional and the innovative.

Sneve, Virginia Driving Hawk (selector)   *6–12+*   X
DANCING TEEPEES: POEMS OF AMERICAN INDIAN   *YEARS*   MS,
YOUTH   SAPAR
  Trans. from Indian languages. Illus. by Stephen Gammell. New York:
     Holiday, 1989.

The songs, stories, chants, lullabies, and prayers in this book were selected from the oral traditions of numerous North American Indian tribes, as well as from anthologies by contemporary tribal poets. The collection reflects the theme of youth and the rite of passage from birth through adolescence. The illustrations are suggestive of the designs found in work by such tribes as the Navaho, Sioux, Crow, Wintu, Apache, and Osage.

Speare, Jean   *5–8*
A CANDLE FOR CHRISTMAS   *YEARS*
  Illus. by Ann Blades. New York: Margaret K. McElderry, 1986.

Full-page, naive-style watercolor paintings in full color were made by this award-winning artist to illustrate a story of a child anxiously awaiting his parent's return on Christmas Eve from their trip to their cattle range. The scenes depicting the family's home as well as those depicting the community (the Indian reservation in the rural Canadian Northwest) during the winter are really quite special, as is this account of family love and responsibility.

Steig, William   5–8
SPINKY SULKS   YEARS
   Illus. by William Steig. New York: Michael di Capua/Farrar, 1988.

Young readers will probably be shocked, but nonetheless amused by the extent to which Spinky pouts because he thinks his parents do not understand him and with the way he choses to tell his family that he is not angry with them anymore without losing his pride. The cartoon-style drawings in pen and ink and full-color, watercolor wash, so recognizable as the work of this well-known, award-winning author and illustrator, are perfect for this wonderfully witty story about family relationships.

Steptoe, John   2–4
BABY SAYS   YEARS
   Illus. by John Steptoe. New York: Lothrop, 1988.

SAPAR

Minimal text combines with realistic pictures in ink and colored pencil to depict this credible account of an infant trying to get his older brother's attention.

Stolz, Mary   4–7
STORM IN THE NIGHT   YEARS
   Illus. by Pat Cummings. New York: Harper, 1988.

In the darkness, during a power outage caused by a thunder and lightning storm, a black grandfather tells his young grandson about his experiences during a frightening storm when he was a child. The realistic, gouache paintings in luminous full-color highlight the mood of this intimate story and help one see the often unappreciated beauty offered by the flashes and slashes of lightning, the sounds of the wind and rain, and the scents of the rain-soaked, garden soil. Compare and contrast the language, illustrations and the mood of this book with those in *Tornado* by Arnold Adoff (Delacorte, 1977) and *Thunderstorm* by Mary Szilagyi (Bradbury, 1985).

Surat, Michele Maria   *5–8*
ANGEL CHILD, DRAGON CHILD   *YEARS*
   Illus. by Vo-Dinh Mai. Milwaukee: Raintree/Carnival Pr., 1983.   *85*

   Oversized impressionistic drawings, rendered in pencil and colored crayons, enrich this competently written text. Together, the words and pictures tell a memorable story of a Vietnamese girl's adjustment to life in the United States, and how a group of school children made it possible for her mother, who was still in Vietnam, to join the rest of the

Illus. 9. Illustration from *Angel Child, Dragon Child*, written by Michele Maria Surat, illustrated by Vo-Dinh Mai, published by Raintree/Carnival Press, 1983.

family in their new home. Vo-Dinh Mai's rendering of the children is wonderful. She portrays them in all shapes and sizes, reminding us that anyone can be the "outsider." (See illustration 9.)

Titherington, Jeanne   4–7
A PLACE FOR BEN   YEARS
   Illus. by Jeanne Titherington. New York: Greenwillow, 1987.

86

   The full-page, full-color illustrations, rendered in colored pencils, add considerable credibility to this predictable, realistic story about a little boy who searched for a place of his own when his baby brother was moved into his bedroom. Compare and contrast how the children in *A Place for Ben* and the children in *Evan's Corner*, written by Elizabeth Starr Hill and illustrated by Nancy Grossman (Holt, 1967), satisfy their need for privacy and what happens to them when they do.

Tsutsui, Yoriko   3–6
ANNA IN CHARGE   YEARS
   Illus. by Akiko. New York: Viking, 1989.

   Double-page, watercolor paintings extend the brief text to give a credible and realistic account of what happens when a young girl is left in charge of her little sister while their mother makes a quick trip to the bank.

Van Vorst, M. L.   2–4
A NORSE LULLABY   YEARS
   Illus. by Margot Tomes. New York: Lothrop, 1988.

   A bedtime poem about a mother and children waiting for the father's return on a wintry night. The double-page paintings embellish the sense of family love and security that prevails and provide a sense of what life was perhaps like during the winter in the far north in Europe at the turn of the century—the expansive wooded terrain, the clothing worn by the rural people, the architecture of a family's home and its furnishings, the attached farm buildings, and the animals (wild and domestic) that inhabited the area.

Viorst, Judith   4–8
ALEXANDER AND THE TERRIBLE, HORRIBLE, NO GOOD,   YEARS
VERY BAD DAY
   Illus. by Ray Cruz. New York: Atheneum, 1972.

   From the time Alexander got up in the morning—with gum in his hair because he went to sleep with gum in his mouth—until he went to bed—when his night-light burned out and he bit his tongue—everything went wrong. Expressive, crosshatched drawings in black and white highlight Alexander's grumpy mood.

Walker, Alice   *9–13+*
TO HELL WITH DYING   *YEARS*   *87*
     Illus. by Catherine Deeter. New York: HBJ, 1988.

Thoroughly accomplished, precise, realistic paintings done in acrylics illustrate a story about a relationship between an elderly neighbor, a little girl, and the other members of her family—a very special relationship based on mutual respect and love as well as tolerance and charity with regard to each other's faults. Told in the first person by the author, the moving story depicts how the little girl often helped keep the old man from dying—until, finally, not even his friends' love and interest could deter Death. A haunting story, to say the least.

Wells, Rosemary   *4–7*
SHY CHARLES   *YEARS*
     Illus. by Rosemary Wells. New York: Dial, 1988.

No matter what they said or did, Charles' parents could not get him to talk to strangers. But when his babysitter falls and is knocked unconscious, he forgets his shyness just long enough to put her at ease and call the emergency service. The black-ink line and full-color, watercolor-wash paintings add considerable charm and insight to this believable tale about a painfully timid and shy (mouse) child.

Williams, Vera B.   *4–8*
MUSIC, MUSIC FOR EVERYONE   *YEARS*
     Illus. by Vera B. Williams. New York: Greenwillow, 1983.

At first, Rosa plays her accordian alone to entertain her grandmother, who is sick and has to stay upstairs in bed. Soon her friends Leora, Moe, and Jenny join her in making music for grandmother. The four girls decide to form a combo which they call the Oak Street Band, and Rosa saves her share of the money the band earns to help her mother pay for the expenses incurred in caring for her grandmother. Each of the expressionistic, watercolor illustrations is framed, and each frame is fashioned from the story elements contained in the illustrations. The details in the illustrations provide a superb sense of place and give a definite personality and ethnicity to Rosa, her family, friends, and community. *Music, Music for Everyone* follows two other books about these same people, written and illustrated by Williams—*A Chair for My*

Mother (Greenwillow, 1982), a 1983 Caldedott Honor book and the 1983 Boston Globe–Horn Book Award for Illustration, and *Something Special for Me* (Greenwillow, 1983).

Winthrop, Elizabeth   *3–7*
BEAR AND MRS. DUCK   YEARS
   Illus. by Patience Brewster. New York: Holiday, 1988.

88
SAPAR

   Children may easily compare their relationships with and their feelings about babysitters with those Bear had about his babysitter, Mrs. Duck. The perky line and watercolor-wash paintings that illustrate this slight animal fantasy add to its appeal and credibility. An especially good story to read to children who are convinced (and rightly so) that no babysitter is the same as mom, but when given the chance will often prove to be interesting and fun to be with.

Yarborough, Camille   *6–12*
CORNROWS   YEARS
   Illus. by Carole Byard. New York: Coward, 1979.

   A nicely written and exquisitely illustrated commentary on some salient experiences shared by black people in the United States. The large-sized, black-and-white, representational drawings truly dramatize and enrich this portrayal of warm family relationships, in which Mama and Grammaw instill in Sister and MeToo pride in their African heritage. Carole Byard received the Coretta Scott King Award in 1980 for the illustrations in this book.

Yashima, Taro (pseud. of Jun Iwamatsu)   *6–12*
CROW BOY   YEARS
   Illus. by Taro Yashima. New York: Viking, 1955.

   A moving story about the shy, withdrawn, little Japanese boy whose unusual talent finally brings him friendship and recognition. The text is brief and the illustrations are colorful, impressionistic paintings suggestive of modern Japanese art.

Yashima, Taro (pseud. of Jun Iwamatsu)   *3–6*
YOUNGEST ONE   YEARS
   Illus. by Taro Yashima. New York: Viking, 1962.

   The brief, simple text and exquisite, impressionistic paintings tell how Bobby, the youngest one, and Momo, his neighbor, become friends. *Momo's Kitten* (Viking, 1961) is another of Taro Yashima's excellent picture books.

Yolen, Jane   5–9
THE GIRL WHO LOVED THE WIND   *YEARS*   *89*
    Illus. by Ed Young. New York: Crowell, 1972

A stunning array of refined Persian miniatures skillfully reflect and extend the content, mood, and writing style of this thought-provoking Oriental tale of a king who wished to protect his beautiful daughter from the harsh realities of life.

Yolen, Jane   6–10
THE SEEING STICK   *YEARS*
    Illus. by Remy Charlip and Demetra Maraslis. New York: Crowell,
        1977.

Drawings done on vellum-surfaced boards with wax crayons and pencil result in damask-like textures and tones to illustrate this tender story about Hwei Ming, a blind princess who lived long ago in China. Many tried but failed to help her; then, with the help of a mysterious old man from the south and his long walking stick, she learns to "see" with her fingers, her mind, and her heart. Before the old man's arrival, when Hwei Ming is blind and insensitive to others and to the world around her, the illustrations are black and white; they are in full color after she learns to "see" and begins to teach other blind children in her city of Peking to see as she does, with the tips of her fingers.

Ziefert, Harriet   5–9
A NEW COAT FOR ANNA   *YEARS*
    Illus. by Anita Lobel. New York: Knopf, 1986.

There is no money to buy Anna a badly needed winter coat, so her mother implements an ingenious plan to provide it: she trades a fine gold watch to a farmer for a bag of wool from sheep; a beautiful lamp to an old woman who spins the wool into yarn (which Anna and her mother dye with ripe lingonberries they pick in the woods); a garnet necklace to a weaver who weaves the red yarn into cloth; and a porcelain teapot to the tailor who makes a coat according to Anna's measurements. Bright, expressionistic line and full-color-wash pictures embellish this charming true story.

Zolotow, Charlotte   *4–6*
A TIGER CALLED THOMAS
   Illus. by Catherine Stock. New York: Lothrop, 1988.

90   A new set of illustrations, impressionistic paintings done with crayon and watercolor, enrich this convincing and sensitive story of a shy child, reluctant to mix with people in the neighborhood into which he and his family have recently moved. During his rounds of trick-or-treating on Halloween he learns that both adults and children in his new neighborhood are anxious to get to know him.

Other People

Alderson, Sue Ann   *4–7*
IDA AND THE WOOL SMUGGLERS   *YEARS*
  Illus. by Ann Blades. New York: Margaret K. McElderry, 1987.

  During pioneer times on an island off the west coast of Canada, Ida
lived on a sheep farm with her family. On her way with some fresh
bread to their neighbors, who had just had a new baby and were much
too busy for baking, Ida foils smugglers' attempts to steal her favorite
ewe and its twin lambs. The full-page (and some double-page), naive-
style illustrations are in clear, full color and were done with watercolor.
They seem a perfect match for this heartwarming pastoral story. The
simplistic style evokes nostalgia for an earlier time, when traits like
love, caring, and honesty, were paramount. (See illustration 10.)

Anderson, Joan   *5–10*
JOSHUA'S WESTWARD JOURNEY   *YEARS*
  Illus. with photographs by George Ancona. New York: Morrow,
    1987.

  In 1836, young Joshua Carpenter and his family travel westward on
the National Road in their horse-drawn Conestoga wagon, leaving
Indianapolis to make a new home. Black-and-white photographs add
vivid details to the fact-filled journal and foster a greater appreciation
and understanding of the family's courageous, challenging, and sometimes frightening trip to their new home, a small town in Illinois.

Anno, Mitsumasa   *7–up*
ANNO'S JOURNEY   *YEARS*
  Illus. by Mitsumasa Anno. New York: Philomel, 1977.

  Mitsumasa Anno's journey through northern Europe needs no
words. He shares with everyone who opens this book his impressions
of the region's geography, its people at work and play, their art, architecture, and literature in detailed line-and-wash illustrations. A look at
any page reveals many treasures, themes, general impressions, and
ideas. Intriguing details from the works of European impressionist
painters, visual puzzles and jokes, on-going children's games, scenes
from well-known folk- and fairy-tales, and a sequence pertaining to a

IDA and the
WOOL SMUGGLERS

Sue Ann Alderson & Ann Blades

Illus. 10. Reprinted by permission of Margaret K. McElderry Books, an imprint of Macmillan Publishing Company from *Ida and the Wool Smugglers* by Sue Ann Alderson, illustrated by Ann Blades. Illustrations copyright © 1977 Ann Blades.

romantic involvement, are to be found in this imaginative and challenging multi-dimensional, wordless picture book.

Baynes, Pauline   6–10
NOAH AND THE ARK   YEARS
 Illus. by Pauline Baynes. New York: Holt, 1988.

 This Old Testament story of faith, rebirth, and regeneration, meticulously illustrated with rich, jewel-tone paintings done with ink and gouache, is replete with action-filled details. The illustrations are reminiscent of ancient, illuminated manuscripts.

Blegvad, Erik   6–12
SELF-PORTRAIT: ERIK BLEGVAD   YEARS   95
    Illus. by Erik Blegvad and others. Reading, Mass.: Addison-Wesley,
    1979.

In this brief, autobiograpical book, Erik Blegvad provides a revealing and impressionistic interpretation of the life that formed his unique, perky drawing style. His verbal comments, study sketches, and finished drawings and paintings offer young readers a glimpse of the thought processes and problem-solving techniques that precede the finished illustrations created by this well-known book artist. He also shares with readers a few illustrations created by some family members and by close friends who are book artists too.

Briggs, Raymond   10–14+
THE TIN-POT FOREIGN GENERAL AND THE OLD IRON   YEARS
WOMAN
    Illus. by Raymond Briggs. Boston: Little, Brown, 1985.

A multi-level picture book, with a deceptively simple narrative about the controversial Falklands War makes a powerful, provocative, satirical anti-war statement. The presence of racist and sexist overtones, especially with regard to Margaret Thatcher and General Galtieri, make it even more controversial. The use of two distinct illustrative styles adds to the savage, satirical tone: evocative charcoal drawings provide a sharp contrast to the gaudy, metallic caricatures that are mixed with them.

Briggs, Raymond   10–16+
WHEN THE WIND BLOWS   YEARS
    Illus. by Raymond Briggs. New York: Shocken, 1982.

A sharp, satirical commentary about the effects of nuclear war is made in this story of a retired couple who confront nuclear war with the same degree of naive optimism that successfully brought them through World War II in England. Extensive use of the Cockney idiom and cultural allusion appears in the text, the bulk of which is presented in a comic strip format. Stark, full-page, impressionistic illustrations, interjected between the cartoon-style illustrations, provide an ominous contrast and add to the build up of tension around the conflict. Be certain to point out to the children (if they fail to notice on their own) two important ways the illustrator uses color: one, his *gradual* replacement of the bright full-color cartoon illustrations with a sickly, gray-green and gray-brown tones and two, the book's pitch-black endpapers. Both add to the statement of doom expressed in the story; both function persuasively to convince the reader to endorse the theme expressed in the story. Compare and contrast uses of color, styles of art, and persuasive techniques in *When the Wind Blows, Hiroshima No Pika*, written and illustrated by Toshi Maruki (Lothrop, 1982), and *Rose Blanche*, written by Christopher Gallaz and Roberto Innocenti and illustrated by Roberto Innocenti (Creative Education, 1985).

Brodsky, Beverly (reteller)   *7–11+*
THE STORY OF JOB   *YEARS*
    Illus. by Beverly Brodsky. New York: Braziller, 1986.

This retelling of the Old Testament story of how God tests Job's faith by letting terrible misfortunes happen to him is a very special picture book! The text for this accomplished piece of writing is illustrated with dramatic and absolutely stunning expressionistic pictures, done in ink and vivid, full-color wash. Expressionism is used to achieve a scale that forcefully conveys the magnitude of Job's relationship to God. Another *tour de force* by an award-winning author and artist. (See illustration 11.)

Bunting, Eve   *6–9*
THE MAN WHO CALLED DOWN OWLS   *YEARS*
    Illus. by Charles Mikolaycak. New York: Macmillan, 1984.

Every night the old man walks in the woods and calls down the owls—a hawk owl, a great gray owl, a great horned owl, a barn owl, and an elf owl. During the day he cares for owls that are sick or injured. Soon, he shares his love for and knowledge about the owls with Con, a young boy from the village. When a stranger, who envied the old man's power to befriend the owls, kills him, the owls come and attack the stranger, forcing him to crawl and then run for safety. Thereafter, the owls, one and all, come to be with the boy, who befriends them and cares for the sick and injured among them as did his beloved mentor and friend. The large drawings done by this notable illustrator were rendered in pencil and reproduced in blue and black. They complement the text perfectly and extend the haunting story, told in precise poetic prose.

Illus. 11. Illustration from *The Story of Job* written and illustrated by Beverly Brodsky, copyright © 1986 by Beverly Brodsky, published by George Braziller, Inc., reprinted by permission of Beverly Brodsky.

Burleigh, Robert   *11–16+*
A MAN NAMED THOREAU   *YEARS*
   Illus. by Lloyd Bloom. New York: Atheneum, 1985.

A thought-provoking and attractive picture book for older readers, this is a brief but fairly comprehensive biographical sketch of Henry Thoreau, the well-known writer and philosopher, independent thinker and individualist whose works have long been studied and whose lifestyle has been idealized over the years. The informative book contains some fine quotes from Thoreau's writings, like examples of his word play that are both serious and fun. Other quotes reveal Thoreau's complex personality and demonstrate how pertinent his ideas are to our own concerns today. The full-page, black-and-white, expressionistic drawings, done in soft pencil, add immeasurably to the mood and theme of the biography, which celebrates deep and simple truths rather than the surface of things. A bibliography of further reading is included at the back of the book, as is a list of Important Dates in the Life of Thoreau.

Carrick, Donald   *6–9*
HARALD AND THE GREAT STAG   *YEARS*
   Illus. by Donald Carrick. New York: Clarion/Houghton, 1988.

   An ingenious young hero, Harald foils the medieval baron's sponsored hunt for a majestic stag. The expertly executed, line and watercolor-wash, expressionistic illustrations offer young readers an authentic and aesthetically pleasing glimpse of the realities of medieval life. Especially effective are the scenes of the lush forest, the animals (dogs, horses, and the stag) involved in the hunt, and the huntsmen of the era. Readers of all ages will find much to think about and discuss in this unique portrayal of an anti-hunting theme. See *Harald and the Giant Knight* (Clarion/Houghton, 1982), in which Harald challenges the medieval practices of tournaments and jousting.

Chaikin, Miriam (adapter)   *8–12*
EXODUS   *YEARS*
   Illus. by Charles Mikolaycak. New York: Holiday, 1987.

   Large, realistic paintings in full color extend and embellish this fine adaptation of the second book of the Bible, which tells how Moses, following the Word of God, led the Israelites out of slavery in Egypt to Canaan. The illustrator makes extensive use of graphic symbols related to the twelve tribes that followed Moses and Aaron out of Egypt as well as other authentic details that reflect the world of the ancient Egyptians. A fine map at the back of the book shows the probable route of the Exodus.

Coalson, Glo   *5–10*
THREE STONE WOMAN   *YEARS*
   Illus. by Glo Coalson. New York: Atheneum, 1971.

   An Eskimo folktale that tells of the good fortune that befell the good and starving Ana and the bad things that happened to Tula, her hard-hearted sister-in-law. Primitive black-and-white paintings reflect the tradition of the Eskimos.

Cohen, Barbara (adapter)   5–9
EVEN HIGHER   YEARS
   Illus. by Anatoly Ivanov. New York: Lothrop, 1987.

   An adaptation of a Jewish folktale, this story is about a Litvak, a
skeptical man who doubts that the rabbi of the village of Nemirov goes
to heaven to speak to God each Friday during Rosh Hashanah, the
Jewish New Year. When the Litvak discovers that the rabbi raises
himself "even higher" than heaven, he becomes one of the rabbi's most
faithful followers. The full-color, realistic paintings provide an excellent sense of ethnicity and peace for this adaptation of *Oyb nisht
nokh hekhert* retold in Yiddish by Isaac Leib Peretz originally in 1851.

Cohen, Barbara   8–12
I AM JOSEPH   YEARS
   Illus. by Charles Mikolaycak. New York: Lothrop, 1980.

   Cohen's retelling of the Old Testament story about Joseph—his life
in Egypt, first as a slave and later as the Pharaoh's adviser, and his
reunion with his father and eleven brothers—is told convincingly in
the first person. The realistic paintings are in full color and effectively
dramatize the well-known story from Genesis.

de Paola, Tomie   3–8
THE FIRST CHRISTMAS   YEARS
   Illus. by Tomie de Paola. New York: Putnam, 1984.

   This version of the nativity is retold through minimal text and six
beautiful, three-dimensional, pop-up scenes that change as the reader
moves the parts indicated by strategically placed arrows. The book is
sturdy in its construction, stunning in appearance, and most certainly
will be a family keepsake or a treasure in the professional book col-
lector's library.

Feelings, Muriel   5–10
MOJA MEANS ONE: SWAHILI COUNTING BOOK   YEARS
   Illus. by Tom Feelings. New York: Dial, 1971.

   A counting book that familiarizes the reader with number concepts
and some basic aspects of East African life. It includes a map which
shows the countries where Swahili is spoken. Stunning, double-
spread, representational paintings evoke an aura of place in this unique
counting book. Named a 1972 Caldecott Honor book.

Field, Rachel   *3–8*
GENERAL STORE   *YEARS*
    Illus. by Giles Laroche. Boston: Little, Brown, 1988.

100   This classic poem about a girl imagining the general store she will own someday is illustrated with detailed, full-color, naive-style paintings. Young readers (and adults) will need to look at the illustrations *many* times to see the fascinating array of things that are for sale in this well-equipped general store.

Fisher, Leonard Everett   *10–16+*
THE ALAMO   *YEARS*
    Illus. by Leonard Everett Fisher. New York: Holiday, 1987.

  Black-and-white photographs, scratchboard illustrations, and meticulously written text document the history of the Alamo, a building in San Antonio, Texas, well-known throughout North America as a fortress during Texas' fight for independence from Mexico. This "shrine of Texas liberty" has also served as a Franciscan mission, a Mexican army barracks as well as a barracks for Confederate soldiers during the Civil War, a United States military supply post, a warehouse, and a general store. An invaluable picture book for older readers.

Forest, Heather (reteller)   *4–7*
THE BAKER'S DOZEN: A COLONIAL AMERICAN TALE   *YEARS*
    Illus. by Susan Gaber. San Diego: Gulliver Books/HBJ, 1988.

  This is a competent retelling of the legend of the origin of the custom among bakers to define a dozen as twelve plus one more. The large, full-color illustrations, done in watercolor and colored pencil, add considerable authenticity and credibility to a story emphasizing that when generosity replaces greed, good fortune follows.

Freedman, Russell   *8–12+*
BUFFALO HUNT   *YEARS*
    Illus. New York: Holiday, 1988.

  A wealth of facts about the buffalo in the 1800s is presented in this excellent, informational book. It explains that the Indians of the Great Plains considered the buffalo a sacred animal and praised its spirit. When they hunted and killed it, they used all of its parts, from head to tail. They used its meat, hide, and bones to subsist; in later years they used only buffalo hides and tongues, selling them to white people at considerable profit. It tells also that white hunters traveling westward in covered wagons, professional hunters hired by the United States Army, and railroad construction crews killed the buffalo for food. Eventually no buffalo remained to roam the Great Plains. This book is illustrated with photographs of a few traditional Indian paintings and designs on robes, masks, lodges as well as reproductions of paintings and drawings done by artists and adventurers who also traveled westward in the 1800s, among them, George Catlin, Karl Bodmer, and Albert Bierstaat.

Fussenegger, Gertrude   *5–9+*
NOAH'S ARK   YEARS
    Trans. from the German by Anthea Bell. Illus. by Annegert Fueh-
      shuber. New York: Lippincott, 1983.

    Full-page, naive-style paintings in rich, jewel tones aptly elaborate and embellish this competent retelling of the Old Testament story of how Noah and the animals survived the flood. It was originally published in 1982 under the title *Die Arche Noah,* by Annette Betz Verlag im Verlag Carl Uebberreuter, Vienna-Munich. Compare and contrast the text and illustrations of this picture book with Peter Spier's *Noah's Ark* (Doubleday, 1977), the 1978 Caldecott Medal winner.

Gackenbach, Dick   *7–10*
THE LEATHERMAN   YEARS
    Illus. by Dick Gackenbach. Boston: Clarion/Houghton, 1977.

    A touching story about an eccentric traveler who came to Mill City, Connecticut, every thirty-four days (Leatherman's Day). He was always on schedule, always wore a leather suit, and never spoke to anyone. People were intrigued by his odd behavior and curious about him and his endless wandering through the Connecticut hills, into New York state, and back again. The real leatherman, Jules Bourclay, was born in France. After experiencing financial and personal disaster, he came to America. His bizarre and lonely journey continued for thirty-one years until 1889, when he was found dead in a cave at Mount Pleasant, New York, and was buried in a pauper's grave. Line-and-wash, three-color illustrations add considerably to the feeling and sensitivity of this story. A very special historical fiction piece for the younger reader.

Gallaz, Christopher and Roberto Innocenti.   *8–12+*
ROSE BLANCHE   YEARS
    Trans. from the French by Martha Coventry and Richard Graglia.
      Illus. by Roberto Innocenti. Mankato, Minn: Creative Education,
      1985.

Rose Blanche, who lived in a small town in Germany during World War II, describes incidents that allude to the war: the presence of German soldiers, their tanks and trucks in the town, soldiers herding people at gun point into the trucks. She tells also how she followed the tracks of one of the trucks, loaded with people, into the forest and discovered many children, emaciated and starving, each wearing a gold star, imprisoned behind electric barbed wire. The text changes to the third person narration, and the reader is told how Rose Blanche sneaks food to the children in the camp each day—first her own lunch, then more and more food from home, growing thinner herself because she is saving her food for the young prisoners. One day Rose Blanche does not come home from school. The reason for her failure to return is devastating. The illustrator's portrayal of the fog on the day she "disappeared" and the use of the lily and other flowers to symbolize what happened to the girl and the end of the war only serve to emphasize the haunting theme of the story. The detailed, surrealistic paintings must be examined very carefully; they offer a number of profound visual comments—about war in general and about children as victims of war in particular—that were omitted or briefly alluded to in the sparse text. Compare the theme of *Hiroshima No Pika*, written and illustrated by Toshi Maruki (Lothrop, 1982), with the theme of this book. *Rose Blanche* was named the 1986 Batchelder Award winner by the Association of Library Service to Children of the American Library Association.

Goble, Paul   *6–10*
DEATH OF THE IRON HORSE   *YEARS*
    Illus. by Paul Goble. New York: Bradbury, 1987.

On August 7, 1867, a group of Cheyenne Indians derailed a Union Pacific freight train traveling from Omaha to Fort McPherson in North Platte, Nebraska. The accomplished artwork that effectively illustrates this account of their brave, defiant act against white men who encroached on their territory, was done in India ink and watercolor. It is important to notice the special beauty and graphic accomplishment of the illustrations in this book, as well as the authenticity of their content—aspects of the terrain, the flora and fauna of the region where the action occurred, and the details of the Indians' clothes, headpieces, and hairstyles, for example.

Hall, Donald   *6–10*
OX-CART MAN   *YEARS*
    Illus. by Barbara Cooney. New York: Viking, 1979.

In October the ox-cart man and his family packed the ox-cart with things they had made or grown during the year. Then he made the long journey to the Portsmouth Market where he sold all the goods, bought provisions that he and his family did not produce on the farm, and returned home to start the cycle once again. The day-to-day life of a nineteenth-century New England family is convincingly and authentically depicted in this lovely picture book. The naive-style illustrations evoke the color and style of primitive paintings done on wood in America during the era that this quiet story takes place. Barbara Cooney received the 1980 Caldecott Medal for her illustrations in *Ox-Cart Man*.

Harrison, Ted   *8–14*
CHILDREN OF THE YUKON   *YEARS*
   Illus. by Ted Harrison. Plattsburgh, New York: Tundra, 1977.

A rare informational book! Bright, flat colors illustrate these stylized paintings, suggestive of the naive school of art, offering a childlike charm and considerable depth and feeling to the emotional yet informative and authoritative array of facts about the history and way of life throughout the year in the various settlements of the Yukon. In the main, the author-artist has emphasized how the Yukon, which is in the northwest corner of Canada and east of Alaska, differs from other parts of North America.

Harrison, Ted   *6–11+*
A NORTHERN ALPHABET   *YEARS*
   Illus. by Ted Harrison. Plattsburgh, N.Y.: Tundra, 1982.

This unique alphabet book depicts cultural aspects of people living across North America, north of the sixtieth parallel and, in some cases, as far south as the fifty-fifth parallel. Each of the flat, bright, full-color, naive-style paintings is filled with things beginning with a single letter of the alphabet pertaining to some aspect of life in the Yukon. The text, in large primary-sized type, offers a basic, simple statement about the picture. It is intended to serve only as a story starter, for each picture tells so much more than the text suggests. Thus, the children are encouraged to look more closely at each picture, to find more things in it beginning with that letter, and to use them to create a more elaborate story. For those who need help with the names of things in the pictures, objects are listed in the back of the book. Also, each picture is framed with a strip of many words pertaining to the Yukon, though they are not shown in the picture. This serves to arouse the curiosity of the readers so they can seek out other books that would provide information about these enrichment words. (See illustration 12.)

Harvey, Brett   *7–10*
CASSIE'S JOURNEY: GOING WEST IN THE 1860'S   *YEARS*
    Illus. by Deborah Kogan Ray. New York: Holiday, 1988.

Illus. 12. Taken from *A Northern Alphabet* © 1982 Ted Harrison, published by Tundra Books.

A little girl describes her family's journey from Illinois to California by wagon during the 1860s. The black, grease-pencil sketches offer a dramatic, impressionistic glimpse of the hardships, dangers, and pleasures experienced by one family, as well as by some other members of the wagon train during the overland journey to the Pacific. The very simple, topograpical map at the beginning of the book shows the route followed by Cassie and her family; it should help readers better appreciate the distance and varied terrain these travelers covered during their migration westward.

Hastings, Selina (reteller)   *7–10*
THE MAN WHO WANTED TO LIVE FOREVER   *YEARS*
   Illus. by Reg Cartwright. New York: Holt, 1988.

   Bodkin wanted to live forever. He almost managed to do just that until he was duped by Death, who eventually "gently led him away." Twelve, full-page, surrealistic paintings in full color and some small paintings reinforce this perceptive folktale. Compare this picture book about the issue of living forever with Natalie Babbitt's classic, fanciful novel *Tuck Everlasting* (Farrar, 1975).

Hort, Lenny (reteller)   *6–10*
THE BOY WHO HELD BACK THE SEA   *YEARS*
   Illus. by Thomas Locker. New York: Dial, 1987.

   Originally this well-known Dutch legend about an irresponsible boy who plugs the leaking hole in the dike and thereby saves his low-lying village from being destroyed by the raging sea was told by Mary Mapes Dodge in her classic novel *Hans Brinker or The Silver Skates*. On this occasion it has been adapted and retold as a story within a story in the personal and informal style of a storyteller. The full-page illustrations that provide an authetic setting in terms of time and place for this legend are in full-color oil paintings, done in the style of the seventeenth-century Dutch masters (Rembrandt and Vermeer) known for their use of sunlight and torchlight in their landscapes and seascapes. A fine picture book.

Houston, Gloria   *5–9*
THE YEAR OF THE PERFECT CHRISTMAS TREE: AN   *YEARS*
APPALACHIAN STORY
   Illus. by Barbara Cooney. New York: Dial, 1988.

A charming story of how a mother and child follow through on the family's commitment to give the community a Christmas tree, which the father, on military duty during the Great War, had tagged for the occasion the spring before he left. Accomplished, expressionistic paintings give the reader a complete sense of what winter is like in an Appalachian mountain valley village and what a mountain home looks like, and help the reader experience, albeit vicariously, a traditional Christmas Eve celebration in a small, community church.

Hutton, Warwick (adapter) *5–10 YEARS*
ADAM AND EVE: THE BIBLE STORY
    Illus. by Warwick Hutton. New York: Margaret K. McElderry, 1987.

Based on the first three chapters of Genesis in the King James version of the Old Testament, this is an eloquent retelling of the story of the first day of creation to Adam and Eve's expulsion from the Garden of Eden. The full-page, expressionistic illustrations, done in pen and ink and full-color watercolor, place most of the action in the garden. The Creator is shown from the rear so the readers can create their own images rather than have one imposed on them.

Kimmel, Eric *5–9 YEARS*
THE CHANUKKAH TREE
    Illus. by Giora Carmi. New York: Holiday, 1988.

This original story, told in the style of a folktale, tells of how the Jewish people of Chelm realize that a peddler has duped them into believing that other Jewish people have Chanukkah trees and convinced them they should have one, too. When they learn that they have been made fools of by this swindler, they are crushed. But by a clever twist of fate, they quite unexpectedly discover a wonderfully satisfying use for their tree. From then on, every year at Chanukkah, one will find a Chanukkah Tree in Chelm: a pine tree decorated with potato latkes and dreidels, lit with Chanukkah candles, and topped with the synagogue door, which has a six-pointed star carved on it. The full-page line, and full-color ink-and-wash, experessionistic illustrations reflect the aura of long ago and far away, as well as the droll humor that pervades this tale.

Kipling, Rudyard *9–12+ YEARS*
GUNGA DIN
    Introd. by Kingsley Amis. Illus. by Robert Andrew Parker. San Diego: HBJ, 1987.

An informative commentary about Kipling and his background offers justification for his writing poetry about the British military serving in India, especially the classic narrative poem "Gunga Din," based on the Indian mutiny of 1857 and a heroic water-carrier at the seige of Delhi in that year. The language of the poem is suggestive of the British Cockney and its rhythms of the music halls in the late 1800s. The illustrations are expressionistic pen-and-ink drawings and full-color watercolor and gouache wash. They give the reader a fine sense of place as well as a genuine feel for the characters involved in this incident—be they the officers, the enlisted men, or, like Gunga Din, the "blackfaced crew" who served as water-carriers and tended the wounded under fire.

Kismaric, Carole (adapter)   *5–8*
A GIFT FROM SAINT NICHOLAS   *YEARS*
   Illus. by Charles Mikolaycak. New York: Holiday, 1988.

A simplified version of the original Flemish story, *A Gift from Saint Nicholas* by Felix Timmermons, this tells of how a poor little girl is unexpectedly given a treasured chocolate ship on St. Nicholas Eve. The full-page, rather stylized, realistic paintings, in rich full color, add a fine sense of time and ethnicity (Old Germany) to this ancient holiday story.

Laird, Elizabeth   *5–10+*
THE ROAD TO BETHLEHEM: AN ETHIOPIAN NATIVITY   *YEARS*
   Foreword by Terry Waite. Illus. New York: Holt, 1987.

This liberal adaptation of the story of the Nativity, as told by a bishop of Cyprus in the fourth century, is illustrated with reproductions of handpainted pictures that Ethiopian artists made over two hundred years ago for manuscripts commissioned by the kings and queens of that African country. Accompanying each illustration is an explanation of the content and the symbolism—for example a person in profile with only one eye showing suggests a wicked person; a person holding a strip of cloth indicates an important person; and persons with their right hands raised demonstrate the traditional gesture of blessing. The text and the illustrations can offer the reader an insight into a rich and ancient but little-known Ethiopian Christian culture.

Langstaff, John (compiler)   *5–10+*
WHAT A MORNING! THE CHRISTMAS STORY IN BLACK   *YEARS*
SPIRITUALS
   Musical arrangements by John Andrew Ross. Illus. by Ashley Bryan. New York: Margaret K. McElderry, 1987.

Bible verses illustrated with full-color, expressionistic paintings done in tempera and reproduced in rich, full color, are alternated with five black spirituals to tell the story of the Nativity. The presence of African motifs in all of the illustrations in this unique picture book, which feature a black Holy Family, will prove an inspiration to all—blacks and nonblacks alike. The musical arrangements are for singing and piano; guitar cords are also suggested. The "Note to Teachers, Parents and Instrumentalists" at the back of the book offers helpful suggestions for interpreting the text and illustrations and for using the book.

Lasker, David   6–9
THE BOY WHO LOVED MUSIC   YEARS
    Illus. by Joe Lasker. New York: Viking, 1979.

This historical fiction in picture book format relates how Joseph Haydn came to compose the "Farewell" Symphony in an easy-to-read story about Karl, a young musician in the orchestra of Prince Esterhazy. The carefully devised, impressionistic paintings are in full color and printed as double-page spreads, each one complementing and extending the wealth of information about the people, customs, and fashions that prevailed in Australia-Hungary during the latter part of the eighteenth century.

Lasker, Joe   8–12
MERRY EVER AFTER: THE STORY OF TWO MEDIEVAL   YEARS
WEDDINGS
    Illus. by Joe Lasker. New York: Viking, 1976.

In a multi-dimensional commentary, the nuptial customs and rites that prevailed in medieval times among the nobility and the peasantry are compared. Beautifully accomplished watercolor paintings combining some of the stylistic elements used by such fifteenth-century European artists as Pisanello, Carpaccio, Rogier van der Wayden, Dürer, and Brueghel extend the brief but well-written text.

Lasker, Joe   8–10
A TOURNAMENT OF KNIGHTS   YEARS
    Illus. by Joe Lasker. New York: Crowell, 1986.

This exciting account about a young knight's first tournament against an experienced knight errant is filled with informative descriptions of the ceremonies, the violence, the rewards, and the tragedies inherent in these traditional events. The watercolor illustrations detail aspects of the duel itself and depict, with a high degree of authenticity, representations of the knights, their weapons, their armor, the clothes worn by the common people and the nobility, the architecture, and so forth. One can acquire a considerable amount of information about the Middle Ages in general as well as about knighthood in particular from this picture book. Compare the images of knighthood and positions taken on the issue of tournaments and jousting in particular depicted in Lasker's picture book with those depicted in *Harald and the Giant Knight* by Donald Carrick (Clarion/Houghton, 1982) and *Medieval Feast* by Aliki (Crowell, 1983).

Lepon, Shoshana   *6–10+*
THE TEN TESTS OF ABRAHAM   *YEARS*
    Illus. by Sigmund Forst. New York: Judaica Pr., 1986.

Following the interpretation of Rashi, the ten tests of Abraham are recalled in rhyme and are illustrated effectively with expressionistic, ink drawings, reproduced in sepia. At the end of the book there are Topics for Discussion, which could provoke some higher order thinking.

Maril, Nadja   *7–11+*
ME, MOLLY MIDNIGHT   *YEARS*
    Illus. with paintings and drawings by Herman Maril. Owings Mills,
        Md.: Stemmer House, 1977.

Molly Midnight tells how she became a special friend and favorite model for Herman Maril, world famous watercolorist and oil painter. She also describes Maril's studio, the working materials he used as well as his techniques for using color, form and space. Many of Maril's most important paintings are reproduced in full color. See the sequel, *Runaway Molly Midnight* by Nadja Maril, with more paintings and drawings by Herman Maril (Stemmer House, 1980). Compare approaches by artists and their works as depicted in these books with those depicted in *All I See*, written by Cynthia Rylant and illustrated by Peter Catalanotto (Orchard, 1988).

Maruki, Toshi   *8–12*
HIROSHIMA NO PIKA   *YEARS*
    Illus. by Toshi Maruki. New York: Lothrop, 1982.

A stirring story of what happened to a little girl, the members of her family, and the residents of Hiroshima when "the flash of Hiroshima" (the atomic bomb) was dropped on that city by the Americans on the morning of August 6, 1945. The full-color, impressionistic and expressionistic paintings will evoke a deep emotional response from the reader. They are in sharp contrast to the very simple, understated, almost emotionless text, making the theme, "it can't happen again if no one drops the bomb," even more forceful. Notice how the illustrations and the narration move repeatedly from the child, to the family, to the multitudes, then back again. That is an effective persuasive technique, whether conscious or not on the part of the author-illustrator. This book, originally published in Japan in 1980 by Komine Shoten Co., Ltd. under the same title, received the Nipon Award for the most excellent picture book of Japan, presented by the Yomiuri Shimbun Press in 1981. The publisher of the English translation was awarded the 1983 Mildred Batchelder Award by the Association of Library Service to Children of the American Library Association.

Mattingly, Christobel   *6–9*
THE ANGEL WITH A MOUTH-ORGAN   *YEARS*
   Illus. by Astra Lacis. New York: Holiday, 1984.

   Each year, just before a glass angel is placed on the top of the family's Christmas tree, a young mother tells her own children how the angel came to symbolize a new beginning for her and her family when she was a child. She explains how it serves as a reminder of their experiences during World War II, when they were forced to flee their home after it was bombed, were separated from their father, and, after many years of wandering and suffering the hardships brought by the war, were all finally reunited. The mother's father found the glass angel in the ruins of a church. He said it kept him company while he searched for his family. This moving account of innocent people as victims of war is told in fine language combined with illustrations done in pen and ink, crosshatched technique, and watercolor wash. Compare and contrast how the words and illustrations in this picture book tell the story of how a family, separated during war, is reunited with how the words and illustrations tell the story in *The Miracle Tree*, written by Christobel Mattingley and illustrated by Marianne Yamaguchi (Gulliver/HBJ, 1985).

Mattingly, Christobel   *8–12+*
THE MIRACLE TREE   *YEARS*
   Illus. by Marianne Yamaguchi. San Diego: Gulliver/HBJ, 1985.

A pine tree, planted on Christmas Day, becomes the symbol of hope and happiness for three Japanese people separated by World War II, each suffering devastating effects from the atomic bomb dropped on the city of Nagasaki. Readers are bound to be fascinated by the gradually unfolding relationship among these three people and the role the tree plays in reuniting them twenty long years after they had been separated by war and, particularly, by the bombing. The exquisite use of language and the poignant, black-and-white charcoal drawings add up to a memorable read, one to be savored. Be certain to notice the green-and-white, over-all pine-tree design on the endpapers—another thoughtful addition by the illustrator, by the art editor, or both to reiterate the symbolism in the story. Compare and contrast the effects of World War II on people as depicted in this book, where the action is in Japan, with *The Angel with a Mouth-Organ,* written by Christobel Mattingly and illustrated by Astra Lacis (HBJ, 1986), where the action is in Europe, or with *Hiroshima No Pika* (Lothrop, 1982), where the action is in Hiroshima, Japan.

McCurdy, Michael   5–9
HANNAH'S FARM: THE SEASONS ON AN EARLY   *YEARS*
AMERICAN HOMESTEAD
    Illus. by Michael McCurdy. New York: Holiday, 1988.

Elegant and masterfully executed, detailed wood engravings, printed in black-and-white, embellish the well-written text about the year-round activities that are typical of a family on a farm in the Berkshire Hills of Massachusetts during the nineteenth century.

McDermott, Beverly Brodsky   10–up
THE GOLEM   *YEARS*
    Illus. by Beverly Brodsky McDermott. New York: Lippincott, 1976.

A retelling of a Jewish legend stressing that hope for a better world is tempered by the reality of humankind's limitations. The large-sized, sophisticated, expressionistic paintings created to illustrate this interpretation of the legend were done in gouache, watercolor, dye, and ink on watercolor paper. Named a 1977 Caldecott Honor book.

Newlands, Anne   7–10
MEET EDGAR DEGAS   *YEARS*
    Illus. New York: Lippincott and National Gallery of Canada, 1989.

A biographical sketch and commentaries about this noted French artist, taken from letters, notebooks, and anecdotes about Degas reported by other people accompany beautiful reproductions of fourteen of his paintings, as well as a study sketch and photograph of the well-known wax sculpture, "The Little 14-Year Old Dancer." A very good first guide to some of Degas' most beautiful art pieces.

Pitseolak, Peter   *7–16*
PETER PITSEOLAK'S ESCAPE FROM DEATH   *YEARS*
  Introd. and ed. by Dorothy Eber. Trans. by Eva Keleotak Deer and
    Lucy Carriere. Illus. by Peter Pitseolak. New York: Delacorte, 1978.

An account of a harrowing walrus hunt during which the Eskimo artist and his stepson Ashevak were caught on a huge ice field that was swiftly moving out to sea. This eloquently written story of their battle against the elements and the full-color illustrations, made with felt pen, crayon, and pencil in the naive-art style, merge into an absolute masterpiece of bookmaking that offers the reader a rare glimpse of a slice of life well-worth seeing and thinking about.

                                                                      9–18
PITSEOLAK: PICTURES OUT OF MY LIFE   *YEARS*
  Ed. by Dorothy Eber. Illus. by Pitseolak. Seattle: Univ.
    of Washington Pr., 1972. Design Collaborative Books/Oxford
    Univ. Pr., paper, 1978.

Written from recorded interviews conducted by Eber, this autobiography of Pitseolak, a noted Eskimo artist, is also a documentary account of how Cape Dorset, a remote point on the Hudson Strait, became an internationally recognized artists' colony. No dates are used in the autobiography; instead Pitseolak relates all events to other important happenings. The text appears in English as well as in syllabics, the phonetic system of writing used by the Eskimos, introduced to them by missionaries in the late nineteenth century. A wealth of Pitseolak's drawings and prints accompany this, her life story told in her own words, a book that belongs in every elementary and secondary school library collection!

Prather, Ray   *5–9*
THE OSTRICH GIRL   *YEARS*
  Illus. by Ray Prather. New York: Scribner, 1978.

In a sampling of East African tradition in a modern setting, detailed, full-color illustrations, done in pencil and wash, extend and enrich a brief, well-written story that unfolds in a manner suggestive of the storyteller. According to the tradition on which this tale is based, each newborn child is placed under a tree and the person returning it to its parents is designated its godfather or godmother and may help in its naming. This picture book is about Oster, also called the Ostrich Girl because she was found under a thorn tree, wrapped in a bundle that looked like an ostrich egg. Most young readers will commiserate with Oster who, when told by the children in the village that her parents had stolen her from the ostriches, runs off into the forest and searches tearfully for her real mother. Before or after reading this story aloud, one might want to play at least a portion of the recording of the Houston Grand Opera production of Scott Joplin's opera, *Treemonisha* (Deutsche Grammophone-Stereo 2707083), the story line of which also has its basis in the same tradition.

Provensen, Alice and Martin   *6–10*
A PEACEABLE KINGDOM: THE SHAKER ABECEDARIUS   *YEARS*
    Illus. by Alice and Martin Provensen. Afterword by Richard Meran
        Barsam. New York: Viking, 1978.

This alphabet in verse (an abecedarius) is very much like those the Shakers created for the practical purpose of teaching their children to read. A successive letter of the alphabet is used at the beginning of each line of the twenty-six line, rhymed verse in which more than one hundred real and fanciful animals are named. The Provensens have offered today's children a truly authentic glimpse of the Shaker's lifestyle and the era in which they flourished. The sense of joy in design and the humor and emphasis on love, so typical of the Shakers, permeate this picture book. A note on Shaker history and education is provided in an afterword by Richard Meran Barsam.

Raboff, Ernest   *9–12*
MARC CHAGALL: ART FOR CHILDREN   *YEARS*
    Illus. Garden City, N.Y.: Lippincott, 1988.

A brief presentation of some facts about this artist: a biographical sketch, about fifteen full-color reproductions of his work, and smaller drawings and designs in black and white. Some of the other picture books in the Art for Children series are about Paul Klee (1988), Pablo Picasso (1987), Rembrandt (1987), and Leonardo da Vinci (1987).

Raskin, Ellen   *6–10*
THE WORLD'S GREATEST FREAK SHOW   *YEARS*
    Illus. by Ellen Raskin. New York: Atheneum, 1971.

Alastair Pflug gets his comeuppance when he takes an assortment of people to the country of Tizuvthee and presents them as "freaks." Full-color illustrations (heavy line decorated with flat color overlays) are perfectly compatible with the text and add much to the thought-provoking, satirical humor of the story.

Rubin, Cynthia Eylce (selector)   6–10+
ABC AMERICANA FROM THE NATIONAL GALLERY   *YEARS*
OF ART
   Illus. San Diego: HBJ, 1989.

This ABC picture book presents, in alphabetical order, selected watercolor paintings from the Index of American Design, a graphic archive of American folk and decorative arts from the colonial period through the nineteenth century. Each page is a visual delight! At the back of the book is a listing of the source of each picture, the medium in which it was originally rendered, and the artist's name.

Sewall, Marcia   7–12+
THE PILGRIMS OF PLIMOTH   *YEARS*
   Illus. by Marcia Sewall. New York: Atheneum, 1986.

Large and full-color gouache, expressionistic paintings and a text written in a style (spelling, grammar, and terminology) suggestive of that used by the English in the 1600s, effectively recreate the day-to-day experiences, thoughts, and activities that were part of the social life and customs of the pilgrims as they traveled across the Atlantic Ocean and experienced their first years in New World. A helpful and extensive glossary of terms used in this chronicle of the early settlers is included at the back of the book.

Sills, Leslie   8–12+
INSPIRATIONS: STORIES ABOUT WOMEN ARTISTS   *YEARS*
   Illus. Niles, Ill.: Whitman, 1989.

The lives of four accomplished women artists, all of whom persevered against many obstacles and pursued their work as they wanted to, are described briefly. These four women artists are Georgia O'Keefe, Frida Kahlo, Alice Neel, and Faith Ringo. In each case, photographs of the women and reproductions of their work, in full color and in black and white are included. A very informative and inspiring book.

Stanley, Diane and Vennema   7–12
SHAKA: KING OF THE ZULUS   YEARS
    Illus. by Diane Stanley. New York: Morrow, 1988.

   This attractive, interesting, and informative picture book biography
is about Shaka, the famous nineteenth-century king of a tiny Zulu clan,   *115*
who built from it a mighty nation made up of an army of the finest
warriors in South Africa, an army revered for its power, endurance, and
discipline. The full-page illustrations detail the terrain and ethnic artifacts (clothing, hairstyles, pottery, jewelry, and fighting gear) of the
people in South Africa in this era. A pronunciation guide for Zulu
words in the order of their appearance is presented at the beginning of
the book; at the back of the book, the map of Africa and the bibliography recommending sources for children interested in further research add to the quality of this significant publication. For another
fine picture book biography by this husband and wife team, see the
1986 ALA Notable Book *Peter the Great* (Morrow, 1985).

Tsuchiya, Yulio   9–12
FAITHFUL ELEPHANTS: A TRUE STORY OF ANIMALS,   YEARS
PEOPLE, AND WAR
    Trans. by Tomoko Tsuchiya Dykes. Illus. by Ted Lewin. Boston:
        Houghton, 1988.

   A highly emotional and disturbing portrayal of grief, fear, and sadness produced by war. The zookeeper at the Ueno Zoo in Tokyo relates
a grim account of why and how three famous performing elephants at
the zoo were allowed to starve to death and all of the other animals in
the zoo were poisoned to death. This true story is illustrated with
expressive watercolor paintings, most of them double-page spreads.
(Notice how the illustrator dwarfs the humans in relation to the elephants, thus emphasizing the animals' vulnerability to zoo keepers.)
This tragic tale was first published in Japan in 1951 by Kin-no-Hoshi-
Sha Co., Ltd., under the title *Kawaiso no zo*. It is read on the Japanese
radio every year to mark the anniversary of Japan's surrender in World
War II. A tomb on the grounds of the Ueno Zoo contains the remains
of the three elephants and other animals that were killed by command
of the Japanese army because it was worried about what would happen
if the animals escaped from their cages if the bombs hit the zoo. Children still decorate the monument with semba-tsuru (paper cranes).
Compare and contrast how the author and illustrator of *Faithful Elephants* made the antiwar statement and portrayed innocent victims of

war with the ways these same themes in the 1983 Batchelder Award book *Hiroshima No Pika,* written and illustrated by Toshi Maruki (Lothrop, 1982) and the 1986 Batchelder Award book *Rose Blanche,* written by Christopher Gallaz and Roberto Innocenti and illustrated by Robert Innocenti (Creative Education, 1985).

Winter, Jeanette   *6–10+*
FOLLOW THE DRINKING GOURD   *YEARS*
  Illus. by Jeanette Winter. New York: Knopf, 1988.

Large, sophisticated expressionistic paintings in rich, jewel tones extend and enrich this well-written story of how a one-legged sailor named Peg Legged Joe, a legendary conductor on the Underground Railroad, helped runaway slaves travel north to freedom in Canada. Compare and contrast the content, genre, and style of illustration in *Follow the Drinking Gourd* with these same elements in *Harriet and the Promised Land,* written and illustrated by the celebrated Jacob Lawrence (Windmill, 1968).

Zemach, Margot   *7–up*
SELF-PORTRAIT: MARGOT ZEMACH   *YEARS*
  Illus. by Margot Zemach. Reading, Mass.: Addison-Wesley, 1978.

In a sensitive and revealing personal statement told through a brief text and full-color, cartoon-style watercolor paintings, this award-winning artist comments about her childhood, her family, and her work as a picture-book artist. She likens illustrating books to creating her own theater and being in charge of everything connected with it. The illustrations in her autobiographical sketch are scenes and sketches from other books she has illustrated. Combined in this book, they form a true composite portrait of the artist "up to the date of publication."

The World
I Live In

Aliki (pseud. of Aliki Brandenberg)   *6–10*
DINOSAURS ARE DIFFERENT   *YEARS*
   Illus. by Aliki. New York: Crowell, 1985.

An informative array of facts about the different types and orders of
dinosaurs gleaned from examining their bones is offered to readers of
this Let's-Read-and-Find-Out Science Book. The text is clearly written,
some of it appearing within balloon shapes like those used in comic
strips, and its vitality and extensive use of comparisons with things in
the children's own world will help readers appreciate the sizes, shapes,
or purposes of various dinosaurs' skeletal parts. The illustrations include detailed, close-up views of skeletal parts and are rendered in
ink line and watercolor wash; larger ink sketches offer an overall, less
detailed view of the skeletons. Compare with *The Trouble with
Tyrannosaurus Rex* by Lorina Bryan Cauley (HBJ, 1988).

Allen, Pamela   *4–7*
HIDDEN TREASURE   *YEARS*
   Illus. by Pamela Allen. New York: Putnam, 1987.

This notable Australian author and illustrator has created a thought-
provoking picture book about the evils of jealousy, greed, and suspi-
cion. A simple text, written in the style of a folktale, and cheerful
illustrations, done in ink and watercolor with pen and brush, tell an
ironic story of what happens when two brothers, partners and friends,
discover a great treasure. The characters in this story are depicted in
cartoon-style drawings, and the settings are portrayed in realistic drawings—all of which add up to an original piece of bookmaking.

Anderson, Sara Lee   *2–3*
NUMBERS   *YEARS*
   Illus. by Sara Lee Anderson. New York: Dutton, 1988.

An attractive picture sequencing of numbers from one to ten. As the
numbers get bigger so do the brilliantly colored cardboard pages on
which the appropriate numbers of objects are pictured.

Arnosky, Jim   *10–15+*
SKETCHING OUTDOORS IN AUTUMN   YEARS
   Illus. by Jim Arnosky. New York: Lothrop, 1988.

   In this picture book, the award-winning author and illustrator provided pencil sketches that capture the interesting line, sharp contrasts,
and variety of tones in the landscapes, foliage, animals, and other
aspects of nature during this season of the year. Included also are
comments by the author-illustrator about how and why he sketched
the illustrations he did. This picture book, and the others in this series,
are the best how-to-do-it books I have ever read! See the other books in
this series, written and illustrated by Arnosky: *Sketching Outdoors in
Winter* (Lothrop, 1988), *Sketching Outdoors in Spring* (Lothrop, 1987),
and *Sketching Outdoors in Summer* (Lothop, 1988).

Atwood, Ann   *8–16*
HAIKU: THE MOOD OF EARTH   YEARS
Photos by Ann Atwood. New York: Scribner, 1971.

   An exquisitely accomplished and perceptive compilation of original
haiku and photographs in full color establishes the "connection between the moods of man and the moods of earth." For more haiku,
compiled and illustrated with photographs by Atwood, see also *My
Own Rhythm: An Approach to Haiku* (Scribner, 1973); *Haiku: Vision in
Poetry and Photography* (Scribner, 1977); and *Fly with the Wind, Flow
with the Water* (Scribner, 1979).

Baker, Jeannie   *5–8*
HOME IN THE SKY   YEARS
   Illus. by Jeannie Baker. New York: Greenwillow, 1984.

   This is a well-written story of a pigeon that leaves its home in a coop
on the roof of an abandoned, burned-out building, gets into a rain-
storm, and flies inside a train where a boy sees it and takes it home.
When the boy's mother tells him he can not keep the pigeon, he places
it on an outside window sill. It finds its way back to its coop, for it was
driven by instinct to be with the other pigeons in its flock. The illustrations, done in collages constructed of natural materials, appear quite
realistic, thus adding considerable credibility to the tale. *Home in the
Sky* was named the Australian Children's Book Council Award (Com-
mended) in 1985. See also *Millicent* (Andre Deutsch, 1980) in which
this author-illustrator uses similar illustrating techniques and offers an

introspective glimpse into an elderly lady's mind as she feeds pigeons in Hyde Park, Sydney, Australia.

Baker, Jeannie   *6–10*
WHERE THE FOREST MEETS THE SEA   *YEARS*
   Illus. by Jeanie Baker. New York: Greenwillow, 1988.   *121*

   While camping with his father in a tropical rain forest, a young boy reflects on the ecological issue concerning the preservation of rapidly diminishing, untamed lands. The last double-page spread depicts the opening scene of beautiful forest of twisted vines and trees, rocks, and animals, but it is overlaid with the hazy image of a resort development. So, readers will have little trouble figuring out what the young narrator (and the author) are forecasting. The illustrations are a sight to behold; they are stunning, relief collages, constructed from such materials as modeling clay, paper, textured materials, natural materials, and paint.

Baker, Leslie   *3–8*
THE THIRD-STORY CAT   *YEARS*
   Illus. by Leslie Baker. Boston: Little, Brown, 1987.

   Alice, the cat that lived on the third floor of a small apartment in the city, managed to get out through an open kitchen window without anyone seeing her. Her escapades during this outing and her subsequent reappearance are described in a sparse, easy-to-read text and are depicted in accomplished, impressionistic, watercolor paintings. This picture book was given the 1988 International Reading Association Children's Book Award (picture book category).

Baskin, Hosea, Tobias, and Lisa   *6–10*
HOSIE'S ALPHABET   *YEARS*
   Illus. by Leonard Baskin. New York: Viking, 1972.

   A sophisticated blend of mind-stretching and imagery-building captions and accomplished, expressionistic paintings of creatures make this a present-day masterpiece of graphic art and literature. A 1973 Caldecott Honor book. See also *Hosie's Aviary* (Viking, 1979).

Baylor, Byrd   *5–9*
GUESS WHO MY FAVORITE PERSON IS?   *YEARS*
   Illus. by Robert Andrew Parker. New York: Scribner, 1977.

   Through a fluid, conversational text and evocative, impressionistic watercolor paintings, readers are introduced to two friends playing a game in which they name their favorite things—favorite colors, things to touch, sounds, places to live, dreams, tastes, and much more. A unique approach to alerting young readers to the importance of specificity in descriptive details, to the many facets of their surroundings, and to respecting the varied responses each of us brings to them.

Baylor, Byrd   7–12+
I'M IN CHARGE OF CELEBRATION   YEARS
    Illus. by Peter Parnall. New York: Scribner, 1986.

    In disciplined and sparse poetic prose the author shares with readers a number of special experiences in the Southwest desert country that she says warranted her private celebrations—"besides the ones they close school for." The sophisticated, expressionistic painting and the use of negative space to form the shapes—characteristics we so readily identify with the name of this notable book artist—are as unique and picturesque as the author's language. A fine model to motivate children (and adults) to be more aware and appreciative of their surroundings, no matter where they live.

Baylor, Byrd   7–12+
THE OTHER WAY TO LISTEN   YEARS
    Illus. by Peter Parnall. New York: Scribner, 1978.

    This is a *very* sophisticated picture book. Imagery-filled prose combined with black-and-yellow, abstract, expressionistic drawings, many of which employ the negative space technique, detail how the narrator hears the hills singing, a feat that she says, after trying and hoping for a long time, "seemed like the most natural thing in the world." Readers are encouraged to listen for the sounds made by the stars in the sky, the rocks murmuring, the wildflower seeds bursting open, the cactus blooming in the dark, and so much more. They are cautioned that it takes a long time and lots of practice to learn. Compare this picture book and the video film version "The Other Way to Listen," narrated by Will Rogers, Jr. (Tucson: Southwest Series, Inc., 1988).

Baylor, Byrd   6–16
THE WAY TO START A DAY   YEARS
    Illus. by Peter Parnall. New York: Scribner, 1978.

    A thought-provoking compilation of verbal and visual statements about how people in times past and present and in different places around the world have honored the coming of each new sunrise. The deceptively simple text is brief and profound, the expressionistic illustrations elegant and sophisticated; together, they offer the reader of this picture book an exhilarating appreciation of each new day, taking it as it comes. A 1979 Caldecott Honor book.

Baynes, Pauline   *5–8*   *123*
HOW DOG BEGAN   *YEARS*
    Illus. by Pauline Baynes. New York: Holt, 1987.

    This very logical explanation about how people discovered that the wolf, when tamed, became the faithful, reliable, and beloved friend now called "dog," is illustrated with full-page, black-and-white drawings suggestive of cave paintings. Compare the text and illustrations of this book about how the dog was domesticated with *The First Dog*, written and illustrated by Jan Brett (HBJ, 1988).

Behfel, Tages   *9–18*
I NEVER SAW ANOTHER BUTTERFLY   *YEARS*
    Illus. with children's drawings. New York: McGraw-Hill, 1964.

    An anthology of poems and full-color drawings created by children confined in the Terezin Concentration Camp from 1942 to 1944, commenting on life in the camp or life in general. Also included is a biographical sketch for each child whose poem or painting appears in the anthology, indicating where the child was born, when she or he arrived at Terezin, and the date of his or her death or departure from the camp.

Biggs, Jonathan (concept) and Janet Harwood (text)   *7–11*
RIDING IN MOTION   *YEARS*
    Illus. by Richard Clifton-Dey. Paper engineering by Jonathan Biggs
        and Ruth Graham. New York: Lippincott, 1988.

    An informative pop-up book intended as a guide to riding, training, and grooming horses. Especially notable are the two- and three-dimensional illustrations depicting various animals related to the horse, the anatomy of horses, and jumping and riding positions. The high-interest content combined with text that is brief but not the least bit condescending or patronizing should provide worthwhile and satisfying fare for reluctant readers.

Bonners, Susan   *5–9*
PANDA   *YEARS*
    Illus. by Susan Bonners. New York: Delacorte, 1978.

A fascinating and authentic portrayal of the panda's life cycle in watercolor paintings done on wet paper. A wild panda of southwestern China is depicted from birth until she is six years old, fully grown, and awaiting the birth of her first cub. The reader of this picture book will want to look again and again at the pictures of the antics of the pandas and the scenes of the icy mountains, wildflower fields, and bamboo thickets.

Branley, Franklyn M.   *5–9*
VOLCANOES   *YEARS*
    Illus. by Marc Simont. New York: Crowell, 1985.

Technical and scientific terminology is defined and explained in a clear and interesting manner in a thoroughly understandable text, embellished by full-color, pen-and-ink line and watercolor illustrations. The result is an excellent introduction to volcanoes for young readers, which focuses on how volcanoes are formed and how the earth is affected when they erupt. Their connection with earthquakes is also explained. This is one of the many fine beginning science books in the Let's-Read-and-Find-Out Science Book series addressed to young children, ages 5 to 9 years.

Brett, Jan   *5–9*
THE FIRST DOG   *YEARS*
    Illus. by Jan Brett. San Diego: HBJ, 1988.

This simplistic account of how humans domesticated the dog, initiating a bond that has lasted over many, many centuries, was inspired by cave paintings and artifacts of the Ice Age. The large-sized, realistic illustrations of the Ice Age landscape and animals of that time period should most certainly be of interest to young readers. The illustrations of the protagonist seem to put him in too recent a time period, yet the animals are all quite well done. Of special interest are the pictures in the margins that frame the double-page spreads, for they contain many examples suggestive of the cave drawings of the Ice Age.

Calhoun, Mary   *5–10*
CROSS COUNTRY CAT   *YEARS*
    Illus. by Erick Ingraham. New York: Morrow, 1979.

A tension-filled saga about a cat that found his way home on cross-country skis after his owners inadvertently left him behind at their mountain cabin. The absolutely stunning, realistic illustrations make this high-spirited fantasy about a persistent and agile cat thoroughly convincing and memorable.

Calmenson, Stephanie   4–6   *125*
WHAT AM I? VERY FIRST RIDDLES   *YEARS*
   Illus. by Karen Gundersheimer. New York: Harper, 1989.

   A fine collection of riddles about every day objects. All are easy to read and fun to guess—over and over again. The illustrations are clean and neat pen-and-ink, line-and-wash pictures.

Carle, Eric   4–9
A HOUSE FOR HERMIT CRAB   *YEARS*
   Illus. by Eric Carle. Saxonville, Mass.: Picture Book Studio, 1987.

   Collage illustrations, vital and colorful, and a brief, but well-written text that takes the form of a cumulative tale tell about a year in the life of a hermit crab.

Carrick, Carol   6–10
DARK AND FULL OF SECRETS   *YEARS*
   Illus. by Donald Carrick. New York: Clarion/Houghton, 1988.

   Christopher quickly overcomes his fear of swimming in the pond after he learns to snorkel and sees what kinds of creatures, plants, and other things are actually in it. No longer afraid of the pond, he goes snorkeling on his own. All is well until he tries to empty the water that has seeped into his mask. When he realizes that he has drifted out too far to stand up while emptying the mask and is unable to tread water, he panics and begins to sink. Luckily his large pet dog, Ben, always anxious to be with Christopher, rescues him. This very credible story is illustrated most effectively in blues and greens with watercolor paintings that are highlighted with ink line and crosshatching.

Chase, Edith Newlin   4–7
THE NEW BABY CALF   *YEARS*
   Illus. by Barbara Reid. New York: Scholastic, 1984.

   Full-color, plasticene, relief pictures embellish this easy-to-read verse of how the new baby calf, from the time it was born in spring to late fall, reacts to life in general and to farm life in particular.

Cobb, Vicki   5–9
GETTING DRESSED   YEARS
      Illus. by Marilyn Hafner. New York: Lippincott, 1989.

Humorous, telling, line and watercolor-wash, cartoon-style illustrations accompany this easy-to-read, interesting account of the historical
background about the things that fasten our clothes—buttons, elastic,
zippers and Velcro, hooks, and snaps. This is a good read whether it is
read only a section at a time or from the beginning to end in one sitting.
It also serves as a fine source to help children notice and appreciate
what we all tend to take for granted and to realize that
the things described in this picture book are unique and amazing
inventions.

Cole, Sheila   5–8
WHEN THE TIDE IS LOW   YEARS
      Illus. by Virginia Wright-Frierson. New York: Lothrop, 1985.

      A slight story serves as a means for presenting a wealth of informa-
tion about what a tide actually is and the kinds of water creatures one
might find on the floor of the ocean, in the sand, and among the water
plants and rocks when the tide is low. The glossary at the back of the
book offers a brief but clear description of each creature named in the
text. The illustrations of the water creatures are simplified, realistic
drawings done in watercolor. Compare with *Very Last First Time*, written by Jan Andrews and illustrated by Ian Wallace (Lothrop, 1985) for
another story about what happens when the tide is low.

Cristini, Ermanno and Luigi Puricelli   5–7
IN THE POND   YEARS
      Illus. by Ermanno Cristini and Luigi Puricelli. Natick, Mass.: Picture
         Book Studio/Neugebauer Pr., 1984. Distributed by Alphabet Pr.

      This is a sophisticated, informative, wordless book about activity
and life in the marshy wetlands—above, around, and beneath the water
of the pond. One has to look long and carefully to find all of the things
that are happening in each of the double-page, realistic paintings,
which are in brilliant, full color. An index of the names and pictures
of each of the fish, birds, animals, and plants sharing this kind of
habitat is at the end of the book and should prove helpful to beginning
naturalists.

de Regniers, Beatrice Schenk, et al. (compilers) *4–12+*
SING A SONG OF POPCORN *YEARS*
  Illus. by nine Caldecott Medal artists. New York: Scholastic, 1988.

A real gem! One hundred twenty-nine poems were culled from the work of renowned poets and are grouped under nine themes: "Fun with Rhymes," Weather, Spooky Poems, Story Poems, Animals, People, Nonsense Rhymes, "Seeing, Thinking and Feeling" Poems, and Free Verse. Each thematic section is illustrated with original artwork by nine different Caldecott winning artists. *Sing a Song of Popcorn*, an expanded and updated edition of *Poems Children Will Sit Still For* (Scholastic, 1969), is a must for every teacher, family or librarian serving children. At the back of the book one will find indexes of titles, first lines, and authors as well as biographical sketches of each of the award-winning book artists whose illustrations appear in this book.

127

Downie, Jill *4–6*
ALPHABET PUZZLE *YEARS*
  Illus. by Jill Downie. New York: Lothrop, 1988.

Whether or not they guess the correct name of the object beginning with each of the particular letters highlighted, young readers are in store for pleasant surprises when they turn each of the windowed pages in this clever alphabet book. Even after they know the right answer to the alphabet puzzle, the children most likely will want to examine each of the detailed colored pencil pictures many times over.

Drescher, Henrik *5–9*
WHOSE FURRY NOSE? AUSTRALIAN ANIMALS YOU'D *YEARS*
LIKE TO MEET
  Illus. by Henrik Drescher. New York: Lippincott, 1987.

A little boy is introduced to a fascinating group of animals (parents and their offspring) found in Australia—climbing kangaroos, wallabies, cuscuses, yellow billy gliders, platypuses, and koalas. The cartoon-style illustrations, showing only part of an animal, and the consistent use of questions about that animal before the answer is given in the text and in the picture sustain the readers' curiosity from the beginning of the book to its conclusion. At the end of the book is a short paragraph on each of the intriguing animals, offering a brief description about what they look like and bits of information about such things as where they live and what they eat.

Ehlert, Lois   3–6
COLOR ZOO   *YEARS*
   Illus. by Lois Ehlert. New York: Lippincott, 1989.

SAPAR
X

128   In this 1990 Caldecott Honor book, one finds a clever use of diecuts: a series of geometrical shapes are cut out and overlaid to suggest the faces of animals. In each case, the particular geometrical shape that is cut out of a page and the animal that is depicted are named. As one turns each page, the geometrical shape and the face gradually diminish in size. For example, one will see a large face of a tiger on the righthand page of the opened book. When that page is turned, a large cutout circle will be seen on the back of that page and that shape is now on the lefthand page of the book. On the new righthand page, one will see the face of a mouse, a bit smaller than the tiger. When that page is turned, one will see a cutout square on what has become the lefthand side of the opened book and on the righthand page one will see a face of a fox, a bit smaller than the face of the mouse. When that page is turned, one will see a cutout shape of a diamond, but a larger face of another animal. As one continues to turn the pages, one is led to another series of geometrical shapes and animals, each gradually diminishing in size, and then to another large face, and so on. Ten different shapes and numerous animals are presented in a stunning spectrum of sixteen colors in this award-winning concept book.

Ehlert, Lois   5–8
PLANTING A RAINBOW   *YEARS*
   Illus. by Lois Ehlert. San Diego: HBJ, 1988.

    A mother and child work together in planting an array of colorful flowers in the garden. They plant bulbs in the fall, order seeds from catalogs in winter, plant seedlings in the spring and summer (sorted by the blazing, primary colors), and gather bouquets of resplendent blossoms. The minimal text is in very large type.

Eisler, Colin   3–8
CATS KNOW BEST   *YEARS*
   Illus. by Lesley Anne Ivory. New York: Dial, 1988.

    A book that calls for repeated examinations, this is a collection of accomplished and detailed, realistic, full-color paintings demonstrating that cats know best where to go to keep warm on cold nights, to keep cool in the heat of the summer, to have their kittens, to groom themselves, to find the best food, to have a good fight or to play. The text is simple and brief. Actually, this is a book to look at rather than to read.

Esbensen, Barbara Juster *8–12*
COLD STARS AND FIREFLIES *YEARS*
    Illus. by Susan Bonners. New York: Crowell, 1984.

In her introductory note the author says that she "paints with words" just as "painters use colors and a brush to put a season on canvas." In this book, she "paints" stunning word pictures, images of sight as well as those of the senses of sound, touch, smell and taste for each of the seasons of the year. The abstract, impressionistic paintings in red and/or black reflect and extend the essence of the poems in this fine collection. No literal or concrete graphics are imposed on the readers of the poetry in this special book.

Fisher, Leonard Everett *3–6*
LOOK AROUND! A BOOK ABOUT SHAPES *YEARS*
    Illus. by Leonard Everett Fisher. New York: Viking/Kestrel, 1987.

A special concept book illustrated with dramatic, uncluttered pictures done in acrylics. The text, which is printed in large-sized primary type, presents a description that defines the basic shapes that are shown alone and then in familiar scenes. In each case young readers are asked to compare and contrast one shape with another and to continue, after they have finished reading the book, to look for the same and other things in which these shapes are found. The crisp, brightly colored illustrations stimulate the children's curiosity about their environment and extend their knowledge about the world around them. (See illustration 13.)

Fitzsimons, Cecilia *5–9*
MY FIRST BUTTERFLIES *YEARS*
    Illus. by Cecilia Fitzsimons. Paper engineering by Ray Marshall. New York: Harper, 1985.

This is a full-color, pop-up field guide to butterflies, classified as migrating butterflies or according to species found in meadows and gardens, hedges and woodland, grasslands, and mountains. At the back of the book is a pop-up guide for other butterflies in America, Europe, and Britain, as well as a page suggesting the format children can use to

Illus. 13. From *Look Around! A Book about Shapes* written and illustrated by Leonard Everett Fisher. Copyright © 1987 by Leonard Everett Fisher. Reprinted by permission of Viking Penguin, a division of Penguin Books USA, Inc.

record butterflies they see. Other pop-up field guide books in this unique series published by Harper are *My First Birds* (1985), *My First Fishes and Other Wildlife* (1987), and *My First Insects, Spiders and Crawlers* (1987).

Fort, Patrick   *3–7*
REDBIRD   *YEARS*
   Trans. from the French. Illus. by Patrick Fort. New York: Orchard, 1988.

This "Eyes at the End of Your Fingers Book" is about a small airplane's encounters with assorted hazards as it attempts to land at an airport. It is told in a simple text in Braille and in clear, black type combined with colorful, raised pictures that are in a very simple, stylized design that can be seen and felt. Although the book is not really appropriate for the totally blind—the stylized illustrations will be quite meaningless unless one has actually seen an airplane (real or model)— it is acceptable for the visually impaired. The illustrations, French text, format, and thermoform technique were copyrighted in 1987 by Editions Laurence Olivier Four, Coen and Chardon Bleu Editions, Lyon.

Gantschev, Ivan   *5–10*
THE TRAIN TO GRANDMOTHER'S   *YEARS*
    Illus. by Ivan Gantschev. Natick, Mass.: Picture Book Studio, 1987.

An account of two children traveling by train from their home in the city to their grandparents' seaside farm that is a masterpiece of graphics. Fold-out pages depict the long train, and die-cut outlines, openings, and overlays reveal the contours of mountains, buildings, and landscapes as well as awesome views of tunnels, a trestle bridge, and the station. The finding of the special stowaway will delight readers as much as it did the young travelers.

Gebert, Warren   *4–7*
THE OLD BALL AND THE SEA   *YEARS*
    Illus. by Warren Gebert. New York: Bradbury, 1988.

An easy-to-read text and stunning, double-page pictures done with acrylic paints are competently combined to tell a satisfying story about how a boy named Roy and his dog, Buddy, spend a full day at the beach building a giant sand castle, watching a passing ship, and then playing with a ball that washed ashore.

Haldane, Suzanne   *5–12+*
PAINTING   *YEARS*
    Illus. with photographs by Suzanne Haldane. New York: Dutton, 1988.

An interesting and well-written text with many exciting, full-color photographs discusses examples of when, why, and how people in the past and present and from all over the world have decorated their faces. Precise and easy-to-follow directions for applying grease paint and water-based makeup, as well as safety tips, are included for designs traditionally associated with North American Indians and designs traditionally associated with the Chinese, Japanese Kabuki, Sudanese, and Southeast Nuba. Designs for animals in art and theatre from diverse cultures, clowns, and original designs are included, too.

Herriot, James   5–9
BLOSSOM COMES HOME   YEARS
   Illus. by Ruth Brown. New York: St. Martin's, 1972, 1988.

Once again the famous country veterinarian tells his reader another charming story about an animal he meets on his rounds. This one is about Blossom, an old cow that was supposed to be sold at the market because it was no longer giving enough milk to justify her keep. When she finds her way back to the farm from the village and into the stall that she has occupied for the past twelve years, the farmer decides to keep her, saying that "when unexpected things happen, they were meant to, and that it works out for the best in the end." The accomplished illustrations, stunning full-color, impressionistic paintings, offer charming scenes of a Yorkshire farm and village life. Other picture books by Herriot are *Only One Woof*, illustrated by Peter Barrett (St. Martin's, 1985), *Christmas Day Kitten*, illustrated by Ruth Brown (St. Martin's, 1986), and *Moses the Kitten*, illustrated by Ruth Brown (St. Martin's, 1984).

Heyduck-Huth, Hilde   4–8
THE STRAWFLOWER   YEARS
   Trans. by Margaret K. McElderry. Illus. by Hilde Heyduck-Huth. New York: Margaret K. McElderry/Macmillan, 1987.

Detailed, realistic paintings rendered in full-color watercolor combine with simple, clear language to tell of the chain of events that occurred when strawflowers, picked by some children to make a bouquet for a snowlady, are taken and used by a woman as table decorations for a party and then thrown out when the woman shakes her tablecloth out the window. Originally published in 1985 under the title *Die Strohblume* by Atlantis Kinderbücher, Verlag Pro Juventute, Zurich. For another in the Treasure Chest Story series, see *The Starfish*, written and illustrated by Hilde Heyduck-Huth (Margaret K. McElderry/Macmillan, 1987), originally published in 1985 by Atlantis Kinderbücher, Verlag Pro Juventute, Zurich, under the title *Der Seestem*.

Hofer, Angelika   1–12+
THE LION FAMILY BOOK   YEARS
   Photographs by Gunter Ziesler. Saxonville, Mass.: Picture Book Stu-
     dio, 1988.

X SAPAR

133

   Studied, full-color photographs and a well-written, thoroughly informative text detail the habits and habitat of a family of lions. The
litter of cubs is shown playing, learning, and growing within an established social order of the family unit based on affection, instinct, and
survival.

Horwitz, Elinor Lander   4–7
WHEN THE SKY IS LIKE LACE   YEARS
   Illus. by Barbara Cooney. New York: Lippincott, 1975.

   A unique blend of imagination and mood is found in this exquisite
prose description of "a bimulous night, when the sky is like lace and
everything strange-splendid . . ." Sage advice on how to celebrate a
bimulous night is included. The wonderful images (appealing to all of
the senses) are created by effective use of language plus charming
full-page illustrations done with watercolor, colored pencil, and crayon
on board, making this a very special picture book.

Hughes, Shirley   3–7
OUT AND ABOUT   YEARS
   Illus. by Shirley Hughes. New York: Lothrop, 1988.

X SAPAR

   Simple, zestful rhymes combine with animated, action-filled realistic drawings, done in mixed media and reproduced in full color, to
depict the wonders and pleasurable activities of the outdoors with
family, friends, or alone in all kinds of weather through the four seasons of the year. A truly special book for family sharing! This book is
good for reading aloud to all children, but particularly to those who are
visually impaired, for the rhymes focus on the physical senses of
sound, touch, and smell in response to one's surroundings.

Kalas, Sybille   5–10
THE GOOSE FAMILY BOOK   YEARS
   Preface by Konrad Lorenz. Trans. by Patricia Crampton. Photographs
     by Sybille and Klaus Kalas. Natick, Mass.: Picture Book Studio,
     1986.

   Seldom does one find an informational book so well written and with
format so beautifully appointed. The informative, accomplished text

combines with interesting photographs in sharp, full color to provide an excellent description of the physical characteristics and behavior patterns of a family of grey geese from the time the eggs are laid to the moment they hatch, then following the baby geese through to adulthood. Note the endpapers; the close-up photographs of goose feathers with light shining through them make an aesthetic statement that should serve to entice the young readers to open the book. The photographs also offer a haunting closing statement, provoking readers to ponder over the fascinating facts about aspects of the grey goose's ways and society. Originally published in 1986 by Neugebauer Press, Salzburg, Austria, under the title *Das Gänse-Kinder-Buch*.

Kalas, Sybille and Klaus   5–9
THE BEAVER FAMILY BOOK   *YEARS*
> Trans. from the German by Patricia Crampton. Illus. with photographs. Natick, Mass.: Picture Book Studio, 1987.

Clear, focused, full-color photographs and an easy-to-read, well-written, and informative text are combined to create an excellent account of the life cycle, habits, and habitat of a family of beavers. This high-quality, factual book was originally published in 1987 by Neugebauer Press in Salzburg, Austria, under the title *Das Biber-Kinder-Buch*.

Keeping, Charles   10–14+
RIVER   *YEARS*
> Illus. by Charles Keeping. New York: Oxford Univ. Pr., 1978.

This is a sophisticated, wordless book for "the visually literate." In each impressionistic and expressionistic line and full-color wash illustration (some of them quite abstract) one sees a river in the foreground of human activity and in the background a hill, a castle, and the sky. The sequence of these pictures, which span the seasons of the year and eras, demonstrates the idea that humanity impinges upon nature, and then nature eclipses humanity over and over.

Kitchen, Bert   4–6
ANIMAL NUMBERS   *YEARS*
> Illus. by Bert Kitchen. New York: Dial, 1987.

A stunning counting book in which large, full-color, realistic paintings depict numerical figures by displaying the adults and the offspring of common and unusual animals. The numbers interpreted are from one to ten and, thereafter, additions of five up to twenty-five. The young animals are arranged in ingenious ways around the adults, challenging the young reader to find them all. At the back of the book there is a listing of facts about each animal, including its name, a statement about the form in which it is born, and, in some cases, how its mother attends to it in its early stages. See *Animal Alphabet* by Bert Kitchen (Dial, 1984) for another exquisite concept book.

Kroll, Steven   5–9
THE HOKEY-POKEY MAN   YEARS
  Illus. by Deborah Kogan Ray. New York: Holiday, 1989.

Illustrations created with pen-and-ink line, colored pencil, and paint are aptly blended with a competently written text to tell how the ice cream cone, invented at the 1904 St. Louis World's Fair, was first introduced in New York City by a Hokey-Pokey Man. The prolific amount of dialogue included in this legend of the invention of the ice cream cone should prove fine fare for Reader's Theatre.

Kuklin, Susan   4–8
TAKING MY DOG TO THE VET   YEARS
  Illus. with photographs. New York: Bradbury, 1988.

Full-color photographs and a factual text detail the various aspects of the medical check-up a veterinarian gave to a little girl's pet Cairn terrier. (Take my word for it, few if any Cairns are as docile at the vet's *or elsewhere* as this one is!) The general procedure described is authentic, and the suggestions given at the back of the book in Keys for a Successful Visit to the Vet should prove helpful to young pet owners.

Larrick, Nancy   3–10+
CATS ARE CATS   YEARS
  Illus. by Ed Young. New York: Philomel, 1988.

An absolutely top-notch picture book in every respect! The forty-two poems about the many aspects of "catness" constitute a superb collection in-and-of itself and include some of the best poets of our time and of times past (John Ciardi, Lillian Moore, Karla Kuskin, Elizabeth Coatsworth, and Aileen Fisher). Each of the illustrations, done on wrapping paper in charcoal and pastel, captures and extends the themes and aura of the poem for which it was created. Furthermore, the poses show the cats as both individualistic and adaptable. (See illustration 14.)

Lattimore, Deborah Nourse   **6–10**

WHY THERE IS NO ARGUING IN HEAVEN   *YEARS*

136   Illus. by Deborah Nourse Lattimore. New York: Harper, 1989.

A retelling of the Mayan creation myth about how the Maize God created a being that was worthy of worshipping the First Creator God properly. Detailed illustrations strongly suggest the designs and symbolism found on the stonework and painted art of the Mayan Indians of Guatemala and parts of Mexico.

Illus. 14. Illustration by Ed Young reprinted by permission of Philomel Books from *Cats Are Cats* by Nancy Larrick; illustrations copyright © 1988 by Ed Young.

Livingston, Myra Cohn   *6–10+*
UP IN THE AIR   *YEARS*
   Illus. by Leonard Everett Fisher. New York: Holiday, 1989.

   Imagery-filled metaphors expressed in artfully crafted triplets exude
the excitement that this award-winning poet felt while in flight. Each   *137*
verse is illustrated with equally accomplished abstract impressionistic,
acrylic paintings of the aerial views. Together, poet and artist offer
readers a memorable literary experience.

Locker, Thomas   *5–10*
WHERE THE RIVER BEGINS   *YEARS*
   Illus. by Thomas Locker. New York: Dial, 1984.

   Fourteen large-sized, full-color, acrylic and watercolor paintings in a
style suggestive of the nineteenth century Dutch landscape artists embellish this well-written text that tells a story of a journey taken by two
boys and their grandfather to find out where the river begins. Notice
how effectively the artist has used light and shading to depict the
varied moods of nature at different times of the day and night and
during a thunder and lightning storm. For other books by this talented
author-illustrator, see *The Mare on the Hill* (Dial, 1985) and *Sailing with
the Wind* (Dial, 1986).

Martin, Bill, Jr., and John Archambault   *3–8*
UP AND DOWN ON THE MERRY-GO-ROUND   *YEARS*
   Illus. by Ted Rand. New York: Holt, 1988.

   The sights, sound, and emotions children experience at the circus
and riding on the merry-go-round are aptly described in simple narrative verse. The illustrations, consisting of historically authentic details, exude the very essence of the thoughts and fantasies one usually
associates with this unforgettable childhood experience. Compare and
contrast the aura of the merry-go-round ride depicted in this book with
that depicted by Donald Crews in *Carousel* (Greenwillow, 1982).

Merriam, Eve   *9–12+*
HALLOWEEN ABC   *YEARS*
   Illus. by Lane Smith. New York: Macmillan, 1987.

   Each letter of the alphabet introduces an accomplished poem about
some mood or attitude associated with Halloween—be it macabre,
violent, spooky, or silly. Each of these twenty-six poems is accom-

panied by an oil painting that complements its very essence, whatever its mood or statement. This is a perfect example of an alphabet book that is not likely to be understood by the early childhood reading audience, but would most probably appeal to many of the older and sophisticated readers.

SAPAR X

Miles, Sally   *3–7*
ALFIE AND THE DARK   YEARS
    Illus. by Errol LeCain. San Francisco: Chronicle, 1988.

    This narrative verse provides a convincing answer to a little boy's question of where the Dark goes when it is light. The full-page, expressionistic watercolor paintings add to the awesomeness that the dark so often holds for children and adults.

Miller, Moira   *7–10*
THE SEARCH FOR SPRING   YEARS
    Illus. by Ian Deuchar. New York: Dial, 1988.

    Detailed, realistic, watercolor paintings, full-page pictures alternating with smaller pictures, enhance and extend this well-written, multilevel story about a boy who pursues answers to "the why and how of things." On the literal level, it is about the boy's persistent efforts to find out where Spring went when Summer came; on a higher level of thinking, it is a mind-jarring allegory about the search for the spiritual meaning of life through seasonal birth, growth, death, and rebirth.

Monfried, Lucia   *3–6*
SEAL   YEARS
    Illus. by Lynne Cherry. New York: Dutton, 1987.

    Double-page, realistic line and wash paintings combine with a brief, easy-to-read text to detail the habits and habitat of the seal. A percentage of the sales of this book and the others in the series by the same author/artist (*Grizzly Bear*, 1987; *Orangutan*, 1987; *Snow Leopard*, 1987) is donated to the World Wildlife Fund in support of its efforts to save endangered species and their habitats around the world. World Wildlife Fund plush toys of the animals focused on in each of these books in the series are also available.

Munro, Roxie   *5–9*
THE INSIDE-OUTSIDE BOOK OF WASHINGTON, D.C.   YEARS
    Illus. by Roxie Munro. New York: Dutton, 1987.

Watercolor paintings depict an array of major sights in our nation's capital from various and dramatic perspectives—the Washington Monument, the Library of Congress, the U.S. Supreme Court, the Bureau of Engraving and Printing, the Organization of American States, the National Air and Space Museum, the East Room of the White House, the Washington Post, RFK Memorial Stadium, the Senate wing of the U.S. Capitol, and the Lincoln Memorial. Notes at the back of the book add important details about these points of interest.

Murphy, Jim   *8–12*
THE LAST DINOSAUR   YEARS
    Illus. by Mark Alan Weatherby. New York: Scholastic, 1988.

A popular hypothesis about how the Age of Dinosaurs gave way to the beginning of the Age of the Mammals is the inspiration for this dramatic account of what life probably was like for the last dinosaurs on earth, the Triceratops. Thirteen spectacular, realistic paintings that cover one and one-quarter page spreads enrich and extend an exciting story about these fascinating creatures and transmit an array of speculations about their food, habits, temperaments, and enemies—be they other animals or the elements—based on the most current research available. Compare the storyline and the role played by the Tyrannosaurus Rex in this story with that in *The Trouble with Tyrannosaurus Rex* by Lorinda Bryan Cauley (HBJ, 1988).

Narahashi, Keiko   *4–7*
I HAVE A FRIEND   YEARS
    Illus. by Keiko Narahashi. New York: Margaret K. McElderry, 1987.

In perky prose a young boy refers to his shadow as "yesterday's night left behind for the day" and to many shapes his shadow takes as it appears in the common and unusual places in the daytime through the nighttime. The large watercolor paintings in the naive-art style reflect the openness and vitality of the little boy's response to this natural phenomenon and to life in general. Furthermore, they encourage readers to look for their own shadows wherever and whenever they can.

Neville, Emily Cheney   *5–8*
THE BRIDGE   YEARS
    Illus. by Ronald Himler. New York: Harper, 1988.

A young boy (and the reader) gets to watch the many machines at work constructing a new culvert bridge across the brook to his house to replace the old wooden bridge that broke. The richly colored paintings, varied in size and shape, enhance this informative story, highlighting the boy's curiosity as well as the warm pleasant relationship between the boy and his parents.

140   Olson, Arielle North   5–10
THE LIGHTHOUSE KEEPER'S DAUGHTER   YEARS
   Illus. by Elaine Wentworth. Boston: Little, Brown, 1987.

Combining incidents that actually happened in lighthouses along the Maine coast, the author has created a thoroughly credible and moving story about a young girl who kept the lighthouse lamps burning for weeks while her father was forced to remain ashore by a violent, winter storm. The realistic, oversized, full-color, watercolor paintings not only provide the beauty of the home and the surroundings, but also capture the starkness and isolation of the island, furthering our admiration for the courage and determination of this young girl. (See illustration 15.)

Oppenheim, Joanne   4–8
HAVE YOU SEEN BIRDS?   YEARS
   Illus. by Barbara Reid. New York: Scholastic, 1986.

Lyrical verse combines with truly unique illustrations, done in full-color, plasticine relief, to depict different types of birds doing different things. Children will find the play with words appealing, and you will hear them repeating the word plays on their own as they examine these pictures over and over again. This is "a must" book for all libraries serving young children.

Parker, Nancy Winslow and Joan Richards Wright   5–10
BUGS   YEARS
   Illus. by Nancy Winslow Parker. New York: Greenwillow, 1987.

A unique informational book to say the least! Each of the many common insects is introduced in the form of a humorous riddle, the bug is shown in the context of a vignette interpreting the riddle, and the answer to the riddle (the name of the bug) rhymes with the last word of the riddle. General information and a brief description of the physical characteristics, habits, and natural environment of each insect is provided in a forthright and easy-to-understand text. Included throughout the text are scientific symbols for the male and female, a line denoting the actual size of the bug, and the three types of insect

Illus. 15. From *The Lighthouse Keeper's Daughter* by Arielle North Olson, illustrated by Elaine Wentworth. Illustrations © 1987 by Elaine Wentworth. By permission of Little, Brown and Company.

metamorphosis: simple, incomplete, and complete. Done in black-pen line combined with full-color, watercolor paints and colored pencils, the illustrations facilitate acquisition of the array of fascinating facts included in this informative picture book.

Peters, Lisa Westberg *5–10+*
THE SUN, THE WIND AND THE RAIN *YEARS*
    Illus. by Ted Rand. New York: Holt, 1988.

A description of the centuries-long geological process of the creation and evolution of the mountain, juxtaposed with a little girl's small-scale sand structures on the beach, explain the concept of the impermanence of mountains and the notion that new mountains are made from the materials of old mountains. The full-page, impressionistic illustrations significantly clarify and extend the brief but explicit text.

Polushkin, Maria   *3–6*
KITTEN IN TROUBLE   *YEARS*
   Illus. by Betsy Lewin. New York: Bradbury, 1988.

   Illustrated appropriately in cartoon-style sketches done in crisp ink and full-color watercolor paint, this fun-filled series of misadventures of Kitten is bound to delight young children. Not only will they begin to anticipate Kitten's antics and join in the refrain of the story "Oh-oh. Kitten's in trouble," but, be assured, most of them will also want it read over and over again—in one sitting!

Pope, Joyce   *8–12+*
KENNETH LILLY'S ANIMALS   *YEARS*
   Illus. by Kenneth Lilly. New York: Lothrop, 1988.

   Children will want to refer to this informational book time and time again to learn more about each of the sixty-two animals and their young, to admire and delight and appreciate their beauty and their uniqueness. Each of the animals and its offspring is depicted in a large, full-color, realistic painting. Its habits and habitats are discussed in an interesting, factual style. A distribution map in the corner of each picture indicates the approximate region(s) of the world where the particular animal lives; a table listing an array of facts and figures about each of the animals and an index appear at the back of the book. This is truly a beautiful and informative picture book.

Poulin, Stephane   *5–8*
HAVE YOU SEEN JOSEPHINE?   *YEARS*
   Illus. by Stephane Poulin. Plattsburgh, N.Y.: Tundra, 1986.

   Young Daniel decides to follow his cat Josephine to find out once and for all where she goes each Saturday. Macabre full-page illustrations in bright, full color depict the many places in the east-end Montreal neighborhood through which Josephine leads Daniel. Black-and-white vignettes in the left-hand corner of each page further embellish the aspects of Daniel's wild chase after his independent cat. The readers of this action-filled story will be as surprised as Daniel is when they find out where Josephine goes each Saturday! This picture book was also published by Tundra in French as *As-tu vu Josephine?* in 1986.

Powzyk, Joyce   6–10   *143*
WALLABY CREEK   *YEARS*
   Illus. by Joyce Powzyk. New York: Lothrop, 1985.

   Striking, realistic, watercolor paintings depict an array of animals that frequent the area in the Australian bush country known as Wallaby Creek. Each animal is shown in its natural habitat along with the creatures and the vegetation it eats. The text is written in a factual essay style that makes use of the popular terminology spoken in this part of Australia.

Prelutsky, Jack   5–8
TYRANNOSAURUS WAS A BEAST   *YEARS*
   Illus. by Arnold Lobel. New York: Greenwillow, 1988.

   Each of the fourteen informative but humorous poems about a dinosaur is illustrated with full-page, stylized, but also what seem to be essentially authentic, pictures made with watercolor, dry mark, and black pen. A unique table of contents at the beginning of the book consists of a miniature picture of each dinosaur described in the poems and a statement indicating when and where each dinosaur lived, its size (body length and height), and number of the page on which a large illustration for each poem can be found.

Radin, Ruth Yaffe   7–11+
HIGH IN THE MOUNTAIN   *YEARS*
   Illus. by Ed Young. New York: Macmillan, 1989.

   Lyrical, poetic prose and elegant, abstract, impressionistic paintings in full color express a child's sense of wonder from the time she wakes up early in the morning as the mist lifts from the mountains, through the day as she runs in the meadow among the alpine flowers and sees a deer among the trees, until dusk, when she and her grandfather follow a mountain road up and down among the clouds, then pitch their tent and build a campfire for the warmth and light it provides. Read this picture book aloud to get the full benefit of the imagery-filled and mood-enhancing text. This is a real gem—in each and every way!

Rand, Gloria   *5–8*
SALTY DOG   *YEARS*
  Illus. by Ted Rand. New York: Holt, 1989.

A well-written, straightforward text and expressionistic paintings in
traditional and liquid watercolor chronicle the growth and adventures
of a dog and the step-by-step construction of a wooden sailboat. Children are bound to enjoy the challenge of finding parallels in the illustrations between the plucky and clever puppy's change into a plucky
and clever full-grown dog and the sailboat's construction through each
stage—from the construction of the frame, to the fitting out, to the
maiden voyage.

Robbins, Ken   *4–7*
BEACH DAYS   *YEARS*
  Illus. with photographs and paintings by Ken Robbins. New York:
    Viking/Kestrel, 1987.

     Varied scenes associated with the beach from morning to night are
highlighted in this concept book. Competently executed, hand-tinted
photographs and full-color paintings dramatize such things as sand
sculpture, wind surfing, sunbathers, real and toy boats, beach and
volley balls, and so much more.

Roy, Ron   *3–7*
WHOSE SHOES ARE THESE?   *YEARS*
  Illus. with photographs by Rose Marie Hausherr. New York: Clar-
    ion/Houghton, 1988.

     Crisp, black-and-white photographs capture readers' attention and
motivate them to guess who wears each of the twenty kinds of shoes,
ranging from running shoes, hip-high, rubber boots, rugged boots,
soccer shoes, snow shoes, and so on. When they turn the page, they will
find the answer and an explanation of why the shoes look the way
they do.

Ryden, Hope   *4–8*
WILD ANIMALS OF AMERICA ABC   *YEARS*
  Photographs by Hope Ryden. New York: Lodestar/Dutton, 1988.

     Stunning, full-page photographs of a unique array of wild animals in
their natural habitat are reproduced in full color in this alphabet book.
Children will probably be familiar with some of the animals, but other

animals are less well-known; all will most likely fascinate them. Brief, informative notes about each animal's habitat and characteristics are included at the back of the book.

Ryder, Joanne   5–8   *145*
MOCKINGBIRD MORNING   YEARS
   Illus. by Dennis Nolan. New York: Macmillan, 1989.

Fifteen imagery-laden, free verse poems describe the animals that one might see (if one really looks and listens) while walking on a sunny morning. Stunning, impressionistic paintings effectively demonstrate the highlights and shadings of the animals, the vegetation in which they are usually found, and the narrator in the sunlight. An excellent book for reading aloud!

Rylant, Cynthia   5–9
ALL I SEE   YEARS
   Illus. by Peter Catalanotto. New York: Orchard, 1988.

Thought-provoking concepts about an artist are offered in this over-sized picture book about how a friendship developed between a young man who painted only whales, because that was all he saw, and a little boy who painted whatever he saw. Large, impressionistic, watercolor paintings (many of them double-page spreads) show the same setting from different perspectives. They also offer the careful reader of visuals excellent lessons in the study of light. A special picture book! Compare the author's definition of an artist and the style of illustration in this book with the theme and style of *An Artist*, written and illustrated by M. B. Goffstein (Harper, 1980).

Sadie Fields Production   7–11+
THE TRAIN: WATCH IT WORK!   YEARS
   Illus. by John Bradley. Design and paper engineering by Ray Mar-
      shall. New York: Viking/Kestrel, 1986.

This unique informational book should delight train enthusiasts of all ages and can provide neophytes with an excellent introduction to the history of trains. Information about the internal workings and the development of trains over more than one hundred years, from nine-teenth-century locomotives to the latest, high-speed electric trains, is presented through various means—a brief, but comprehensive text; three-dimensional, pop-up pictures; moving diagrams, lift-up flaps, and more. The discussion and the illustrations about railroad signaling are excellent. Signals used in the United Kingdom, France, Italy, Germany, and the United States are depicted so the reader can easily compare and contrast them. An easy-to-assemble model of the French TGV, the world's fastest electric train, is included in a pocket at the back of the book.

Serfozo, Mary   *2–6*
WHO SAID RED?   *YEARS*
  Illus. by Keiko Narahashi. New York: Margaret K. McElderry, 1988.

Double-page, naive-style, watercolor paintings elaborate a dialogue that a boy and girl have about colors. Most young readers will join in with the boy, who insists that he is interested in the color red and constantly rejects the other hues the girl offers.

Seymour, Peter   *4–7*
HOW THINGS GROW   *YEARS*
  Illus. by Carole Etow. Designed by David A. Carter. New York: Lodestar/Dutton, 1988.

By turning the wheels, readers will see in a five-step, visual sequence how eight different things grow from start to finish. The five steps in the life cycle of each of the eight things (butterfly, apple, pine tree, deer, sunflower, chicken, corn, and frog) are illustrated with full-color, realistic pictures. The information is summarized pictorially and verbally. An early, developmental stage (not necessarily the first stage) is shown on the top of a flap; underneath it is the word for the name of the thing in the stage that is pictured as well as the name of the thing in its mature stage. Another Turn-the-Wheel Book series book is *How Things Are Made* by the same author-artist-designer team (Lodestar/Dutton, 1988).

Shefelman, Tom   *6–9*
VICTORIA HOUSE   *YEARS*
  Illus. by Tom Shefelman. San Diego: Gulliver/HBJ, 1988.

Line and watercolor-wash illustrations detail this account of the moving of an old, deserted, Victorian house from the country to an empty lot in the city, where it is refurbished and then happily occupied by a husband and wife architect team and their son.

Siebert, Diane   *6–10*
HEARTLAND   *YEARS*
   Illus. by Wendell Minor. New York: Crowell, 1989.

   The central theme of this celebration of the Midwest in America's
heartland is "a land where, despite man's power, nature reigns." Real-   *147*
istic paintings in brilliant, lush colors and fine, rhymed verse are
effectively combined to convey this theme. Also, see *Mojave* by this
author-artist team (Crowell, 1988).

Simon, Seymour   *5–7*
SHADOW MAGIC   *YEARS*
   Illus. by Stella Orami. New York: Lothrop, 1985.

   An easy-to-read text effectively combines with simple, realistic, line
and full-color-wash illustrations to provide a straightforward and interesting explanation of what shadows are and how they are formed.
Easy-to-follow directions for how to make a sundial and shadow pictures are included in this picture book. It is quite likely to be a very
popular book; in fact, it may be necessary to have more than one copy
of it in each classroom!

Simon, Seymour   *8–12+*
VOLCANOES   *YEARS*
   Illus. with photographs. New York: Lothrop, 1988.

   Spectacular, full-color photographs combined with a concise text
that is informative and easy to understand should help young readers
appreciate the significance of volcanoes and the good and bad things
that have resulted from these scientific wonders—in the long distant
past as well as in the here-and-now. Other books in this elegant series,
each one as worthwhile and beautiful as the other, are *The Galaxies*
(1988), *Mars* (1987), *Uranus* (1987), *The Sun* (1986), *Stars* (1986),
Jupiter (1985), *Saturn* (1985), and *Icebergs and Glaciers* (1987).

Smith, Ivan   *8–10+*
THE DEATH OF A WOMBAT   *YEARS*
   Illus. by Clifton Pugh. New York: Scribner, 1972.

   By way of effective use of language and creative illustrations, one
sees vividly what happens to wild life caught in a raging fire that
started when heat from the rays of the summer sunlight built up in a

brown bottle that was carelessly tossed among dried leaves and undergrowth on the dry bushland of the Australian outback. The animals are depicted in large-sized, fine-line, expressionistic drawings; the fast-spreading, explosive temples of flame and muddy smoke are depicted in black-and-white, abstract, impressionistic paintings. Compare the action, language and theme expressed in this picturebook with those in *Wildfire,* written by Evans B. Valens, Jr., and illustrated by Clement Hurd (Philomel, 1963).

Somme, Lauritz and Sybille Kalas   *6–10*
THE PENGUIN FAMILY   YEARS
    Trans. by Patricia Crampton. Illus. with photographs by Sybille Kalas. Saxonville, Mass.: Picture Book Studio/Neugebauer Pr., 1988.

Full-color photographs combine with a detailed and descriptive text to offer a thorough and authentic portrait of a colony of Chinstrap penguins on Bouvet Island in the Antarctic Ocean. Following from one spring to the next, we are told of their mating and see the eggs they lay through the summer, watch the hatching and the care provided by both the male and female penguins until late fall, when the offspring are fully adult and all leave the island to return again in spring. Originally entitled *Das Pinguin—Kinder-Buch,* this was published in 1988 by Neugebauer Press, Salzburg, Austria.

Steele, Mary Q.   *3–9+*
ANNA'S GARDEN SONG   YEARS
    Illus. by Lena Anderson. New York: Greenwillow, 1989.

Fourteen poems about vegetables, fruits, and herbs commonly planted in people's gardens are illustrated with perky pen-and-ink and watercolor-wash paintings. Originally published in Sweden in 1987 by Rabén & Sjögren as *Majas Lilia Grona,* with text and illustrations by Lena Anderson.

Steele, Mary Q.   *4–8*
ANNA'S SUMMER SONGS   YEARS
    Illus. by Lena Anderson. New York: Greenwillow, 1988.

The imagery-filled poems were written to be paired with the watercolor paintings about children and their experiences and associations with trees, flowers, ferns, and fruits. First published in 1984 in Sweden by Rabén & Sjögren as *Majas Alfabet,* with poems and illustrations by Lena Anderson.

Stolz, Mary   9–14+
ZEKMET THE STONE CARVER: A TALE OF ANCIENT   *YEARS*
EGYPT
    Illus. by Deborah Nourse Lattimore. San Diego: HBJ, 1988.

An array of pictures done with watercolor, pencil, and "ponce" in a   *149*
style reminiscent of Egyptian art combine with a convincing, albeit
fictitious, account of the origin of the Sphinx, which remains to this
day an everlasting monument to an Egyptian pharaoh. Each picture is
framed with hieroglyphics, some of which retell the part of the story
written about and illustrated on that page. Note the images on each of
the endpapers. They are taken from the borders that frame the pictures
in this book and are translated. Both the text and the artwork demonstrate that the members of this author and artist team have acquired
considerable knowledge about ancient Egyptian culture and history
and are dedicated to excellence in each of their crafts.

Szilagyi, Mary   4–7
THUNDERSTORM   *YEARS*
    Illus. by Mary Szilagyi. New York: Bradbury, 1985.

The illustrations in this very credible story (thirteen double-page
spreads and a few smaller pictures) are done with colored pencil in
rich, full color. They enhance and extend the brief text to tell about the
reactions of a little girl and her dog to a sudden storm, complete with
thunder, lightning, wind, and rain. Compare the descriptions and reactions to the thunderstorm as depicted in the text and illustrations in
this picture book with those in *Tornado,* written by Arnold Adoff and
illustrated by Ronald Himler (Delacorte, 1977), and *Time of Wonder,*
written and illustrated by Robert McCloskey (Viking, 1957).

Tejima (pseud. of Keizaburo Tejima)   6–9
FOX'S DREAM   *YEARS*
    Trans. from the Japanese by Susan Matsui. Illus. by Tejima. New
       York: Philomel, 1987.

In this life-cycle story a vixen (and the reader) observes a fox who
lives alone through the cold winter until spring comes. Twenty large,
double-spread, woodblock prints are combined with sparse, poetic
prose to create an enchanting and evocative, albeit somewhat anthro-

pomorphic, story of the stages and phases of a fox's life. Originally published in 1983 by Fukutake Publishing Company in Tokyo, Japan, *Fox's Dream* was awarded Special Mention in the "Fiera di Bologna" Graphic Prize at the 1986 Children's Book Fair in Bologna, Italy.

Tejima (pseud. of Keizaburo Tejima)   6–9
OWL LAKE   *YEARS*
   Trans. from the Japanese. Illus. by Tejima. New York: Philomel,
      1987.

   Magnificent, dramatic, over-sized, black woodblock prints illustrate this simply told story of an owl family that lives deep in the mountains that surround a lake. The setting remains the same, but shifts in perspective and subtle changes in the colors of the sky and lake—from sunset to night and from moonlight to dawn—offer beautiful contrasts as one observes the mother and father owl finding food and feeding their owlet. Each of the prints would make an attractive picture for framing, but together they comprise a masterpiece in book art. *Owl Lake* won the Japan Prize for Outstanding Picture Books in 1983. It was published originally in 1982 by Fukutake Publishing Company in Japan under the title *Shemafuro no mizuumi.*

Thayer, Ernest L.   9–15
CASEY AT THE BAT: A BALLAD OF THE REPUBLIC SUNG   *YEARS*
IN THE YEAR 1888.
   Illus. by Wallace Tripp. New York: Coward, 1978.

   This famous poem about the celebrated baseball player who struck out at the crucial moment of the game is depicted as a clever joke. The cartoon-style illustrations that alternate between full color and black and white and the assemblage of animals that make up the teams will provide fun for readers young and old. Casey is a bear, the umpire a swine-like creature, the pitcher a wolf, the fans are dogs of all breeds, rabbits, tigers, pigs, skunks, and more. The source for this version of Casey was *The Annotated Casey at the Bat* by Martin Gardner (Potter, 1967). Compare and contrast Tripp's illustrations for Thayer's vintage piece of Americana with those done by Leonard Everett Fisher (Watts, 1964). The mood of the piece changes drastically by use of different illustrations. Tripp has created a comedy by illustrating with cartoon-style animals, whereas the feeling created by Fisher is consistently more serious. (See Illustrations 16 and 17.)

Illus. 16. Illustration by Wallace Tripp reprinted by permission of Coward, McCann and Geoghegan from *Casey at the Bat* by Ernest Lawrence Thayer; illustrations copyright © 1978 by Wallace Tripp.

Illus. 17. From the book *The First Picture Book Edition of Casey at the Bat* by Ernest L. Thayer and illustrated by Leonard Everett Fisher. Copyright © 1964 by Franklin Watts, Inc. Reprinted with permission of the publisher, Franklin Watts.

Thayer, Ernest L.   *9–15*
THE FIRST BOOK EDITION OF "CASEY AT THE BAT"   YEARS
    Intro. by Casey Stengel. Illus. by Leonard Everett Fisher. New York:
      Watts, 1964.

152   A very special picture book version of the well-known, classic, narrative poem about the celebrated baseball player who struck out at the
crucial moment in the game is illustrated with exquisitely crafted
scratchboard drawings in black and white. Compare and contrast the
illustrations of this picture book version of Ernest Thayer's famous
poem with *Casey at the Bat: A Ballad of the Republic Sung in the Year
1888,* illustrated by Wallace Tripp (Coward, 1978). (Illustrations 16
and 17.)

van der Meer, Ron and Alan McGowan   *7–adult*
SAILING SHIPS   YEARS
    Illus. by Borge Svensson. Paper engineering by John Strejan and
      David Rosendale. New York: Viking, 1988.

    Young and old readers alike will find this book about sailing ships
through thousands of years an invaluable and truly beautiful factual
book. Six beautiful, large paintings, dramatically enhanced by three-
dimensional paper engineering, are combined with an informative text
and many diagrams and drawings to trace the development of sailing
ships from the Roman Corbita (A.D. 230) to the Australia II, a twelve-
meter yacht that won the America's Cup race in 1983. Each of the
endpapers is different and each adds more important information.
There is also a short but worthwhile bibliography at the end of the book
for further reading by nautical enthusiasts.

Wahl, Robert   *2–6*
FRIEND DOG   YEARS
    Illus. by Joe Eivers. Boston: Little, Brown, 1988.

    In this picture book one will find an upbeat story about the antics of
a toddler and his puppy. Their exuberant activities from daytime to
bedtime, at which time both are thoroughly tired out, are aptly illustrated with expressionistic line and wash paintings in clear and rich
colors.

Williams, Vera B.   *7–11*
STRINGBEAN'S TRIP TO THE SHINING SEA   YEARS
    Illus. by Vera B. Williams. New York: Greenwillow, 1988.

Snapshots and postcards, arranged chronologically in an album by the boys' grandfather, record Stringbean's account of his trek with his older brother from Kansas to the Pacific coast. Each illustration suggests the ambience as well as the geography of each locale. A masterful blending of text and illustrations.

Yolen, Jane   *4–8*
OWL MOON   *YEARS*
   Illus. by John Schoenherr. New York: Philomel, 1987.

Impressionistic, poetic prose and impressionistic paintings in pen and full-color watercolor tell a quiet winter's night story of father and daughter walking into the woods under a full moon to see and to hear the great horned owl. The poetic prose makes it especially effective for reading aloud. This accomplished mood book was named the 1988 Caldecott Medal winner.

Ziefert, Harriet   *3–6*
SARAH'S QUESTIONS   *YEARS*
   Illus. by Susan Bonners. New York: Lothrop, 1988.

Sarah and her mother play "I Spy" as they take a walk on a sunny, summer day. The child's questions about the things she sees will serve as a fine model for the young readers of this picture book, encouraging them to be more alert and curious about their world. The mother's responses to Sarah's questions will, no doubt, satisfy and please readers as they obviously did Sarah. The fresh, bright, full-color, impressionistic paintings seem a perfect match for this glimpse of intimacy between mother and daughter.

Zolotow, Charlotte   *2–6*
SLEEPY BOOK   *YEARS*
   Illus. by Ilse Plume. New York: Harper, 1988.

Easy-to-read, poetic prose and realistic, ink and pastel drawings in full color depict how animals, insects, birds, and children sleep in their own unique way.

Zolotow, Charlotte   *4–9*
SOMETHING IS GOING TO HAPPEN   *YEARS*
   Illus. by Catherine Stock. New York: Harper, 1987.

There is usually a definite sense of anticipation before a big snow, and each member of the family in this very credible here-and-now story wakes up with that feeling. Their excitement with the coming of the first snow on a cold November day is expressed most effectively through accomplished use of language and beautifully crafted, impressionistic watercolor paintings.

154

THE
IMAGINATIVE
WORLD

Abolafia, Yossi   *4–7*
A FISH FOR MRS. GARDENIA   *YEARS*
   Illus. by Yossi Abolafia. New York: Greenwillow, 1988.

Children are bound to delight in this account of the series of mis-adventures that finally leads to an elderly man's serving his new friend (an elderly woman he met at the park) a tasty fish dinner that he thinks is chicken. The full-page, cartoon-style, black-pencil line and water-color-wash illustrations are an excellent match for this slapstick tale.

                                             7–11+
AESOP'S FABLES   *YEARS*
   Illus. by Heidi Holder. New York: Viking/Kestrel, 1981.

The detailed, realistic illustrations in this unique picture book were done in pen and India ink and in watercolor wash applied with brush and sponge. This is a studied balance of large, full-page pictures and double-page spreads. Be certain to notice the details in the borders that frame each picture, for they add important nuances to each of the nine fables that are illustrated. The editors of Viking Press obtained the text from several sources, but primarily from works by Boris Anzyhasheff and Sir Robert L'Estrange.

[handwritten margin note: order for molly ?]

Agee, Jon   *5–8*
THE INCREDIBLE PAINTING OF FELIX CLOUSSEAU   *YEARS*
   Illus. by Jon Agee. New York: Farrar, 1988.

Felix Clousseau, once an unknown painter, quickly becomes fa-mous, and then infamous, when the figures in his paintings come to life. A delightful surprise is in store for young readers when they see how a dog, the subject of Clousseau's painting that hung in the King's Palace, catches a notorious jewel thief who tries to steal the crown. The expressionistic paintings are done with full-color wash and outlined with thick, black ink. Older children might be interested in translating the French captions that appear throughout the illustrations.

Ahlbom, Jens   5–8
JONATHAN OF GULL MOUNTAIN   YEARS
    Trans. from the Swedish by Barbara Lucas. Illus. by Jens Ahlbom.
    Stockholm: Rabén & Sjögren, 1987.

    Full-color, expressionistic, watercolor paintings combine with a
well-written text to tell a convincing, fanciful tale of how Jonathan,
born without wings, and his best friend Sara devise a glider that enables Jonathan to participate in all the activities of the other winged
people in his world. The story ends with Jonathan and his father
drawing and constructing "something," and only the thoughtful, sensitive person will know what and for whom that "something" is. Originally published in Swedish under the title *Jonathan pa Masberget* by
Rabén & Sjögren, 1986.

Aksakov, Sergei   5–10
THE SCARLET FLOWER   YEARS
    Trans. from the Russian by Isadora Levin. Illus. by Boris Diodorov.
    San Diego: HBJ, 1989.

A retelling of the Russian variant of "Beauty and the Beast." The
illustrations, beautifully crisp and detailed, are done in ink, colored
pencil, and paint. They can be likened to those in Lucy Maxym's book
Russian Lacquer, Legends and Fairy Tales (Manhasset, N.Y.: Siamese
Imports, 1981).

Andersen, Hans Christian   6–12
THE LITTLE MATCH GIRL   YEARS
    Illus. by Blair Lent. Boston: Houghton, 1968.

Intricately detailed, muted color illustrations add to the magic of this
classic story of the death and redemption of the little match girl.

Andersen, Hans Christian   5–9
THE NIGHTINGALE   YEARS
    Trans. from the Danish by Anthea Bell. Illus. by Lisbeth Zwerger.
    Natick, Mass.: Picture Book Studio/Neugebauer Pr., 1984. Distrib-
    uted by Alphabet Pr.

Full-page pictures done in pen and ink and full-color, watercolor
wash illustrate this classic fairy tale about the heroic little bird who
asked only for the freedom to sing and bring joy to everyone regardless
of their status. Copyrighted in 1984 by Verlag Neugebauer Press (Salz-

burg) under the title *Nattergalen*; original title: *Die Nachtigall*. Compare and contrast the translation and the illustrations in this retelling of Andersen's classic to the retelling translated by Eva Le Gallienne and illustrated by Nancy Elkholm Burkert (Harper, 1965); to the adaptation by Alan Benjamin and illustrated by Beni Montresor (Crown, 1985); and to the adaptation by Anna Bier and illustrated by Demi (HBJ, 1985).

Andersen, Hans Christian   *6–12*
THE NIGHTINGALE   *YEARS*
   Trans. by Eva Le Gallienne. Illus. by Nancy Ekholm Burkert. New
      York: Harper, 1965.

Exquisite, jewel-tone, double-spread paintings in three colors, in a style suggestive of Chinese art, illustrate the enduringly popular story of the emperor and the nightingale; a drab, ordinary-looking bird that sang so beautifully.

Andersen, Hans Christian   *5–9*
THE SNOW QUEEN   *YEARS*
   Trans. and adapted by Anthea Bell. Illus. by Bernadette Watts. Fael-
      lander, Switzerland: North-South Books, 1987. Distributed by Holt.

This classic fairy tale tells of a little girl's long, perilous, and magical journey to rescue her beloved friend who was abducted and turned into ice by the Snow Queen. The full- and double-page impressionistic drawings are done in ink and pastels and are reproduced in rich, full color. They highlight the aura of fantasy and enchantment that pervades this literary statement on the power of love and persistence. Published in 1987 by Nord-Sud Verlag, Mönchalftorf, Switzerland, under the title *Die Schneekönigin*. Compare and contrast the text and illustration of this retelling of *The Snow Queen* with the version created by Naomi Lewis and illustrated by Errol Le Cain (Viking, 1968, 1979) or that told and illustrated by Edmund Dulac (Hodder & Stoughton, n.d.).

Andersen, Hans Christian   *6–9*
THE SWINEHERD   *YEARS*
   Trans. from the Danish by Anthea Bell. Illus. by Lisbeth Zwerger.
      New York: Morrow, 1982.

A satirical statement about a society of shallow people, who neither recognize nor care for true beauty, is told in this story of a prince who poses as a swineherd in order to learn the true character of the princess he desires. The full-page illustrations, done in pen-and-ink line and watercolor wash, interpret the satirical tone of this tale most effectively. Copyrighted in 1982 by Verlag Neugebauer Press, Salzburg, Austria, this retelling was published under the title *Svinedrengen*. First published in German under the title *Der Schweinehirt*.

Andersen, Hans Christian   5–10
THUMBELINA   YEARS
    Trans. from the Danish by Richard and Clara Winston. Illus. by Lisbeth Zwerger. New York: Morrow, 1980.

Full-page, meticulously detailed, representational illustrations in richly colored ink and wash highlight the sensuous imagery and contrasting moods expressed in this romantic story of how a tiny girl, exploited by creatures stronger and more aggressive than herself, eventually found happiness in the world of flowers. This picture book is an elegant and artistic achievement!

Andersen, Hans Christian   6–9
THE TINDERBOX   YEARS
    Illus. by Warwick Hutton. New York: Margaret K. McElderry, 1988.

Expressionistic paintings, appreciatively varied in shape, size, and placement on the page, are done in pen and ink and watercolor wash and embellish this competent translation of the well-loved fantasy of how a soldier, with the help of a magic tinderbox, finds not only a fortune and a princess imprisoned by the king, but also wins the princess' hand in marriage.

Andersen, Hans Christian   5–8
THE UGLY DUCKLING   YEARS
    Trans. by Anne Stewart. Illus. by Monika Laimgruber. New York: Greenwillow, 1985.

This original, classic fairy tale about the ugly duckling, unloved and ostracized by the other animals, that turns out to be a beautiful swan, is retold in elegant prose. The full-color illustrations—eleven striking, full-page pictures and many smaller pictures varying in size and placement on each page—are rendered in ink and watercolor wash. They enhance the range of emotions and details of the action and reflect the sentimental and romantic tone of this well-known story. Originally published in 1982 by Artemis Verlag (Zurich and Munich) under the title *Den grimme aelling*. Compare and contrast the language as well as the tone of the illustrations in this version of *The Ugly Duckling* with that told by Marianna Mayer and illustrated by Thomas Locker (Macmillan, 1987).

Arnold, Tedd   *3–5*
NO JUMPING ON THE BED   *YEARS*
   Illus. by Tedd Arnold. New York: Dial, 1987.

   A wonderfully zany, chain-reaction-type story, ending in a way that is bound to move the reader to beg for an immediate repeat. It is an unforgettable tale of how a boy's habit of jumping on his bed leads to his falling through floor after floor of a tall apartment house, collecting the occupants below him on the way until they all reach the basement. The bright, animated, expressionistic paintings were done with pencil and full-color, watercolor washes.

Arnold, Tedd   *4–8*
OLLIE FORGOT   *YEARS*
   Illus. by Tedd Arnold. New York: Dial, 1988.

   Ollie, who has a most unreliable memory to say the least, is on his way to market to buy "a joint of beef, a wedge of cheese, and a loaf of bread, if you please." But he soon forgets what he is supposed to buy. Instead, he remembers only what he heard uttered by the last person he met, and when he repeats whatever he heard last to whomever he meets next, he manages to offend that person mightily. Fortunately, and quite by accident, he says the right thing to the right person and is rewarded with money and a jingle that help him to remember what he was sent to buy at the market in the first place. But he is faced with the ultimate challenge—to remember his way home. The full-page, stylized, expressionistic illustrations, done in colored pencil and full-color watercolor wash, reflect so well the jovial tone of this wonderfully modern simpleton's tale.

Aruego, Jose (reteller)   *4–6*
ROCKABYE CROCODILE   *YEARS*
   Illus. by Ariane Dewey. New York: Greenwillow, 1988.

   A crocodile helps two elderly boars (one cheerful and kind, the other mean and selfish) realize what they must do to get him to supply them with all the fish they can eat. Black-ink line and watercolor and gouache wash were used to create the cartoon-style illustrations for this effective retelling of a classic Philippine fable.

Asbjornsen, Peter C. and Jorgen Moe   *7–14*
EAST OF THE SUN AND WEST OF THE MOON   YEARS
   Illus. by Kay Nielsen. Garden City, N.Y.: Doubleday, 1977.

Trolls who can assume any shape and who are synonymous with the blind forces of nature, are ever-present in these six Norse folktales. Among the themes that recur in these stories is one that involves the subservient beast who, by magic or other means, protects or permits the protagonist to benefit from some of the advantages of the animal world. Another pervasive theme, suggestive of the Greek myth of Cupid and Psyche, is about the maturing of love through a hazardous search or mission. Although this is not a picture book in the truest sense, the thirteen full-page, watercolor paintings and the many monochromatic sketches capture the dangers, intrigues, and enchantments of these classic folktales from Europe's North Countries, making this a profusely illustrated storybook worthy of note. This edition was originally published in England in 1976 by Hodder & Stoughton Children's Books (Leicester) and Gallery Five (London).

Asch, Frank and Vladimir Vagin   *4–8*
HERE COMES THE CAT!   YEARS
   Illus. by Frank Asch and Vladimir Vagin. New York: Scholastic, 1989.

The very brief text for this almost wordless picture book is written in Russian and English. The detailed, double-page line and jewel-tone wash paintings considerably embellish the fictional elements (especially the setting and the action) of this story about creatures who were once arch enemies and became fast friends.

Aylesworth, Jim   *5–9*
HANNA'S HOG   YEARS
   Illus. by Glen Rounds. New York: Atheneum, 1988.

Expressive ink drawings in heavy line and full color transmit the brazen humor of this incredible tale of how Hanna Brodie makes clever use of a rake, a bit of rope, and her own voice to convince her neighbor who has stolen her beloved hog as well as a number of her chickens that he was being attacked by a bear. A funny story!

Bang, Molly   5–8
DAWN   YEARS
   Illus. by Molly Bang. New York: Morrow, 1983.

In this variant of the Japanese folktale "The Crane Wife," the story
takes place in nineteenth-century New England. A wounded Canadian   *163*
goose, rescued by a poor shipbuilder, returns as a beautiful woman.
The two are married, and a little girl is born to them. The woman
surprises her husband with a set of beautiful and strong sails for the
sailboat he made for his family. When a man comes and asks the
shipbuilder to make him a racing schooner equipped with sails like
those the woman made for their sailboat, the woman most reluctantly
agrees to weave them—on the condition that her husband never come
into the room while she weaves the sails. Fearful his wife will not finish
them by the time they are due, the shipbuilder breaks his promise.
Looking in on her, he sees that she is the Canadian goose he rescued
years before. She disappears after that and only their daughter remains
with him. The full-page, realistic illustrations alternate with full-color
paintings and black-and-white pencil and ink drawings. A careful look
at the details in the full-color illustrations and in their frames will
reveal any number of clues that the woman is a Canadian goose. Seek
and thou shalt find! The text is done in exquisite hand calligraphy by
G. G. Laurens. Compare Molly Bang's version of the Japanese folktale
with *The Crane Maiden*, retold by Miyoko Matsutani, English translation by Alvin Tresselt and illustrations by Chihiro Iwasaki (Parents,
1968) and *The Crane Wife*, retold by Sumiko Yagawa, translated from
the Japanese by Katherine Paterson, and illustrated by Suekichi Akaba
(Morrow, 1981).

Bang, Molly   6–11
THE GREY LADY AND THE STRAWBERRY SNATCHER   YEARS
   Illus. by Molly Bang. New York: Four Winds, 1980.

This allegory, depicting how the Grey Lady escapes the Strawberry
Snatcher, is filled with surprises, lively humor, and suspense. Its unusual colors and its characters are ethnically indeterminate, but the
whole is strongly suggestive of a folktale from India. The skillfully
executed, impressionistic illustrations, so full of meticulous, often star-
tling details, offer an exciting visual treat to the readers of this wordless
book.

Barber, Antonia   *5–10*
THE ENCHANTER'S DAUGHTER   *YEARS*
    Illus. by Errol LeCain. New York: Farrar, 1987.

    Lavish, full-page fantasy paintings place this fairy tale in ancient China. They add an aura of elegance and charm to the well-told story. The Enchanter's beautiful daughter was tired of living with her father, who never talked to her. He was too busy looking in his books for the secret of eternal youth, which he wanted to find before age and death robbed him of all his power and possessions. How the daughter managed to escape from this sterile and lonely place and reunite with her mother and brother should fascinate and satisfy most of the young readers of this very beautiful picture book.

Birch, David   *6–10*
THE KING'S CHESSBOARD   *YEARS*
    Illus. by Devis Grebu. New York: Dial, 1988.

    The full-color, expressionistic pictures, prepared with black ink, watercolor, and colored pencil, reiterate the humor and setting of this predictable tale set in ancient India. The King insisted his wise man be paid for the services he performed. The wise man asked to be paid in rice, the amount of which was to be doubled each day for each square of chessboard. The King was too proud to admit he was unable to compute the amount of rice this would total and agreed to the wise man's request. Even the most reluctant math students should be tempted to work out the geometrical progression in weights for each of the payments that the wise man's request would amount to.

Bryan, Ashley (reteller)   *6–10*
THE DANCING GRANNY   *YEARS*
    Illus. by Ashley Bryan. New York: Atheneum, 1977.

    Granny Anika, a happy old lady who loves to dance and sing, finds rhythm in everything she does. Spider Ananse, a lazy trickster, keeps plundering Granny's vegetable garden of corn, beans, peas, potatoes, and beets. When Ananse returns to find nothing left in the garden, Granny Anika grabs him around the waist and leads in the dance to the spider's own tune. To this day, according to the narrator, they are dancing still! Sophisticated, pen-and-ink sketches in the impressionistic style add to the levity of this retelling of the West Indies folktale.

Buffet, Jimmy and Savannah Jane Buffett   *6–9*
THE JOLLY MON   *YEARS*
 Illus. by Lambert Davis. San Diego: HBJ, 1988.

 Large-sized, brilliant, full-color, acrylic paintings add a healthy
amount of realism and drama to this fantasy about how a loyal dolphin
saved the life of a talented, Caribbean guitar singer after pirates seized
his boat and threw him into the sea. The realism of the paintings
conveys a sense of the actuality of the danger *and* the fulfillment of
trust that overcomes it. (See illustration 19.)

165

Bunting, Eve   *5–8*
CLANCY'S COAT   *YEARS*
 Illus. by Lorinda Bryan Cauley. New York: Warne, 1984.

Illus. 18. Illustration from *The Jolly Mon* by Jimmy Buffett and Jane Buffett, copyright
© 1988 by Lambert Davis, reprinted by permission of Harcourt Brace Jovanovich, Inc.

Full-page, stylized illustrations—full-color wash paintings alternating with black-and-white pencil drawings—reflect the droll and exaggerated humor in a story about how a friendship between a tailor and a farmer, who were no longer speaking to each other, was renewed slowly but surely "with care and attention." Although few young readers will be able to predict the farmer's response to the tailor, who keeps putting off the return of his coat, they are bound to enjoy not only the outcome of the tale, but also the many ingenious uses the tailor makes of the farmer's coat before working on it as he had promised.

Burningham, John *4–7*
AVOCADO BABY *YEARS*
    Illus. by John Burningham. New York: Crowell, 1982.

This is a refreshingly humorous tall tale about the amazing feats the Hargraves' baby can do because he lives on a diet of avocado pears. The full-color, expressionistic drawings, done in ink and watercolor wash, add just the right amount of credibility. Be certain to notice the end papers that depict the baby engaging in even more escapades, exhibiting unusual strength and agility among a maze of botanically accurate avocado plants—from the sprouted seed to the mature flowering plant, the fruit, and another sprouting seed.

Burningham, John *3–6*
MR. GRUMPY'S OUTING *YEARS*
    Illus. by John Burningham. New York: Holt, 1971.

Economical text and skillfully executed, crosshatched drawings that alternate with impressionistic, watercolor paintings tell about an outing held on Mr. Grumpy's boat by rambunctious animals and children.

Carlson, Natalie Savage *7–10*
THE GHOST IN THE LAGOON *YEARS*
    Illus. by Andrew Glass. New York: Lothrop, 1984.

A great story to read aloud on Halloween or any other time. The fact that it is divided into five short chapters should make it especially appealing to the transitional reader. The first two nights that Timmy and his father tried to catch catfish in the haunted lagoon, the pirate's ghost kept them from catching anything. He cut their line, dragged Timmy and his pole into the water, and finally confronted Timmy and his father and told them to stay away. How Timmy scared the ghost on Halloween night and learned about the buried treasure the pirate's ghost was hiding will most certainly please readers. The expressive, black-and-white, crosshatched pencil drawings are perfect for this ghost story; they make it even more delightfully titillating—not frightening, but definitely more fun!

Cauley, Lorinda Bryan   6–10   *167*
THE TROUBLE WITH TYRANNOSAURUS REX   *YEARS*
   Illus. by Lorinda Bryan Cauley. San Diego: HBJ, 1988.

A fascinating and unique blend of a fanciful tale and realistic illustrations. A wealth of factual information about the dinosaurs that lived in the Cretaceous period can be found just by looking at the detailed, colored pencil drawings and checking the glossary of pictures with the phonetic pronunciation guide that accompanies it. Peaceful dinosaurs outwit and humiliate the great Tyrannosaurus Rex before he eats them all. Finding these prehistoric animals should prove to make this a very popular book indeed, one children will read and look at many times.

Chapman, Carol   5–8
BARNEY BIPPLE'S MAGIC DANDELION   *YEARS*
   Illus. by Steven Kellogg. New York: Dutton, 1988.

Superstition has it that if you blow the puffy, white, dandelion seed away, your wish will come true. Unfortunately, Barney Bipple fails to follow Miss Miske's sage advice, wishing for complicated things rather than the simple ones she suggested. His wishes are granted, but the results are far from pleasant. The detailed, ink-line and watercolor-wash, cartoon-style illustrations add wonderfully to the humor and credibility of this outlandish fantasy.

Chorao, Kay   5–8
CATHEDRAL MOUSE   *YEARS*
   Illus. by Kay Chorao. New York: Dutton, 1988.

Detailed, realistic, pencil and watercolor illustrations extend and enrich this well-told story of a friendship between a stone sculptor and a homeless mouse in a cathedral. Children will be intrigued with the home the man makes for his little mouse friend.

Chouinard, Roger and Mariko   4–7
THE AMAZING ANIMAL ALPHABET   *YEARS*
   Illus. by Roger Chouinard. Garden City, N.J.: Doubleday, 1988.

Humorous, alliterative captions in crisp, bold print and full-page, detailed, action-filled, humorous illustrations done in ink, clear, bright watercolors, and colored pencil combine to offer young readers a refreshing, highly imaginative application of the alphabet.

Clark, Ann Nolan (reteller)   *4–9*
IN THE LAND OF THE SMALL DRAGON   YEARS
   Illus. by Tony Chen. New York: Viking, 1979.

This retelling of the Vietnamese variant of "Cinderella," based on a story told to Clark by Dang Manh Kha, is illustrated in double-page, exquisitely detailed, realistic pictures. They are done in pen-and-ink and full-color, watercolor wash alternating with detailed, pen-and-ink wash in monochromatic shades of black and gray. Compare and contrast the text and illustrations in Clark's retelling with those in the Chinese variant of "Cinderella," *Yeh-Shen*, retold by Ai-Ling Louie and illustrated by Ed Young (Philomel, 1982); the French variant, *Cinderella*, based on Perrault's version, retold and illustrated by Errol LeCain (Faber & Faber, 1972); and the German story, *Cinderella*, based on the Grimm brothers' version, retold and illustrated by Nonny Hogrogian (Greenwillow, 1981).

Clément, Claude   *8–12*
THE PAINTER AND THE WILD SWANS   YEARS
   Trans. from the French by Robert Levine. Illus. by Frédéric Clément.
      New York: Dial, 1986.

Teiji, a famous Japanese painter, stops painting after he sees a flock of exquisitely beautiful swans fly overhead, because he insists that he has to see the birds again in order to capture their beauty on canvas. As he follows the birds across a treacherous lake to the island where they rest, a block of ice hits his boat and capsizes it. Teiji manages to swim to the shore of the island where he sees the beautiful swans again, but he dies of exposure to the icy water and the winter elements. Although he never does paint the birds, he dies knowing that just seeing them is enough, for, as he says, "Such beauty is rare and impossible to capture on canvas." The ice and snow that cover his body gradually change to feathers and large wings, and he flies away "with his brothers" where winter is milder. This transformation, elegantly depicted in words and pictures, is thoroughly hypnotic in its effect. The acrylic paintings, in tones of blue-gray and white with hints of red and yellow, are breathtaking in their beauty and are strongly suggestive of classic Japanese brush paintings. The entire format of the book is a work of art—the crisp type; the delicate, Japanese calligraphy that tells one swan's story; the studied and varied placement of the paintings, which are of different sizes and shapes; the effects of the cold colors and shading. All add up to an example of fine bookmaking. Originally published by Duculot Paris-Gembloux in 1986, the book was entitled *Le peintre et les cygnes sauvages*. It received the French Foundation Grand Prize for Children's Literature.

Cohen, Caron Lee   *5–10+*
THE MUD PONY   *YEARS*
    Illus. by Shonto Begay. New York: Scholastic, 1988.

A folktale based on an ancient "boy-hero story" told among the Skidi band of the Pawnee Indians of the Great Plains. It tells how a boy, accidentally left behind by his family when they break camp to hunt for buffalo, is reunited with them, saves them and other members of the tribe from an approaching enemy, and helps them to capture the buffalo, which provides the food they need through the winter months. The symbolism evidenced in the Skidi's lore, the oneness the Skidi feel with nature, and their emphasis on the virtue of persistence and the spirit of humility are all authentically reflected in the text and in the superb, full-color, expressionistic paintings that combine to tell this folktale. Compare and contrast this picture-book retelling of the Skidi "boy-hero story" with the 1982 Caldecott Honor book *Where the Buffaloes Begin*, retold by Olaf Baker and illustrated by Stephen Gammell (Warne, 1981).

Cole, Joanna   *1–4*
ANIMAL SLEEPYHEADS: 1 TO 10   *YEARS* X
    Illus. by Jeni Bassett. New York: Scholastic, 1988.   SAPAR

This satisfying bedtime counting book for sleepyheads is illustrated with "sweet" cartoon-style-line and full-color, watercolor paintings.

Corbalis, Judy   *5–10*
PORCELLUS, THE FLYING PIG   *YEARS*
    Illus. by Helen Craig. New York: Dial, 1988.

What a fun-filled picture book! The cartoon-style illustrations, done in pen-and-ink line and full-color, watercolor wash, are jam-packed with wonderfully detailed facial expressions and actions. The language offers readers one clever word pun after another as well as other kinds of plays with and plays on words. Porcellus, a piglet determined to earn enough money for an operation to remove two ugly bumps on his back, gets a job as a watchpig at a piggy bank. He becomes a hero when he rescues his little sister, who is held hostage by the notorious Al Porcone, turns Porcone and his henchmen over to the police, and returns the stolen money to the strong room of the bank. *Porcellus, the Flying Pig* is a hero tale of the first order; it will be remembered and laughed about for a long time.

Craft, Ruth   *4–9*
THE DAY OF THE RAINBOW   *YEARS*
   Illus. by Niki Daly. New York: Viking/Kestrel, 1989.

   This is an upbeat tale of three people who lost important things on a hot summer day. Readers will smile as do the persons in the story, who find their things at the end of a rainbow that appears after the cooling rain comes down. Colorful, poetic prose, filled with appropriate similes and metaphors, and rich, detailed, impressionistic paintings in full color capture the hustle and bustle of these diverse, urban people.

Crossley-Holland, Kevin   *11–16+*
BEOWULF   *YEARS*
   Illus. by Charles Keeping. New York: Oxford Univ. Pr., 1987.

   An eighth-century, Anglo-Saxon classic has been competently rewritten in poetic prose, making it accessible to upper-elementary and middle school students. The illustrations for this story of Beowulf and his fight with two gross monsters are sophisticated, expressionistic drawings, done in sepia ink. They will attract and hold the interest of most readers, and they certainly extend and embellish the action, setting, characterization, and mood of the story.

Dahl, Roald   *10–16*
DIRTY BEASTS   *YEARS*
   Illus. by Rosemary Fawcett. New York: Farrar, 1984.

   Each of the nine narrative poems (all of them clever, some of them a bit gross) tells how beasts outwit an unsuspecting human. The full-page, surrealistic, jewel-tone illustrations are perfectly compatible with the absurd, macabre poems. *Dirty Beasts* is certain to be a favorite with

Illus. 19. Reprinted by permission of Macmillan Publishing Company from *The Little Wooden Farmer* by Alice Dalgliesh, illustrated by Anita Lobel. Illustrations copyright © 1968 Anita Lobel.

children in upper-elementary and middle schools. See also Roald Dahl's *Revolting Rhymes* (Farrar, 1982).

Dalgliesh, Alice   *3–6*
THE LITTLE WOODEN FARMER   *YEARS*
   Illus. by Anita Lobel. New York: Macmillan, 1930, 1968, and 1988.

   This reissue of the classic picture book is illustrated with full-color, line and wash paintings suggestive of Swedish folk art decorations. It is a captivating story about how a friendly steamboat captain helps a wooden farmer and his little wooden wife, who live in a neat, wooden farmhouse near a river, find all the animals they need to make their farm "the nicest farm in the world." The use of an indigenous style of illustration is intended to help children recognize that love, desire for a place of one's own, and friendship are evident among all people. (See illustration 19.)

Day, Alexandra   *5–10+*
FRANK AND ERNEST   *YEARS*
   Illus. by Alexandra Day. New York: Scholastic, 1988.

   Anyone interested in language, especially "a secret language" or word plays, will thoroughly enjoy this story of what happened when two animals answered an ad and agreed to run a restaurant while its owner was on holiday. Examples of their restaurant language and its counterpart in "standard English" include "burn one, take it through the garden and pin a rose on it," for a hamburger with lettuce, tomato, and onion; "Eve with a lid and moo juice," for a piece of apple pie and a glass of milk; and "Paint a bow-wow red" and "a nervous pudding," for a hot dog with ketchup, and jello. The large, full-page, realistic illustrations, done in full-color wash, add to the credibility and humor of this unique picture book. Be certain to notice each of the four end pages; they contain a full glossary of the restaurant language Frank and Ernest use when they call the orders out to their cook.

Day, Edward C. (reteller)   *6–9*
JOHN TABOR'S RIDE   *YEARS*
   Illus. by Dirk Zimmer. New York: Knopf, 1989.

A retelling of John Tabor's far-fetched tale of his meeting with a mysterious old man and his fantastic ride on a whale. Based on an entry in a journal written by seaman J. Ross Browne, published in *Etchings of a Whaling Cruise* (1846), the tale was used later by Herman Melville in his novel *Moby Dick*. The action-filled, cartoon-style drawings, done in pen-and-ink line with crosshatching and in full-color wash, reflect perfectly the humorous and hair-raising aura of this fantastic yarn. Notice the map on the end pages designating the route taken by Tabor when he was on the whaling ship and on the whale.

De Mejo, Oscar   *5–9*
THERE'S A HAND IN THE SKY   *YEARS*
   Illus. by Oscar De Mejo. New York: Pantheon, 1983.

Highly stylized, expressionistic drawings, done in pen-and-ink and gray, watercolor wash, extend and enrich a brief, well-crafted text to tell an unusual but credible, fanciful tale about what happens when a ghost tells two children to attend a masked ball held in a mansion near their home, and a hand in the sky gives them a note that instructs them to enter the mansion through a secret passage. A fun, fanciful mystery for those who enjoy reading picture books!

de Beaumont, Madame Leprince   *6–12*
BEAUTY AND THE BEAST   *YEARS*
   Trans. from the French and adapted by Diane Goode. Illus. by Diane
     Goode. New York: Bradbury, 1978.

Elegant, delicate, beautifully structured watercolor paintings on parchment, which alternate between full color and black and white, dramatize the imaginative language of this version of the well-known tale of magic, kindness, and love.

Devlin, Wende and Harry   4–8   **173**
CRANBERRY MYSTERY   *YEARS*
   Illus. by Harry Devlin. New York: Parents' Magazine, 1978.

In this lighthearted, mystery story set in Cranberryport, Mr. Whiskers and Maggie use their ingenuity and cunning to catch the thieves who stole a priceless copper kettle, a gold weather vane, and a carved figurehead named Annabelle. The cartoon-style illustrations, some full-color, line-and-wash paintings, and others black-and-white, pen-and-ink silhouettes, help to evoke the special atmosphere of suspense required by a story of intrigue and adventure. A recipe for an easy-to-make, tasty cranberry pie-pudding is provided (tested by the Food Department of Parents' Magazine). Other titles in the Cranberryport series by Wende and Harry Devlin are *Cranberry Christmas* (Parents' Magazine Pr., 1976), *Cranberry Halloween* (Four Winds, 1982) and *Cranberry Thanksgiving* (Parents' Magazine Pr., 1971).

Diamond, Donna (adapter)   6–10
SWAN LAKE   *YEARS*
   Introd. by Clive Barnes. Illus. by Donna Diamond. New York: Holiday, 1980.

The elements of good and evil in the Russian fairy tale about the tragic love of Odette, the graceful Swan Queen, and Siegfried, the handsome prince, have been retained in this picture-book adaptation of the classical ballet version of the story. The six double-page and two full-page pencil drawings are strongly suggestive of the great master Monet. Each provides a stunning interpretation of the major incidents in this fantasy; together, they give the feeling of watching a performance of the ballet by an accomplished, professional troupe.

Edens, Cooper (selector)   *Infancy–8+*
THE GLORIOUS MOTHER GOOSE   *YEARS*
   Illus. New York: Atheneum, 1988.

This collection of Mother Goose and other traditional nursery rhymes is illustrated by artists important in the history of children's literature in English-speaking countries and still well-loved and respected (Arthur Rackham, Walter Crane, Kate Greenaway, L. Leslie Brooke, William Donabey, Mary Royt, and many others). A fine illustrated anthology for today's children as well as the children's literature scholars. Compare and contrast the selections, especially the selection of illustrations, in *The Glorious Mother Goose* with those in *Tail Feathers From Mother Goose: The Opie Rhyme Book,* compiled by Iona and Peter Opie and illustrated by many of the world's most distinguished contemporary illustrators (Little, Brown, 1988).

Esbensen, Barbara Juster (reteller)   5–9
THE STAR MAIDEN: AN OJIBWAY TALE   *YEARS*
   Illus. by Helen K. Davie. Boston: Little, Brown, 1988.

The Star Maiden, tired of wandering in the sky, came to earth to live among the people as a water lily. The full-page, full-color, expressionistic, watercolor paintings are framed with designs and symbols suggestive of those used traditionally by the Cherokee Indians. The traditional clothes worn by these Native Americans in past times along with aspects of the terrain, and the flora and fauna of the mid-states region where the Cherokee lived (Michigan and Minnesota, among other places) are also authentically portrayed in the pictures. This is a retelling of "The Star and the Lily" from *The Traditional History and Characteristic Sketches of the Ojibway Nation*, an 1850 work by Ojibway Chief Kah-ge-ga-gah-bowh, who later took the name George Copway.

THE FANTASTIC BOOK OF BOARD GAMES   7–12+
   Illus. New York: St. Martin's, 1988.   *YEARS*

Originally published in England in 1985 under the title *The Great Games Book*, this is a collection of fourteen unique board games. Each game is ready for use. All the readers need are dice, counters, paper and pencil, and the willingness to play the games and take the time to examine the incredibly detailed pictures throughout the book. Each set of pictures reflects the theme or motif of each game. Among the established artists who created the games are Angela Barrett, Quentin Blake, Tony Blundell, Catherine Brighton, Peter Cross, Satoshi Kitamura, Shoo Rayner, Tony Ross, Ralph Steadman, John Talbot, Fulvio Testa and Joseph Wright. Most are British.

Fisher, Leonard Everett   5–9
THESEUS AND MINOTAUR   YEARS
  Illus. by Leonard Everett Fisher. New York: Holiday, 1988.

  Superbly executed, dramatic and sophisticated, expressionistic
paintings in rich, full color are perfectly suited to this carefully written   *175*
retelling of the well-known Greek myth about the hero Theseus and his
fierce battle with Minotaur, the half-man, half-bull monster. The combination of fine language and accomplished graphics brings characters
and action to life!

Foreman, Michael   8–11+
WAR AND PEAS   YEARS
  Illus. by Michael Foreman. New York: Crowell, 1974.

  Wonderfully imaginative and original, surrealistic collages, watercolor paintings, and an easy-to-read but satirical text are expertly
blended to tell a multi-level fable. Because of a lack of rain, plants
could not grow, and King Lion and his animals have no food. When a
neighboring kingdom refuses to give King Lion food from its stockpiles,
an all-out war breaks out. How world peace and good will win in the
end amounts to an hilarious story on the literal level and a biting,
satirical comment about sharing and goodness on a higher level. A
mind-jarring, but fun story—well worth reading *and* discussing carefully.

Foreman, Michael   5–10
WINTER'S TALES   YEARS
  Illus. by Freire Wright. New York: Doubleday, 1979.

  Some of the luminous watercolor illustrations are surrealistic in
style, others are elegantly impressionistic; all dramatically complement this unusual, diverse collection of six spirited Christmas stories.

Fox, Mem   4–7
POSSUM MAGIC   YEARS
  Illus. by Julie Vivas. New York: Abingdon, 1987.

  Once upon a time, but not very long ago, Grandmas Poss fed Hush
some "people food" that made her invisible. When Hush asked Grandma Poss to make her visible again, Grandma realized that she had
forgotten the spell to make Hush reappear. The two possums traveled
all over the continent of Australia in search of the right food. Persis-

tence paid off; when Hush ate a "vegemite" sandwich in northern Australia her tail became visible; when she ate "pavlova" in Perth her legs appeared; and when she ate the "lamington" in Hobart, Hush became visible from head to foot. The cartoon-style, full-color illustrations, done in ink and watercolor, detail this charming saga perfectly. A brief glossary is provided for those who think children will need more specific information than just the names of each of these foods. See *Grandma Poss Cookbook* (Omnibus Press, Adelaide, Australia: 1988) for easy-to-make recipes for the people foods Hush ate in her attempt to become visible. It is a perfect companion volume to *Possum Magic*.

Freeman, Don   4–7
A POCKET FOR CORDUROY   *YEARS*
   Illus. by Don Freeman. New York: Viking, 1978.

   Pen-and-wash illustrations in full-color highlight the adventures of the appealing, lovable toy bear. After he hears Lisa's mother tell Lisa to empty her pockets before putting her clothes into the washing machine, Corduroy, as resourceful as always, decides to find something with which to make a pocket for his green pants. His adventures at the laundromat and the fact that he does get a pocket will please his many young fans.

French, Fiona   8–11
FUTURE STORY   *YEARS*
   Illus. by Fiona French. New York: Bedrick, 1987.

   Glitzy, fairly surrealistic paintings in flat psychedelic colors are combined with a minimal text that consists primarily of messages from a starship in which the crew attempts to rescue the survivors of a dying planet. Everything about this book—the plot, the style of the art work, the postures and expressions of the astronauts, and even the style of writing—suggests an aura of insensitivity and controlled emotions that does not speak well for the future, specifically for the year 2301, the time when the action takes place.

Garfield, Leon   12–16+
THE WEDDING GHOST   *YEARS*
   Illus. by Charles Keeping. New York: Oxford Univ. Pr., 1987.

   In this very clever blend of elements from "Sleeping Beauty" and Shakespeare's "Twelfth Night," one will find a haunting, multi-level comment about people's concept of the real and the ideal, the homely, and the romantic. The expressionistic, black-and-white, line-and-wash drawings embellish the nineteenth-century English setting and the mysterious and sinister overtones of this fantasy. To say this picture book would be a memorable read would be a gross understatement.

Gedin, Birgitta   5–9
THE LITTLE HOUSE FROM THE SEA   YEARS
  Trans. from the Swedish by Elizabeth Dyssegaard. Illus. by Petter
    Pettersson. New York: Rabén & Sjögren, 1988. Distributed by Far-
    rar.

Unsophisticated, impressionistic seascapes in full-color watercolor illustrate this story of how a house made out of timber from the ship-wrecked *Ida Sina* and situated on the highest cliff of a rocky island, longed to be a boat so it could explore the horizon and beyond. Originally published in 1986 in Sweden by Rabén & Sjögren under the title *Det lilla huset frin havet.*

Gerstein, Mordecai   7–11+
THE MOUNTAIN OF TIBET   YEARS
  Illus. by Mordecai Gerstein. New York: Harper, 1987.

This charming picture book provides some fine food for thought: if you were offered the chance to live again, in any form and in any place you'd like, what choice would you make? The choice made by the main character in this story of reincarnation should not surprise the thoughtful adult, but it might well surprise young readers. The illustrations, done in watercolor and gouache, are quite in keeping with the Tibetan setting of the story, for many of them suggest the Chinese symbol of the universe, the mandala. In this case each choice offered the man for his reincarnated life is enclosed in a separate circle: the various planets, creatures, racial groups, countries, parents, gender.

Ginsburg, Mirra (reteller)   4–8
THE CHINESE MIRROR   YEARS
  Illus. by Margot Zemach. San Diego: HBJ, 1988.

Children will undoubtedly be delighted to recognize what the characters in this story do not—that the object the characters looked into was a mirror and that the images they saw were their own. This retelling of a droll Korean folktale is effectively illustrated in watercolor paintings in a style that was "inspired by the paintings of two eighteenth century Korean genre painters, Sin Yun-bok and Kim Hong-do."

Goble, Paul   *6–9*
THE GIRL WHO LOVED WILD HORSES   *YEARS*

178   Illus. by Paul Goble. New York: Bradbury, 1978.

A distinguished book in every sense. Fine use of language, excellent design, and stunning illustrations are expertly combined in this 1979 Caldecott Medal winner to tell the story of a Native American maiden who loved horses and understood them in a special way. The maiden accepted an Appaloosa stallion's invitation to live with his herd, and because she communicated with the horses and understood them so well, she eventually turned into one of them. This original fairy tale is illustrated with colorful, full-page, stylized paintings, containing authentic details suggestive of the Plains Indians—the horseback Indians of the Great Plains of North America.

Goble, Paul (reteller)   *6–10*
HER SEVEN BROTHERS   *YEARS*
Illus. by Paul Goble. New York: Bradbury, 1988.

Illustrated with full-color paintings made by using pen, India ink, and watercolor, this story is an authentic retelling of the Cheyenne legend in which a girl and her seven brothers become the stars that make up the Big Dipper. The pictures are filled with many allusions and direct references to the folk art, the cultural traditions, and the flora, fauna, and terrain associated with the Cheyenne Indians and the Great Plains region of the United States where they lived.

Goldin, Barbara Diamond   *4–10*
JUST ENOUGH IS PLENTY: A HANUKKAH TALE   *YEARS*
Illus. by Seymour Chwast. New York: Viking/Kestrel, 1988.

Large, brightly colored, acrylic paintings embellish this fine retelling of the original folktale. A family with barely enough money to buy food and celebrate Hanukkah, the Jewish Festival of Lights, invites a poor peddler, who comes to the door, to join their table. A very special picture book!

Goodall, John S.   *4–8*
NAUGHTY NANCY GOES TO SCHOOL   *YEARS*
Illus. by John S. Goodall. New York: Margaret K. McElderry/Atheneum, 1985.

Nancy begins school reluctantly. It takes little or no time for her to live up to the reputation she earned in *Naughty Nancy* (Greenwillow, 1975), the first book of this amusing series by John Goodall. She misbehaves in the classroom, on the school playground, and during the field trip, shocking and delighting her fellow classmates. The spirited little girl becomes the school's hero when she rescues a nonswimmer who is stranded in his inner tube in deep water. The detailed, realistic, watercolor paintings and the carefully planned and appropriately placed half-pages so typical of John Goodall warrant repeated examination by young readers.

Goodall, John S.   *5–8*
PADDY UNDER WATER   YEARS
    Illus. by John S. Goodall. New York: Margaret K. McElderry/Atheneum, 1984.

This wordless adventure story uses full-color, very detailed watercolor paintings and half pages to advance the action. Paddy Pork has some harrowing experiences and finds a chest full of treasures in the wreck of an ancient ship that King Neptune showed him. Like all of Goodall's wordless books, this one is good for use in original storymaking. Some other wordless stories about Paddy Pork are *Paddy's New Hat* (1980), *Paddy Pork's Holiday* (1976), and *Paddy Pork-Odd Jobs* (1983), to name but a few.

Goodall, John S.   *7–11*
SHREWBETTINA'S BIRTHDAY   YEARS
    Illus. by John S. Goodall. San Diego: HBJ, 1971.

An appealing, happy story without words tells how Shrewbettina prepared for and celebrated her birthday. The watercolor illustrations are subdued but richly detailed. They combine with an innovative alternation of half- and full-width pages to provide the reader with an added element of surprise.

Grahame, Kenneth   *6–10*
THE RIVER BANK FROM WIND IN THE WILLOWS   YEARS
    Illus. by Adrienne Adams. New York: Scribner, 1977.

The delicate, representational, watercolor paintings beautifully visualize the details of this story about the rowboat ride Mole and Rat take down the river. The text is lengthier and the language more mature than is usually found in picture books in this format, but the book is excellent for reading aloud to beginning readers. This excerpt from the classic fantasy *Wind in the Willows* (originally illustrated by Ernest H. Shepard in 1931) might well serve as the beginning for many more read-aloud sessions from the rest of this well-known animal fantasy. Other picture-book renditions of complete chapters from *Wind in the Willows* are *The Open Road,* illustrated by Beverly Gooding (Scribner, 1980) and *Wayfarers All,* also illustrated by Beverly Gooding (Scribner, 1981).

Grimm, Jacob and Wilhelm *6–12*
THE BROTHERS GRIMM: POPULAR FOLK TALES *YEARS*
    Trans. by Brian Alderson. Illus. by Michael Foreman. Garden City, N.Y.: Doubleday, 1978.

Although this is not a picture book, it is a stunning illustrated book with a full-color, full-page painting and a small, black-and-white sketch for each of the thirty-one popular folktales retold in it. And, as Alderson states in his afterword, he offers his readers "something of the unself-conscious directness and the colloquial ease" so characteristic of the nineteenth-century storytellers from whom the Grimms originally collected the tales. See also the mate of this collection, *Hans Andersen: His Classic Fairy Tales,* translated by Eric Haugaard and illustrated by Michael Foreman (Doubleday, 1978). Both are just the thing for the family library.

Grimm, Jacob and Wilhelm *5–8*
RUMPELSTILTSKIN *YEARS*
    Retold by Paul O. Zelinsky. Illus. by Paul O. Zelinsky. New York: Dutton, 1986.

A fine retelling in words and pictures of the well-known German folktale. Brought to the castle because her father falsely bragged to the king that she could spin straw into gold, a miller's daughter outwits the little man (an imp-like creature) who agrees to do the spinning for her if, when she becomes queen, she will give him her first born child. The story is illustrated with accomplished, detailed, oil paintings suggestive of Renaissance masters. Especially noteworthy is the artist's use of color and shading to convey the opulence of the setting and the texture of the costumes worn by the characters. The Association for Library Services to Children of the American Library Association honored the artist for the illustrations by awarding him the 1987 Caldecott Honor award. Compare and contrast aspects of this picture book with other versions—*Duffy and the Devil,* a Cornish tale retold by Harve Zemach and illustrated by Margot Zemach (Farrar, 1973) and named the 1974 Caldecott Medal winner; *Tom Tit Tot,* a British version retold and illustrated by Evaline Ness (Holt, 1965) and named a 1966 Caldecott Honor book; and *Rumpelstiltskin,* a German version by the Grimm brothers, retold and illustrated by Donna Diamond (Holiday, 1983).

Grimm, Jacob and Wilhelm   *4–7*
TOM THUMB   *YEARS*
   Illus. by Felix Hoffmann. New York: Margaret K. McElderry/Atheneum, 1973.

A special interpretation of the famous fantasy of a very tiny, quick-witted boy whose adventures and misadventures take him "in a mouse hold, in a snail shell, down a cow's throat, and in the wolf's belly." He arrives back safe and sound with his mother and father, who love him dearly and who he loves dearly in return. The expressionistic art work by this well-known Swiss book artist is done in warm, full-color pen and ink and pencil. Compare and contrast the story line and the illustrations in this book with the story line and illustrations in *Thumbelina* by Hans Christian Andersen, retold and illustrated by Lisbeth Zwerger (Morrow, 1980).

Hastings, Selina (reteller)   *6–10*
THE SINGING RINGING TREE   *YEARS*
   Illus. by Louise Brierley. New York: Holt, 1988.

In a Slavic tale of ill fortune and sorrow, simplified spite and evil, and love and sacrifice, a handsome Prince, smitten with the awesome beauty of an indulged, arrogant Princess, makes a dangerous quest for the music of those with love in their hearts. The full-page details add much to the fairy tale's aura of charm and enchantment. Despite, or perhaps because of its predictability, the story will be read and reread and the illustrations examined again and again. Compare and contrast the theme and illustration of *The Singing Ringing Tree* with Oscar Wilde's *The Nightingale and the Rose,* illustrated by Michael Foreman and Freire Wright (Oxford Univ. Pr., 1981).

Hazen, Barbara Shook   *5–8*
THE KNIGHT WHO WAS AFRAID OF THE DARK   *YEARS*
   Illus. by Tony Ross. New York: Dial, 1989.

Humorously sophisticated, cartoon-style, line-and-wash drawings enhance this romantic tale of bravery, detailing how Sir Fred, a knight who was "knee-bumping, heart-thumping afraid" of the dark and the fair Lady Wendylyn, who was "terrified of bugs and all slithering things that creep and crawl," overcame their fears because of their love for each other.

Hearn, Lafcadio   7–11+
THE VOICE OF THE GREAT BELL   YEARS
   Retold by Margaret Hodges. Illus. by Ed Young. Boston: Little, Brown, 1989.

Sophisticated, accomplished, impressionistic illustrations, done in pastels and watercolor, enrich this retelling of the Chinese folktale about a bell maker's daughter who sacrificed her life so that the castings of the Great Bell for the emperor would be flawless. Originally entitled "The Soul of the Great Bell" and published in Hearn's collection of stories entitled *Some Chinese Ghosts* (Boston: Roberts Brothers, 1887).

Heine, Helme   4–6
KING BOUNCE THE FIRST   YEARS
   Illus. by Helme Heine. London: Neugebauer Pr., 1982. Distributed by Alphabet Pr.

King Bounce the First forgets all his worries by bouncing on his bed and is then able to sleep peacefully. When his ministers and his people learn he behaves in such an unkingly manner, he is told he must stop bouncing. Near death because he cannot sleep, the King asks the minister to grant him a last request, which, predictably, is to bounce once more. The ending will delight one and all, just as it did the king and the whole kingdom. The full-color, double-page pictures created by this award winning author-illustrator from Germany have an aura of naivety and vitality that is unmatched by any other collage artist. First published in Austria by Neugebauer Press in 1976 under the title *Konig Hupf Der I.*

Heine, Helme   5–8+
THE PEARL   YEARS
   Illus. by Helme Heine. New York: Margaret K. McElderry/Atheneum, 1985.

The same theme as John Steinbeck's classic *The Pearl* is presented in this simple picture-book, cautionary tale that depicts the "other side of good fortune." The story of why Beaver tossed the treasured pearl mussel back into the lake is illustrated with humorous, expressive, and stylized, watercolor paintings. The visual portrayal of the Beaver as likeable and thoughtful balances the serious moral of the tale. (See illustration 20.) Published originally under the title *Die Perle* by Ger-

Illus. 20. Reprinted by permission of Margaret K. McElderry Books, an imprint of Macmillan Publishing Company from *The Pearl* by Helme Heine copyright © 1984 Gertraud Middlehauve Verlag Koln. English translation copyright © 1985 J. M. Dent and Sons, Ltd., London.

traud Middelhave Verlag, Cologne in 1984; the English translation was copyrighted in 1985 by J. M. Dent & Sons, Ltd. of London.

Heyer, Marilee

184 THE FORBIDDEN DOOR

5–9
YEARS

    Illus. by Marilee Heyer. New York: Viking/Kestrel, 1988.

    The full-page fantasy art, suggestive of antique tapestries, is perfect for this story about what happens when a little girl, who has always lived underground, discovers the Forbidden Door to the Outside. The picture book account of how the girl shatters the power of the evil monster Okora and frees her relatives from their long imprisonment will intrigue most young readers. Few children are likely to be satisfied with just one reading of this picture book fantasy.

Hill, Susan
CAN IT BE TRUE?

4–7
YEARS

    Illus. by Angela Barrett. New York: Viking/Kestrel, 1988.

    Thomas Hardy's classic poem "The Oxen" was the inspiration for this story in which everyone and everything from "field and farm, city and town" hears about the newborn Jesus and together stop whatever they are doing (be it good or evil) to go to the stable to see him. The accomplished, poetic prose combines with detailed and exquisitely executed expressionistic paintings, done in warm, rich colors, in an elegant and memorable Christmas story.

Hirsh, Marilyn
ONE LITTLE GOAT: A PASSOVER SONG

4–8
YEARS

    Illus. by Marilyn Hirsh. New York: Holiday, 1979.

    One Little Goat (Had Gadya) is a song that is often sung by families at the end of the Passover seder. Amusing action-filled, cartoon-style drawings are used in this picture book adaptation to depict children dramatizing this cumulative-type song on a stage. The author-artist has included a musical score and a brief history of the song as well as a commentary on Passover.

Hissey, Jane
LITTLE BEAR'S TROUSERS

4–6
YEARS

    Illus. by Jane Hissey. New York: Philomel, 1987.

Little Bear lost his trousers and in the process of searching for them discovered that his friends Sailor, Dog, Camel, Duck, Rabbit, Zebra, and Bramwell Brown had all used them in very "un-trouserly" ways. All of the characters in this pleasant little story are toys, and all are illustrated with crayon in realistic, full-color drawings. The characters look much like toys but are nonetheless expressive. See *Old Bear* by Jane Hissey (Philomel, 1986), the first book in this series.

Hogrogian, Nonny   *4–7*
THE CAT WHO LOVED TO SING   *YEARS*
   Illus. by Nonny Hogrogian. New York: Knopf, 1988.

   Full-color, line-and-wash pictures in the expressionistic style focus on an animated and definitely charming cat who loves to sing and trades many things, one for another, until he finally gets a mandolin. To the delight of all, especially the cat himself, he strums the mandolin and goes on his way. Children will spontaneously join in the refrain, which begins, "Trala/lala. I gave my thorn and got some bread./I lost the bread and gained a hen./I gave the hen for some nice red yarn . . . /Tra lala lala." The musical score for the "Cat Song" at the back of the book is an added bonus. It will encourage children's participation in the telling and retelling of this story, inspired by an Armenian folktale.

Holder, Heidi   *9–12+*
CROWS   *YEARS*
   Illus. by Heidi Holder. New York: Farrar, 1987.

   A beautiful and unique counting book for older readers inspired by an old rhyme that spoke of seven superstitions about crows. Adding five more, the author-artist uses a total of twelve superstitions as the basis for a moving love story about Millie, a faithful mink, and Willie, an adventurous weasel. Each full-page illustration, enclosed in a symbol-laden illuminated frame, consists of fascinating details depicting the stages of the relationship of this unusual couple. On facing pages are pictures of one to twelve crows, also framed. Underneath these is a substory about a rabbit. The pictures deserve repeated, careful examination, for each examination will reveal more about the characters, the fairyland in which they live, and their possessions. The influence of the fantasy art techniques and styles of Arthur Rackham and Nancy Elkholm Burkert are recognizable but the results are decidedly unique to Holder. At the back of the book is an excellent key to the symbols used in the visuals as well as some interesting notes about the text and the animals; a bibliography of references used for the text and illustrations is also included.

Holme, Bryan   *8–up*
ENCHANTED WORLD: PICTURES TO GROW UP WITH   YEARS
   Illus. New York: Oxford Univ. Pr., 1979.

The ninety-six illustrations (forty-four in color) demonstrate the power of a picture to cast the spell of magic and stimulate imaginative thinking. By showing some of the ways artists of various eras and from different countries (Brueghel, da Vinci, Degas, Picasso, Calder) have interpreted fanciful subjects, readers of all ages can see the wide variety of techniques that may be used. They will also appreciate the diversity of vision the artists reveal in these illustrations of tales and subjects associated with the "enchanted world." Truly a valuable book to include in a school or public library collection!

Hooks, William H.   *4–12*
MOSS GOWN   YEARS
   Illus. by Donald Carrick. New York: Clarion/Houghton, 1987.

This romantic story blends aspects of "Cinderella" and *King Lear*. Candice is forced to work as a scullery maid in a white-pillared mansion owned by the handsome Young Master whom she eventually marries. Her benefactor is the gris-gris woman, a swamp witch who gives her a magical moss gown that changes into a golden gown; when the Morning Star fades, the gown turns back into dull, gray moss. The expertly executed, full-page, full-color, line and watercolor paintings suggest elements of the tidewater section of eastern North Carolina during the Victorian era. This is an excellent read-aloud selection for primary grade children, useful as well for independent reading by transitional readers. Fine fare for the study of narrative literary conventions by students in the middle- and upper-elementary grades.

Hutchins, Pat   *4–7*
WHERE'S THE BABY?   YEARS
   Illus. by Pat Hutchins. New York: Greenwillow, 1988.

It is a gross understatement to say that Baby Monster is sweet when he is asleep! The complete and utter mess made by this monstrous child is depicted by the award-winning author-illustrator in simple narrative rhyme and double-page, cartoon-style drawings done in watercolors and ink. Most everyone reading this zany picture book—children, grandparents, teachers, and even parents—will be excited, shocked, and amused. Be assured few children will be satisfied with one reading in a sitting.

Ishii, Momoko   5–9
THE TONGUE-CUT SPARROW   YEARS
    Trans. from the Japanese by Katherine Paterson. Illus. by Suekichi   *187*
    Akaba. New York: Lodestar/Dutton, 1987.

    Illustrated in the style of the traditional Japanese brush paintings, this story relates how a cut-tongue sparrow cured an old woman of her greediness and rewarded her kind, humble husband with precious treasures. There are a number of Japanese terms retained in the re-telling to add a Japanese flavor; a glossary and a pronunciation guide are provided in the back of the book. Originally published in Japan in 1982 by Fukuinkan Shoten, Publishers Inc., Tokyo, under the title *Shita-kiri suzume.*

Kamen, Gloria (reteller)   6–9
THE RINGDOVES   YEARS
    Illus. by Gloria Kamen. New York: Atheneum, 1988.

    This story about true friendship, a retelling of one of the classic Indian fables of Bedpai (forerunners of Aesop's Fables), tells how animals who are natural enemies band together to save each other from a hunter. The illustrations of the hunter and the unlikely group of loyal friends (a flock of doves, a crow, a mouse, a turtle, and a gazelle) have a rather fanciful aura about them. They are done in rich, clear jewel tones.

Kellogg, Steven   4–8
THE MYSTERIOUS TADPOLE   YEARS
    Illus. by Steven Kellogg. New York: Dial, 1977.

    Each year Louis receives a birthday present for his nature collection from his Uncle McAllister who lives in Scotland. In this thoroughly fantastic tale, Alphonse, the tadpole that the lad's generous relative caught in Loch Ness and sent to Louis for his birthday grows into a Loch Ness monster during the course of a year. On his next birthday Louis receives another present, an egg, for his collection. And, shortly after its arrival, a strange-looking, duck-like animal hatches from it. So, new fantastic adventures may be created by the readers of this imaginative and original tale. The detailed, cartoon-style illustrations for which Kellogg is so well-known add considerably to the humor of this refreshing whimsy. One examination will definitely not reveal the wonderfully zany and action-filled details in the illustrations.

Kellogg, Steven   5–8
PREHISTORIC PINKERTON   YEARS
Illus. by Steven Kellogg. New York: Dial, 1987.

Cartoon-style illustrations, done in full color in ink- and pencil-line and watercolor-wash, add considerable depth to a brief, easy-to-read story about Pinkerton's chaotic visit to the dinosaur section of the museum. Other books about this nutty Great Dane include *Tallyho, Pinkerton!* (Dial, 1982), *Pinkerton, Behave!* (Dial, 1979), and *A Rose for Pinkerton* (Dial, 1981), all written and illustrated by Steven Kellogg.

Kimmel, Eric   6–9
HERSHEL AND THE HANUKKAH GOBLINS   YEARS
Illus. by Trina Schart Hyman. New York: Holiday, 1989.

The realistic and detailed paintings, in vibrant full colors, significantly enhance the scary mood of this 1990 Caldecott Honor book. This is an original tale of how Hershel of Ostropol outwitted the Hanukkah goblins that haunted the synagogue and prevented the villagers from celebrating Hanukkah and lighting the menorah candles, a tradition followed by the Jewish people to commemorate their victory thousands of years ago over the Syrians, thereby winning their right to worship as they wanted.

Kismaric, Carole (adapter)   6–9
THE RUMOR OF PAVEL AND PAALI   YEARS
Illus. by Charles Mikolaycak. New York: Harper, 1988.

This adaptation of a Ukrainian folktale tells how kind and generous Paali receives good fortune so he and his wife can live contentedly the rest of their lives, while Pavel, his cruel and greedy twin brother, meets a horrifying fate. He is turned into an evil spirit and never seen again. The cross hatched, realistic paintings in rich, full color are suggestive of the Ukrainian setting and the traditional folk designs on clothing, furniture, and artifacts associated with this ethnic group.

Kojima, Naomi   4–9
THE CHEF'S HAT   YEARS
Illus. by Naomi Kojima. San Francisco: Chronicle Books, 1989.

Andre's gourmet cooking is acknowledged by the Emperor by the gift of a crisp, white, and magnificently tall hat, which Andre promises he will never, ever take off. The results of this promise (for Andre is the kind of person who keeps his promises!) are hilarious, and the resolution of the dilemma proves quite satisfying to Andre and to the reader. All ends well, especially for Andre and the Emperor. Simple, but very telling, precise, line and watercolor-wash sketches reflect and greatly extend the absurdities of this humorous tale.

Kroll, Steven   5–8
LOOKING FOR DANIELA   *YEARS*
    Illus. by Anita Lobel. New York: Holiday, 1988.

A poor street performer who won the heart of the daughter of a wealthy merchant by juggling, tightrope gymnastics, and guitar playing is rewarded with gold and a beautiful cape after he rescued her from bandits who kidnapped her. Cartoon-style, line-and-watercolor paintings in full color enhance this tale of innocent romance and adventure.

La Fontaine   6–10
THE RICH MAN AND THE SHOEMAKER   *YEARS*
    Illus. by Brian Wildsmith. New York: Oxford Univ. Pr., 1979.

Impressionistic, gouache paintings in rich colors extend this brief retelling of the well-known fable of how the poor but happy shoemaker found his newly acquired wealth too burdensome and gave the gold back to the rich man.

Lewis, J. Patrick   5–9
THE TSAR AND THE AMAZING COW   *YEARS*
    Illus. by Friso Hinstra. New York: Dial, 1988.

Were it really possible! In the heart of a faraway Russian village an old peasant couple, Maria and Stefan, are restored to the "green time of their lives" (their thirties) after they drink their cow's magic milk. The three children they had tragically lost (one by drowning, one by the plague, and one who disappeared when she wandered too far from home in the birch forest) are returned to them. Expressionistic line and watercolor-wash paintings contribute to the credibility of this spellbinding, fanciful tale.

Lindgren, Barbro   4–8
A WORM'S TALE   *YEARS*
    Trans. by Dianne Jonasson. Illus. by Cecilia Torudd. New York: Rabén & Sjögren. Distributed by Farrar, 1988.

A unique tale about a friendship between a polite and proper, but lonely gentleman and an earthworm. The cartoon-style, watercolor illustrations add wonderfully humorous and charming details to the adventures shared by this unlikely pair of friends. Originally published in Sweden by Rabén & Sjögren under the title *Sagan om Karlknut: En Historia*.

Lionni, Leo   5–9
SIX CROWS   YEARS
    Illus. by Leo Lionni. New York: Knopf,1988.

This fable about how a farmer and six crows realize that they can resolve their differences by talking things over instead of fighting about them is illustrated with large-sized, brilliant collages. Although the illustrations appear graphically simplistic and the story appears inconsequential at first, further thought and examination of both will reveal their sophistication.

Littledale, Freya (reteller)   4–7
PETER AND THE NORTH WIND   YEARS
    Illus. by Troy Howell. New York: Scholastic, 1988.

Full-page, line-and-gouache, realistic paintings in full color combine with effective prose to offer a sense of reality to this well known Norse folktale about Peter who retrieves the three magic gifts given to him by the North Wind—a cloth that gave the little boy and his mother food, a goat that gave them milk, and a stick that did exactly what it was told to do.

Louie, Ai-Ling (reteller)   5–10
YEH-SHEN   YEARS
    Illus. by Ed Young. New York: Philomel, 1982.

The complete Hsueh Chin T'oo Yun edition of the Chinese "Cinderella" story recorded from the Ch'ing dynasty (1644–1912) is shown in the Chinese characters on a block-printed page. Following this is a portion of that story, retold in English and accompanied by Ed Young's pastel and watercolor illustrations set in panels like those of the Chinese folding, painted screen. The details in the pictures (the style of clothing and jewelry worn by the characters and their hairstyles, for instance) establish the story's setting "before the time Chin (222–206 BC)." Be certain to notice an image of a fish in each illustration; the magic in this version of the Cinderella motif comes from the bones of the fish that Yeh-Shen loved and her stepmother killed. Compare aspects of the Chinese "Cinderella" story (the source of magic, how the heroine meets and eventually marries the hero, how the heroine and the slipper are reunited, and what happens to the heroine's stepmother and stepsisters) with other variants, including *In the Land of Small Dragon,* a Vietnamese version told by Dang Manh Kha to Ann Nolan Clark and illustrated by Tony Chen (Viking, 1979); *Cinderella,* a French version adapted from Perrault's "Cendrillon" of 1697, retold by John Fowles and illustrated by Sheila Beckett (Little, Brown, 1974); *Cinderella,* a German version by the Grimm brothers, retold and illustrated by Nonny Hogrogian (Greenwillow, 1981); and *Tattercoats,* an English version retold by Flora Anni Steel and illustrated by Diane Goode (Bradbury, 1976).

Mahy, Margaret   *6–9*
17 KINGS AND 41 ELEPHANTS   *YEARS*
   Illus. by Patricia McCarthy. New York: Dial, 1987.

The narrative told in quatrain verse is extended and enriched by batik paintings on silk reproduced in full-color, double-page spreads. The lush jungle scenes as well as the humor expressed in the verses and illustrations will intrigue and fascinate most young readers over and over and over.

Malotki, Ekkehart   *7–12+*
THE MOUSE COUPLE   *YEARS*
   Illus. by Michael Lacapa. Flagstaff, Ariz.: Northland, 1988.

This accomplished translation of a Hopi Indian folktale about a father's search for a suitable husband for his only daughter is told in the true style of the Hopi storyteller and is illustrated with seventeen oversized, sophisticated, and stylized paintings in full color. The illustrations and the decorations throughout this exceptional picture book exude every facet of Hopi tradition—their lifestyle; the symbols on their clothing, tools, pipes; the architectural style of their homes; and the stylized design of the mouse, which is on practically every page. Most importantly, Lacapa's illustrations have blended the traditional with contemporary found in Hopi culture. (See illustration 21.) A "must purchase" for every school and public library interested in presenting multi-cultural views and values, past and present. Compare and contrast the style of storytelling and illustrations used to tell the

Illus. 21. Artwork by Michael Lacapa, copyright 1988 by Northland Publishing, from *The Mouse Couple,* retold by Ekkehart Malotki. Reprinted with permission.

story of *The Mouse Couple* with those in *Little Joe: A Hopi Indian Boy Learns A Hopi Indian Secret,* written and illustrated by Terry Latterman (Pussywillow, 1985).

Manes, Stephen   *6–9*
LIFE IS NO FAIR   *YEARS*
   Illus. by Warren Miller. New York: Dutton, 1985.

The full-color, watercolor, cartoon-style drawings are a perfect
match for this collection of vignettes (some droll, some witty, some   *193*
macabre) about what happened when people's worst fears came true.
In one example a little boy worried that he would never make friends
when his family moved from his old neighborhood. He was quite right
to be concerned, for they moved into a house on a cliff large enough to
hold only one structure. In another, a little boy refused to eat his
vegetables, so his parents told him he would never grow up to be big
and strong. He grew up to be little and strong. As the author said, "They
were half right." A fun book!

Mariana (pseud. of Marian Foster Curtis)   *3–6*
MISS FLORA McFLIMSEY AND THE BABY NEW YEAR   *YEARS*
   Illus. by Mariana (recreated by Caroline Walton Howe). New York:
      Morrow, 1951, 1961, 1988.

Reissued in a larger format, illustrated entirely in full-color watercolors instead of the original alternation of full-color and black-and-
white paintings. This is an endearing story about a loveable little doll,
Miss Flora McFlimsey, who feels lonely because she is not included in
the New Year's Eve party with other dolls. Then she gets an unexpected
visitor, namely the Baby New Year. She is quite cheerful by the time the
Old Year ends and she hears the revellers in the "Big House" nearby
calling "Happy New Year" and singing "Auld Lang Syne." The illustrations are simple and uncluttered, giving focus to Miss Flora McFlimsey
and her emotional changes through the course of the story. (See illustration 22.) All of the Flora McFlimsey stories, inspired by the nineteenth-century poem about the original Miss Flora by William Allen
Butler, have fascinated children for generations. Six other stories about
this wistful heroine focus on how she celebrates various special days,
including her birthday, Easter, May Day, Valentine's Day, Halloween,
and Christmas Eve.

Marshak, Samuel   *5–9*
THE PUP GREW UP   *YEARS*
   Trans. from the Russian by Richard Pevear. Illus. by Vladimir Ra-
      dunsky. New York: Holt, 1989.

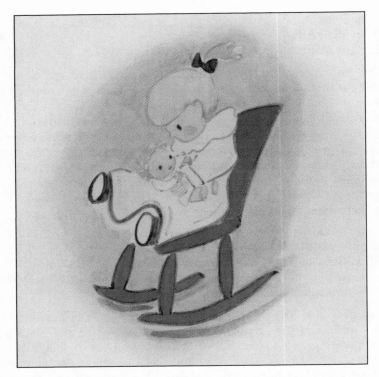

Illus. 22. *Miss Flora McFlimsey and the Baby New Year* by Mariana © 1951, 1961, 1988 by Marian Foster. Reprinted by permission of Lothrop, Lee and Shepard (a division of William Morrow and Company).

A humorous narrative poem and bold, comic, surrealistic paintings, strongly suggestive of those used by commercial artists in the late 1920s and early 1930s, are a perfect match to tell this tale of how a Pekinese puppy, supposedly traveling by train with its owner, "grows up" into Great Dane. This clever spoof about bureaucracy was originally published in the Soviet Union.

Martin, Rafe   5–9
FOOLISH RABBIT'S BIG MISTAKE   YEARS
  Illus. by Ed Young. New York: Putnam, 1985.

An oversized book with free-flowing, double-page, impressionistic illustrations in full-color pastels that dramatize this humorous, cumulative Jataka folktale. A foolish rabbit announces hysterically that the earth is breaking up, when in actual fact the sound he heard was the noise made by an apple falling to the ground from the branches of the tree above him. This ancient Buddhist tale retold in rhythmic prose should be compared with retellings of versions of the well-known folktales "Henny-Penny," "Chicken-Little," and "The Sky Is Falling."

Mayer, Marianna (reteller)   6–10
IDUNA AND THE MAGIC APPLES   *YEARS*
   Illus. by Laszlo Gal. New York: Macmillan, 1988.

   The kind, fun-loving, and witty goddess Iduna, guardian of the magic apples that keep all those who eat them ever young, was betrayed and then rescued by the god Loki, a selfish mischief-maker who frequently changes his shapes and loyalties. Ethereal illustrations, rendered in a resin-color wash with egg tempera, exquisitely detail the action, shifting settings, and changing moods described most competently in the text. Neither the text nor the illustrations leave any doubt about which characters in this ancient Norse myth are good and which are evil.

Mayer, Marianna (reteller)   6–10+
THE TWELVE DANCING PRINCESSES   *YEARS*
   Illus. by Kinuko Y. Craft. New York: Morrow, 1989.

   Once radiant, open, and warm-hearted, twelve young princesses grow pale, cold, and haughty as they suffer under an evil spell that forces them to dance each night until they wear holes in their shoes. A handsome young gardener enables them to break the spell in this competent retelling of the popular fairy tale.

Modesitt, Jeanne   3–6
VEGETABLE SOUP   *YEARS*
   Illus. by Robin Spowart. New York: Macmillan, 1988.

   This animal fantasy is illustrated with large-sized, expressive, impressionistic, watercolor paintings in rich, full color. When two rabbits discover they have run out of carrots, which they planned to have for their first lunch in their new home, they set out to borrow some from their new neighbors. None of the neighbors have carrots, but each of them gladly gives them some other vegetable. Reluctant to try food they have not eaten before, the rabbits decide to throw everything into the big cooking pot and make soup of it. The results are much to their liking, and the way they celebrate should prove as pleasing to the readers as it is to the rabbits. An easy-to-follow recipe for vegetable soup is provided at the end of the book, but readers are cautioned to get an adult's help. There is a considerable amount of dialogue used in this well-written text, making it especially good for use in readers' theatre activities with children who have achieved an independent reading level.

Moore, Inga (reteller) 3–6
FIFTY RED NIGHTCAPS YEARS
   Illus. by Inga Moore. San Francisco: Chronicle, 1988.

Impressionistic watercolor paintings illustrate this story of how a little boy on his way to the market retrieves caps the monkeys take from him while he naps in the cool shade of the forest. Compare and contrast the specific events and the illustrations in this retelling with those in *Caps for Sale: A Tale of a Peddler, Some Monkeys and Their Monkey Business*, retold and illustrated by Esphyr Slobodkina (William R. Scott, 1957).

Myers, Odette (reteller) 4–7
THE ENCHANTED UMBRELLA YEARS
   Illus. by Margot Zemach. San Diego: Gulliver/HBJ, 1988.

When an elderly maker of umbrellas dies, his selfish nephew gives the old man's faithful young helper only a ragged umbrella. As luck would have it, the umbrella has magical powers that outwit villains who strike out against the lad, protecting him from dangers and ultimately leading him to a country whose people make him their king. The watercolor paintings, done in the expressionistic art style, add considerable depth and wit to this retelling of a French folktale. A short history of the umbrella is included at the end of the book.

Noble, Trinka Hakes 5–9
MEANWHILE BACK AT THE RANCH YEARS
   Illus. by Tony Ross. New York: Dial, 1987.

Some people have all the luck, and Elna has a generous share. While waiting back at the ranch for her husband Rancher Hicks to return from his eighty-four mile trip to Sleepy Gulch in search of excitement, she strikes oil, inherits a fortune, gets discovered by a Hollywood producer, is visited by the President, and more. The zany, cartoon-style illustrations, done in pen and ink and watercolor wash, are perfect for this tall tale.

Oakley, Graham   5–9+
HETTY AND HARRIET   *YEARS*
   Illus. by Graham Oakley. New York: Macmillan, 1982.

   A multi-leveled fable. On the literal level it is a slight animal fantasy,
about two chickens in search of Utopia, and is a classic example of the   *197*
pecking order, a practice well established in the farmyard. On the
higher level it is a clever, albeit rather savage, exposé of contemporary
society and human relationships. This is a fine book to use for teaching
about such literary conventions as satire, character portrayal, and cir-
cular story structure. The full-color, line-and-wash paintings contain
any number of amusing details and are a perfect complement to the
story's satirical tone.

Obrist, Jurg   5–9
THE MISER WHO WANTED THE SUN   *YEARS*
   Illus. by Jurg Obrist. New York: Margaret K. McElderry/Atheneum,
      1984.

   Written in the style of a folktale, this is an original story of how a
deceitful, miserly man learned from the tailor and his daughter that the
sun was for everyone to enjoy and that he had to make fair payment for
services rendered. The bold, full-color, surrealistic paintings are quite
in keeping with the imaginative tale. Translated from the German, the
book was published in 1983 by Artemis Verlags, Zurich and Munich.

Opie, Iona and Peter (compilers)   *Infancy–8+*
TAIL FEATHERS FROM MOTHER GOOSE: THE OPIE   *YEARS*   X
RHYME BOOK
   Illus. Boston: Little, Brown, 1988.   SAPAR

   This collection of rhymes chosen from the Opie Collection of Children's Literature housed at Oxford University Press is illustrated by
many of the world's most distinguished contemporary illustrators—
Maurice Sendak, Shirley Hughes, Ron Maris, Quentin Blake, Barbara
Firth, Errol LeCain, Michael Foreman, and others. It is a fine illustrated
collection of poetry for today's children as well as the children's literature scholars. Compare and contrast the selections especially of the
illustrations, in *Tail Feathers from Mother Goose: The Opie Rhyme Book*
with those in *The Glorious Mother Goose*, selected by Edens Cooper and
illustrated with pictures by artists important in the early history of
children's literature.

Osborne, Mary Pope (reteller)   5–9+
BEAUTY AND THE BEAST   *YEARS*
 Illus. by Winslow Punny Pels. New York: Scholastic, 1987.

198   There is always room for another retelling of a popular fairy tale if the
rendition is unique and reflects quality. Both characteristics describe
this retelling of the well-known fairy tale in which a kind, beautiful
young woman's unconditional love releases a handsome, and sensitive
prince from the spell that made him a repulsively ugly beast. The
full-size, expressionistic paintings in rich color give this version a
modern, but not current aura that is seldom seen in visual interpretations of stories set "long ago and far away." Compare and contrast the
text and illustrations of this picture book version with: *Beauty and the
Beast* retold by Madame Leprince de Beaumont and translated and
illustrated by Diane Goode (Bradbury, 1978) and *Beauty and the Beast*
retold by Rosemary Harris and illustrated by Errol LeCain (Doubleday,
1979).

Paxton, Tom (reteller)   5–9
AESOP'S FABLES   *YEARS*
 Illus. by Robert Rayevsky. New York: Morrow, 1988.

 Ten Aesop's fables are retold in verse and are illustrated in witty,
action-filled, full-color, ink-and-watercolor paintings.

Pierce, Meredith Ann   7–9
WHERE THE WILD GEESE GO   *YEARS*
 Illus. by Jamichael Henterly. New York: Dutton, 1988.

 Delicate realistic paintings in full color add to the fanciful elements
of this story of how a heedless child, dreamy and careless, is transformed into a responsible child during her search to find out where the
wild geese go. Observant children will probably notice that the motifs
that appear at the very beginning of this story are repeated throughout,
establishing a logic for the dream fantasy and strengthening the mood
and symbolism that are so pervasive.

Porazinska, Janina   5–9
THE ENCHANTED BOOK   *YEARS*
 Trans. from the Polish by Bozena Smith. Illus. by Jan Brett. San
  Diego: HBJ, 1987.

 Told in the style of an experienced and accomplished storyteller, this
Polish folktale is reminiscent of the Bluebeard motif. It tells how the

youngest and most industrious of the miller's three daughters is able to save herself, her two sisters, and eighteen other young maidens from an evil enchanter because she alone is able to read. The fourteen full-page, accomplished, lavishly detailed, watercolor paintings were inspired by Polish paper cuts and folk motifs. They reflect the ethnic aspects of this story of mystery and magic nicely.

Preussler, Otfried   5–9
THE TALE OF THE UNICORN   YEARS
   Trans. from the German by Lenny Hort. Illus. by Gennady Spirin.
   New York: Dial, 1989.

   This fable tells of three brothers' search for a precious unicorn. They think his horn of ivory, hooves of purest gold, and his crown of diamonds will bring them great wealth. Only the youngest endures the trials of fire, ice, and darkness to find the unicorn, but he chooses not to kill it because he thinks it is too beautiful to destroy. Brilliantly accomplished, oversized, impressionistic paintings in full color add to the long ago and far away setting and aura of the fantasy. Notice the end pages. The four panels highlight the trials that challenged the hero very effectively. This picture book was published in West Germany in 1988 by K. Thienemanns Verlag, Stuttgart, a *Dans Marchen vom Einhorn*.

Rodanas, Kristina   5–9
THE STORY OF WATI DAD   YEARS
   Illus. by Kristina Rodanas. New York: Lothrop, 1988.

   Full-page, detailed, realistic paintings in rich, full color extensively enrich the forthright, imagery-filled language used to tell a fascinating tale about the chain of events that happened when Wati Dad, an old grasscutter from India, purchased a bracelet with a beautiful pearl carefully inlaid at its center. This story would be especially good for use in creative dramatics.

Rogers, Paul   4–8
TUMBLEDOWN   YEARS
   Illus. by Robin Bell Corfield. New York: Greenwillow, 1988.

   Tumbledown is an archetypal village where everything is broken. No one feels driven to fix anything—until they are told the Prince is coming for a visit. They scurry to repair things, managing to get everything in order except their ramshackled village hall with its creaking door, shaky old steps, and wobbly railing. The villagers' reaction to their fixed-up world and the Prince's reaction to the village hall are bound to delight the readers of this good-humored book. The full-color pictures, done in pastels and watercolor, give a fine sense of specificity to the good-natured people in the charming, rural community.

200 Ross, Tony   5–8
HUGO AND ODDSOCK   YEARS
    Illus. by Tony Ross. Chicago: Follett, 1978.

A wonderfully nutty fantasy! Hugo, a larder-mouse made a sock horse (and named it Oddsock, of course) out of an old golf sock that belonged to Uncle Townmouse, some old rags, which he stuffed into the sock, some stiff cloth for the ears, and a short pole. Most children will be awed and certainly amused by the cartoon-style illustrations showing the mice walking on snow stilts and showing Hugo and Oddsock's adventures when they fly off to Lostsockland, inhabited by weird animals made from, what else, socks or long stockings. As expected from this author-artist, the book is loaded with visual and verbal puns. Don't be a bit surprised if readers of this unique fantasy decide to make sock horses, too.

Ross, Tony (reteller)   5–8
THE THREE PIGS   YEARS
    Illus. by Tony Ross. New York: Pantheon, 1983.

Tony Ross's witty, tongue-in-cheek text and action-filled, cartoon-style, ink-and-watercolor sketches in full color offer a sophisticated modern retelling of a classic tale. The three pigs decide to build their own houses in the spacious, sunny countryside because they are fed up with living on the 39th floor of a high-rise apartment and with city life in general. As in the traditional tale, two pigs are gobbled up by the grumpy, old wolf, and the third pig, who builds his house of bricks, gets to eat the wolf who falls from the chimney into the pot of boiling water. Compare and contrast this lighthearted retelling of the classic tale with *Three Little Pigs*, retold and illustrated by Erik Blegvad (Margaret K. McElderry/Atheneum, 1980), and *Three Little Pigs*, retold and illustrated by John Wallner (Viking/Kestrel, 1987).

Roth, Susan L.   5–9
KANAHENA: A CHEROKEE STORY   YEARS
    Illus. by Susan L. Roth. New York: St. Martin's, 1988.

Sophisticated collages suggestive of Jean Dubuffet are made from natural materials (leaves, grasses, cotton, and cornmeal). An old Cherokee woman tells a young child this Cherokee Indian legend about how Terrapin (a turtle) tricked the wolves who threatened to kill him by using a wicked wolf's ears as spoons to eat Kanahena (cornmeal mush or hominy). In addition to a well-told folktale, original to this group of native Americans from the Southern Appalachian Mountain area, young readers of this picture book will find a fascinating and logical account of why the turtle has scars on his shell and a recipe for Kanahena, along with some variations.

Sales, Francesc   6–9
IBRAHIM   *YEARS*
    Trans. from the Catalan by Marc Simont. Illus. by Eulalia Sariola. New York: Lippincott, 1989.

Ibrahim was tempted to give up his job in his father's stall at the market in Marrakesh for the freer life of the desert nomad. But a genie of the well told him two things in his dreams: "freedom is something you carry in your heart" and "dreams can also set you free." This bit of advice caused Ibrahim to decide to continue to work as a vendor in his family's stall and to live by the words of the genie of the well. The full-page, expressionistic, watercolor paintings capture the aura of a Moroccan marketplace.

San Souci, Robert D.   5–9
THE TALKING EGGS   *YEARS*
    Illus. by Jerry Pinkney. New York: Dial, 1989.

Using soft black pencil, colored pencils, and watercolor, the illustrator created realistic pictures depicting a rural southern United States setting for this Cinderella-type tale of a kind sister who is rewarded with riches because she followed the instructions of an old witch and the girl's greedy sister who is chased by hoards of whip snakes, frogs, yellow jackets, and an old gray wolf when she disobeys the old woman. *The Talking Eggs* was named a 1990 Caldecott Honor book by the Association of Library Service to Children of the American Library Association.

Schneider, Elisa   4–7
THE MERRY-GO-ROUND DOG   *YEARS*
    Illus. by Elisa Schneider. New York: Knopf, 1988.

Full-color, expressionistic pictures done in collage and watercolor enhance the charm and credibility of this story about an imaginative little girl who finds the tail of an old brown wooden merry-go-round dog and transforms it into a wooden bird. When the merry-go-round opens again in spring the dog, without a tail, is part of it. The little girl's way of keeping her new much-loved, wooden bird and providing a tail for her much-loved, old brown merry-go-round dog will delight and intrigue young and old readers alike. Be certain to look carefully at the tiny circus scenes that appear on the end pages.

Scott, Sally (adapter)   5–9
THE THREE WONDERFUL BEGGARS   *YEARS*
   Illus. by Sally Scott. New York: Greenwillow, 1987.

This story about how three beggars, after predicting that the hard-hearted merchant named Mark the Rich would lose his fortune, save Vassili, the seventh son of a poor man, from Mark's repeated attempts to kill him. This adaptation of a version of a Serbian tale that was included in the 1901 edition of Andrew Lang's *The Violet Fairy Book* is illustrated with brightly colored and textured paintings that strongly suggest the Russian setting, ancient Russian clothing, and architecture.

Seuss, Dr. (pseud. of Theodor Geisel)   5–9
THE 500 HATS OF BARTHOLOMEW CUBBINS   *YEARS*
   Illus. by Dr. Seuss. New York: Random, 1938.

A fast-paced, funny tale of a little boy who is unable to keep a hat off his head when the king passes by. The hats stop duplicating with the 500th hat, one so elegant the King buys it for 500 pieces of gold. Typical Dr. Seuss drawings illustrate this wonderful fantasy.

Seuss, Dr. (pseud. of Theodor Geisel)   5 & up
HORTON HATCHES THE EGG   *YEARS*
   Illus. by Dr. Seuss. New York: Random, 1940.

Hilarious, cartoon-style illustrations and verse tell about Horton the elephant who faithfully sits on the egg in the Mayzie bird's nest so she can take a rest.

Seuss, Dr. (pseud. of Theodor Geisel)   6–9
THE KING'S STILTS   *YEARS*
   Illus. by Dr. Seuss. New York: Random, 1939.

In this fun-filled fantasy, a rhythmical text and cartoon-style illustrations in red and black tell of the wild hubbub that occurs when the King's stilts disappear. Eric, the page, finds them and all rejoice. Good for creative dramatization.

Sherman, Josepha (reteller)   7–11
VASSILISA THE WISE: A TALE OF MEDIEVAL RUSSIA   YEARS
   Illus. by Daniel San Souci. San Diego: HBJ, 1988.

Vassilisa, posing as a Tartar ambassador, courageously uses her wisdom and cleverness to rescue her merchant husband from the dark dungeon he was thrown into because he angered Prince Vladimir. The highly decorative, detailed, over-sized watercolor paintings establish, with a aura of authority and drama, a specific sense to the era, action, and personalities that make up this Russian folktale.

Shi, Zang Xiu (adapter)   6–10
MONKEY AND THE WHITE BONE DEMON   YEARS
   Trans. from the Chinese by Ye Pin Kuei and rev. by Jill Morris. Illus. by Lin Zheng, Fei Chang Fu, Xin Kuan Liang, and Zhang Ziu Shi. New York: Viking/Kestrel, 1984. Publ. in association with Liaoning Fine Arts Publishing Co., China.

An adaptation of the sixteenth-century novel *The Pilgrimage to the West* by Wu Cheng Eng, this picture book tells of a monk's travels far and wide with his disciples in search of the ancient Buddhist sculptures. The cluttered, very detailed, and action-filled, cartoon-style illustrations are in bright, clear colors. They are quite typical of those found in many of the picture books published currently in China.

Shute, Linda (reteller)   5–8
CLEVER TOM AND THE LEPRECHAUN   YEARS
   Illus. by Linda Shute. New York: Lothrop, 1988.

This is a story of how a clever leprechaun (a solitary fairy) outsmarted Clever Tom Fitzpatrick, who thought he had put the leprechaun in a position that would force him to reveal the hiding place of his gold. The cartoon-style, watercolor paintings give this fantasy a specific sense of place. Some helpful information about the origin of the story and about leprechauns is included in source notes at the back of the book.

Steptoe, John   6–9
MUFARO'S BEAUTIFUL DAUGHTERS: AN AFRICAN TALE   *YEARS*
    Illus. by John Steptoe. New York: Lothrop, 1987.

204   In a modern African "Cinderella" story, one of two sisters is declared
by the king as "The Most Worthy and Beautiful Daughter in the Land"
and, thus, his queen. Both of the girls are beautiful, but as with all
variants of this motif, one is selfish, bad tempered and indulged, while
the other is kind, considerate and sweet. The basis upon which the king
makes his choice is bound to fascinate the young readers. The details
in the full-color, realistic paintings (style of architecture, styling and
designs on the clothes and jewelry worn by the characters, the flora and
fauna found in the region, for example) place the setting of this fairy
tale in an area near the Zimbabwe ruins. For its illustrations it was
named the 1988 Caldecott Honor book by the Association of Library
Service to Children of the American Library Association.

Stevens, Janet (reteller)   3–6
THE THREE BILLY GOATS GRUFF   *YEARS*
    Illus. by Janet Stevens. San Diego: HBJ, 1987.

    This retelling of a fantasy of how the three billy goats get past the
ugly troll that was guarding the bridge and preventing them from eating
the hillside grass is dramatically illustrated with wonderfully humorous and detailed paintings done in watercolor, colored pencil, and
pastel.

Stevenson, James   6–9
THE WORST PERSON IN THE WORLD AT CRAB BEACH   *YEARS*
    Illus. by James Stevenson. New York: Greenwillow, 1988.

    Meet the worst person in the world (referred to as "the worst" in this
story). He is the epitome of the anti-hero. This crabby, old man meets
a hostile and cruel mother and son while he is vacationing at a seaside
lodge where, to his delight, it is often cold and foggy in the daytime and
there are very large mosquitoes and lots of jelly fish. Also, the other
guests are not in the least friendly and cheerful. The circumstances
under which he meets the annoying mother and son should surprise
and please the readers as it did "the worst." It should surprise no one,
however, that the cartoon-style, full-color, pen and watercolor-wash
sketches, so characteristic of this famous artist, are perfectly compatible with this zany story. The first story about "the worst" is *The Worst
Person in the World* (Greenwillow, 1978).

Stock, Catherine
ALEXANDER'S MIDNIGHT SNACK: A LITTLE ELEPHANT'S
ABC

3–7

Illus. by Catherine Stock. New York: Clarion/Houghton, 1988.

Nicely detailed, cartoon-style, watercolor paintings embellish this
story about the ludicrous combinations of snacks, presented in alphabetical order, that are consumed by a little elephant, who gets up
in the middle of the night intending only to get a glass of water. A fun
alphabet book! The ending is a shocker and should evoke all kinds of
ideas about the price Alexander will have to pay for his feast.

Trivas, Irene
EMMA'S CHRISTMAS

5–9
YEARS

Illus. by Irene Trivas. New York: Orchard, 1988.

Here is an offbeat interpretation of this well-known Christmas song
"The Twelve Days of Christmas." Humorous, action-filled, expressionistic watercolor paintings in full-color document the chaos that
occurred when a prince courts Emma, a farm girl, by sending her gifts
on the twelve days of Christmas.

Trosclair (pseud. of J. B. King, Jr.)
CAJUN NIGHT BEFORE CHRISTMAS

8–12+
YEARS

Ed. by Howard Jacobs. Illus. by James Rice. Gretna, La.: Pelican,
1976.

This very clever parody of Clement C. Moore's classic poem, "The
Night before Christmas," is told in a Cajun dialect that is as authentic
as is possible to suggest in a written form in terms of pronunciation and
intonation. Full-page, pen-and-ink, crosshatched drawings in black
and white alternate with pen-and-ink, crosshatched full-color, watercolor paintings to depict in a thoroughly accurate but witty manner the
alligators (instead of the reindeer), the Louisiana bayou people and
their culture, the homes along the marshy waterways, and the swampy
terrain. An excellent book to read aloud. Compare and contrast the
language and the illustration of this clever parody with *The Night before
Christmas* by Clement C. Moore as illustrated by Tasha Tudor (Rand
McNally, 1975), Arthur Rackham (Weathervane/Crown, 1976), and
Tomie de Paola (Holiday, 1980).

Ungerer, Tomi
THE THREE ROBBERS

Illus. by Tomi Ungerer. New York: Atheneum, 1962.

How lucky today's children are that this longtime favorite has been reissued! Three fierce robbers dressed in black capes, victimized people in the dark of night, and then took their loot to a hideout in a cave high in the mountains. One night they stopped a carriage that had only one passenger, an orphaned girl who was on her way to live with a wicked aunt. The robbers carried her to their hideout where she saw their great wealth and asked them how they would use it. Charmed by her manner and presence, the robbers decided to put their treasure to good use: they gathered up all the lost, unhappy, and homeless children they could find, bought a castle where they could all live, and dressed them in red caps and capes. All lived happily and lovingly ever after. The very simple, cartoon-style illustrations, most of them night scenes, are absolutely delightful and dramatize this tongue-in-cheek, Robin Hood-type tale to perfection.

van Laan, Nancy (reteller)
RAINBOW CROW

Illus. by Beatriz Vidal. New York: Random, 1989.

A retelling of a Lenaape Indian folktale. To help the animals engulfed by snow keep warm until the warm weather returns, Crow (Raven) sacrifices his beautiful rainbow-colored feathers and sweet voice to bring the gift of fire down from the Great Sky Spirit. Large, full-color paintings illustrate this pourquoi tale from the northeastern United States.

Waddell, Martin
ALICE THE ARTIST

Illus. by Jonathan Langley. New York: Dutton, 1988.

Alice happily adds to her picture the things her friends suggest, but a disgruntled tiger rips the canvas off the easel and eats it up. Alice proceeds to paint another picture but this time she does it her own way. The reader's eyes move from one clear, perky line and watercolor-wash illustration to another as if watching an animated film.

Waddell, Martin
THE PARK IN THE DARK

Illus. by Barbara Firth. New York: Lothrop, 1989.

Pencil-line and watercolor-wash illustrations detail the capers of three toy animals in the dark park while their owner is fast asleep in his bed.

Wagner, Jenny

THE BUNYIP OF BERKELEY'S CREEK

4–8

YEARS

Illus. by Ron Brooks. New York: Bradbury, 1977.

What do bunyips look like? Even the bunyip did not know. But its search for an identity ended happily shortly after it came up out of the bottom of the black mud and heaved itself on to the bank of Berkeley's Creek. This version of a tale about a mythological creature typical of Australian lore is so exquisitely illustrated with detailed, black-and-white, pen-and-ink drawings and rich, full-color paintings that it was given the Best Australian Picture Book of the Year Award for 1974.

Wallace, Ian

MORGAN THE MAGNIFICENT

5–8

YEARS

Illus. by Ian Wallace. New York: Margaret K. McElderry, 1988.

Morgan is absolutely fearless of heights; she walks straight and sure—on her hands and on her feet—across the peak of the barn roof; with her eyes closed, she walks across the highest beam of the barn. What happens when she walks across the highwire of the circus is something quite different. How she manages to get to that point is of special interest as well. It would be a gross understatement to say that her behavior, accomplishments, and association with her idol "Amazing Anastasia," the daring highwire artist, would impress the young reader of this tale. The double-page, watercolor paintings offer stunning views of farm life and the circus, but the aerial views, seen through Morgan's eyes when she takes her perilous walks, are very special.

Watson, Richard Jesse (reteller)

TOM THUMB

4–9

YEARS

Illus. by Richard Jesse Watson. San Diego: HBJ, 1989.

This is a mighty big book for a story about such a tiny character. Nonetheless, the results are really very good. Detailed, large, realistic illustrations combine with a good retelling of this ever-popular tale to bring to life the adventures of Tom Thumb, a courageous, witty hero who was just about the size of his father's thumb.

Wersba, Barbara   *12–16+*
X AMANDA, DREAMING   *YEARS*
   Illus. by Mercer Mayer. New York: Atheneum, 1973.

208   This absolutely superb picture book epitomizes the ultimate in elegance—in its sensuous, poetic prose and in its accomplished, surrealistic paintings, so strongly suggestive of Dali. Read the text aloud to
fully benefit from its dream-like images of sight, sound, and touch and
its range of emotions—happiness, fear, sadness, and joy. And, look at
the full-page, muted illustrations while listening to the poetic prose for
an even fuller appreciation of what this talented author-and-illustrator
team created. A rare picture book, in every way.

West, Colin   *3–6*
I BOUGHT MY LOVE A TABBY CAT   *YEARS*
   Illus. by Caroline Anstey. San Francisco: Chronicle, 1988.

   A nonsense rhyme tells of the menagerie of animals the bride-to-be
gave to the intended groom and the clothes he made for them. The
logical ending should delight young readers as will the perky, brightly
colored, humorous, expressionistic, pastel illustrations.

Wettasinghe, Sybil   *4–8*
THE UMBRELLA THIEF   *YEARS*
   Illus. by Sybil Wettasinghe. Brooklyn: Kane/Miller, 1987.

   This is a fun story about a man from a small village on the island of
Sri Lanka. It is illustrated in heavy, pen-and-ink and full-color, expressionistic drawings that are quite in keeping with this island in the
Indian ocean off Southern India. Originally published in Japan in 1986
under the title *Kasa Doroboh* by Fukutaka Publishing Co. (Tokyo).

Wilde, Oscar   *9–14+*
THE HAPPY PRINCE   *YEARS*
   Illus. by Jean Claverie. New York: Oxford Univ. Pr., 1980.

   Gilded all over with thin leaves of fine gold, with eyes made of bright
sapphires, and a large red ruby on its sword-hilt, the statue of the Happy
Prince was placed on a tall column on a hill overlooking the city, where
many people came to admire it for its elegance and beauty. From this
point the statue Prince could see all the ugliness and all the misery of
the city. Moved by what he saw, he asked a swallow to bring each of the
precious stones and leaves of gold that decorated him to specific poor

people who could get the money they needed if they sold the precious items. Stripped of these beautiful decorations the statue looked shabby, so the city leaders declared that it be removed from its pedestal and melted down; the leaders also said that the swallow, found dead at the base of the statue, should be thrown on the dust-heap. How the Happy Prince and the swallow were eventually rewarded for their sacrifices makes for a moving conclusion. The full-page, expressionistic, watercolor paintings add an aura of sophistication to this classic, romantic fairy tale.

Wilde, Oscar 6–9
THE SELFISH GIANT YEARS
 Illus. by Michael Foreman and Freire Wright. New York: Methuen, 1978.

A classic fairy tale, created by Oscar Wilde for his own children, was originally published in 1888. In this picture-book edition, fantasy art, done in clean, full-color, watercolor paintings, embellishes the diverse moods of the story of a giant who forbids children to play in his garden because he wants it for himself. Realizing that only when children are present can he enjoy the garden, he eventually welcomes them back. Seeing one waif crying because he is unable to climb the trees as the other children do, the giant picks him up and puts him in the tree. Years later, the child (a Christ figure) rewards him for his kindness with eternal happiness in Paradise.

Willis, Val 5–8
THE SECRET IN THE MATCHBOX YEARS
 Illus. by John Shelley. New York: Farrar, 1988.

A fun and awesome fantasy of what happens when Bobby Bill's secret (a tiny dragon) gets out of the matchbox and grows and grows until it gets to be gigantic. How Bobby manages to get the dragon down to its original size and place it in the matchbox again should delight young readers. The fifteen full-color, double-page, expressionistic illustrations are loaded with a wonderful array of details, and each picture is framed with more pictures that add even more information about the students' and their teacher's reaction to this incredible dragon.

Wisniewski, David 6–10+
THE WARRIOR AND THE WISE MAN YEARS
 Illus. by David Wisniewski. New York: Lothrop, 1989.

Told in the style of a folktale, this is an original story of how twins (alike in every respect except that one was the greatest warrior in the land, the other was the greatest wise man) tried to accomplish their father's challenge to bring him the five universal elements: earth, water, fire, wind, and clouds. The cut-paper illustrations are remarkable accomplishments. They have the almost three-dimensional effect of shadow puppets, and, except for a few instances when the artist took artistic license in adapting designs of the weapons, their details are true to those used in the Japanese decorative arts. This is an excellent picture book to use in teaching critical thinking, especially those aspects that pertain to the characteristics of literary genre and authenticity.

Wolkstein, Diane   *6–10*
WHITE WAVE   *YEARS*
     Illus. by Ed Young. New York: Crowell, 1979.

How the moon goddess White Wave saved a young Chinese farmer from starvation is simply and gracefully told in this traditional Taoist tale of magic, illustrated with exquisite, impressionistic, black-and-white drawings. The theme of the story, the mystery of a small shrine in the hills of southern China, is explained succinctly and characteristically by the storyteller: "When we die, all that remains is the story." A truly beautiful picture book in every detail.

Wood, Audrey   *4–7*
HECKEDY PEG   *YEARS*
     Illus. by Don Wood. San Diego: HBJ, 1987.

Told in the style of a classical folktale and reportedly inspired by a sixteenth-century game children still play today, this original, dramatic story is about how a mother breaks a spell to save her seven children (named after the days of the week) from being eaten by Heckedy Peg, a witch who turned them into different kinds of foods. The artist's use of contrasting light and dark tones throughout the full-page, detailed, full-color oil paintings is suggestive of the Dutch and Flemish masters.

Wood, Audrey   *3–6*
THE NAPPING HOUSE   *YEARS*
     Illus. by Don Wood. San Diego: HBJ, 1984.

Cumulative rhymes detail what happened when "a wakeful flea bit the slumbering mouse on a snoozing cat on a dozing dog on a dreaming child on a snoozing granny on a cozy bed in a napping house," where everyone *was* sleeping. Full-page, animated, oil paintings in jewel tones that change ever so subtly reflect the changing moods—from a quiet, peaceful sleepy scene to one of incredible commotion and turmoil.

Yamashita, Haruo   *4–7*
MICE AT THE BEACH   *YEARS*
  Trans. from the Japanese. Illus. by Kazuo Iwamura. New York: Morrow, 1987.

The Mouse family, consisting of Mama and Daddy Mouse and their seven children, celebrate the end of the school year and the beginning of the sumer with a day at the beach. Tired from keeping track of his family while they are at the beach, Daddy Mouse falls asleep on a big rock and is not aware when the tide comes in. He wakes up to find himself stranded on the rock far from shore, for he does not know how to swim. Mama Mouse's solution to Daddy Mouse's predicament will please the readers of this humorous tale as much as it did the Mouse children. The double-page, line and watercolor-wash cartoon-style illustrations are wonderfully expressive and action-filled, each one containing many details that call for repeated, careful examination. First published in Japan in 1983 by Child Honsha, Tokyo, under the title *Nezumi No Kaisuiyoku*.

Ying, Pan Cai (adapter)   *6–9*
MONKEY CREATES HAVOC IN HEAVEN   *YEARS*
  Trans. by Ye Pin Kuei and rev. by Jill Morris. Illus. by Xin Kuan Liang, Zhang Xiu Shi, Fei Chang Fu, and Lin Zheng. New York; Viking, 1987. Publ. in association with Liaoning Fine Arts Publishing House, China.

This is a lively story about the havoc created in Heaven by the shapeshifter Monkey King, which led to his imprisonment in a mountain for five hundred years. He was released to guard Tripitaka, a monk on a journey to the West in search of the Buddhist holy scriptures. During their journey, Monkey King rid the world of many evil spirits and performed numerous good deeds. The content of the detailed, full-color paintings provides a fine glimpse of sixteenth-century China, the setting for the episode in *The Pilgrimage to the West*, the classic novel upon which this tale of the fearless Monkey King is based.

Yolen, Jane   7–10+
PIGGINS   YEARS
    Illus. by Jane Dyer. San Diego: HBJ, 1987.

Piggins, a very proper butler for Mr. and Mrs. Reynard, turns detective and identifies the culprits who stole Mrs. Reynard's diamond lavaliere when the lights went out during an elegant dinner party. The crisp, elaborate, cartoon-style illustrations are in full-color and were done in colored pencil and watercolor. They extend the droll humor of this clever, Edwardian era, mystery-detective story very well. Note text and visual allusions to memorable characters in classic and modern literature and in televeision series. In addition to allusions to Sherlock Holmes stories and the television series "Upstairs, Downstairs," consider these: Pierre Lampin (world-famous explorer, who in his youth stole into a farmer's garden and made too much noise) and his three unmarried sisters, otherwise known as Peter Rabbit, Flopsey, Mopsey and Cottontail; Mr. Reynard Fox (inventor of contraptions), otherwise known as Reynard, the fox; Professor T. Ortoise (famous for his conversation), otherwise known as Tortoise, the turtle; and Mr. and Mrs. Ratsby (greedy and deceitful rats), otherwise known as *The Great Gatsby*. *Piggins* is an excellent selection for reading aloud (for independent reading, too). It also provides fare for fun-filled, critical-thinking activities. Other episodes about Piggins are *Piggins and the Royal Wedding* (1989) and *Picnic With Piggins* (1988).

Yorinks, Arthur   5–8
HEY, AL   YEARS
    Illus. by Richard Egielski. New York: Farrar, 1986.

Named the 1987 Caldecott Medal winner, this is an upbeat story of how Al, a janitor, and his faithful dog, Eddie learn that there is no place like home. The effectively executed detailed and action-filled, cartoon-style illustration are done in pen and ink and full-color, watercolor wash.

Young, Ed   5–10
LON PO PO: A RED-RIDING HOOD STORY FROM CHINA   YEARS
    Trans. from a collection of Chinese folktales by Ed Young. Illus. by
    Ed Young. New York: Philomel, 1989.

Ed Young's modern, fairly abstract impressionistic paintings are done in full-color pastels and watercolor and seem to suggest the Tao (pronounced *Dow*) influence. The illustrations, typified by rhythmic energy and vitality and spirited emotion, are presented in panel art. The overall effect is an elegant sophistication and drama, giving an aura of authenticity to this casual translation of the folktale about three children who outwit a hungry wolf pretending to be their grandmother. Compare and contrast Ed Young's use of media, illustration techniques, and art style in *Lon Po Po* and in *Yeh-Shen: A Cinderella Story from China* (Philomel, 1982). Notice, too, how in each book the artist uses his art to express the *idea* about the many levels of feeling he gives to the settings for these tales rather than a specific and personal view of them. *Lon Po Po: A Red-Riding Hood Story from China* was named the 1990 Caldecott Medal winner by the Association of Library Service to Children of the American Library Association.

Ziefert, Harriet   *3–5*
GOOD NIGHT, EVERYONE!   *YEARS*
    Illus. by Andrea Baruffi. Boston: Little, Brown, 1988.

A bit of slight fantasy that even the youngest can enjoy. Tired, Harry wanted to go right to sleep, and he expected his toys to do likewise. Not only did they choose to play instead, but they also refused to be quiet when he told them to be quiet. Harry's way of handling these poorly behaved toys is certain to please all. The double-page, cartoon-style illustrations in this lively, bedtime story are in bright, full colors.

Index

Compiled by Jane Durkott

This is an index to titles as well as illustrators and writers (authors, editors, compilers, etc.) named in the alphabetical lists in each section as well as in the annotations and in the introduction, Choosing Picture Books.

219

223

225

Patricia J. Cianciolo is a professor of children's and adolescent literature at Michigan State University in East Lansing. She holds a doctorate in curriculum from Ohio State University and a master's degree in child development from the University of Wisconsin, Milwaukee. Patricia Cianciolo has published numerous articles on children's literature, presented papers and workshops at the state, national, and international level, and has served as a visiting faculty member at universities in 14 countries. She has also served on several children's literature award committees.